Classifying Drinking Water Contaminants

for Regulatory Consideration

Committee on Drinking Water Contaminants

Water Science and Technology Board

Board on Environmental Studies and Toxicology

Division on Earth and Life Studies

National Research Council

NATIONAL ACADEMY PRESS
Washington, D.C. 2001

NOTICE: The project that is the subject of this report was approved by the Governing Board of the National Research Council, whose members are drawn from the councils of the National Academy of Sciences, the National Academy of Engineering, and the Institute of Medicine. The members of the committee responsible for the report were chosen for their special competences and with regard for appropriate balance.

Support for this project was provided by the U.S. Environmental Protection Agency under Grant No. X-826345-01-0.

International Standard Book Number: 0-309-07408-8

Library of Congress Control Number: 2001093985

Classifying Drinking Water Contaminants for Regulatory Consideration is available from the National Academy Press, 2101 Constitution Avenue, N.W., Washington, D.C. 20418; (800) 624-6242 or (202) 334-3422 (in the Washington metropolitan area); Internet <http://www.nap.edu>.

THE NATIONAL ACADEMIES
Advisers to the Nation on Science, Engineering, and Medicine

National Academy of Sciences
National Academy of Engineering
Institute of Medicine
National Research Council

The **National Academy of Sciences** is a private, nonprofit, self-perpetuating society of distinguished scholars engaged in scientific and engineering research, dedicated to the furtherance of science and technology and to their use for the general welfare. Upon the authority of the charter granted to it by the Congress in 1863, the Academy has a mandate that requires it to advise the federal government on scientific and technical matters. Dr. Bruce M. Alberts is president of the National Academy of Sciences.

The **National Academy of Engineering** was established in 1964, under the charter of the National Academy of Sciences, as a parallel organization of outstanding engineers. It is autonomous in its administration and in the selection of its members, sharing with the National Academy of Sciences the responsibility for advising the federal government. The National Academy of Engineering also sponsors engineering programs aimed at meeting national needs, encourages education and research, and recognizes the superior achievement of engineers. Dr. William A. Wulf is president of the National Academy of Engineering.

The **Institute of Medicine** was established in 1970 by the National Academy of Sciences to secure the services of eminent members of appropriate professions in the examination of policy matters pertaining to the health of the public. The Institute acts under the responsibility given to the National Academy of Sciences by its congressional charter to be an adviser to the federal government and, upon its own initiative, to identify issues of medical care, research, and education. Dr. Kenneth I. Shine is president of the Institute of Medicine.

The **National Research Council** was organized by the National Academy of Sciences in 1916 to associate the broad community of science and technology with the Academy's purposes of furthering knowledge and advising the federal government. Functioning in accordance with general policies determined by the Academy, the Council has become the principal operating agency of both the National Academy of Sciences and the National Academy of Engineering in providing services to the government, the public, and the scientific and engineering communities. The Council is administered jointly by both Academies and the Institute of Medicine. Dr. Bruce M. Alberts and Dr. William A. Wulf are chairman and vice chairman, respectively, of the National Research Council.

Preface

Most people would agree that protecting our drinking water supply by regulating the maximum allowable content of hazardous contaminants is desirable. What is of considerable debate is which contaminants should be regulated, how many should be regulated, and what process will be used to select them. The U.S. Environmental Protection Agency (EPA) currently has enforceable National Primary Drinking Water Regulations for more than 80 inorganic and organic chemical, radionuclide, and microbial contaminants and groups of related contaminants under the Safe Drinking Water Act (SDWA). The 1996 SDWA Amendments were intended to further this protective approach by requiring EPA to periodically develop a list of contaminants that are currently unregulated and may pose a health risk. The agency must then select from each list—called the Drinking Water Contaminant Candidate List, or CCL—at least five contaminants for regulatory decisions every five years. In addition to supporting the mandated development of drinking water regulations, each CCL is intended to be the source of priority contaminants for the EPA's drinking water program as a whole and, to include research, monitoring, and guidance development. However, the specifics of developing the CCL and the manner in which the five or more contaminants are ultimately selected for regulatory decisions are not specified in the legislation.

The EPA requested assistance from the National Research Council (NRC) in addressing these difficult issues. This project has been conducted in two phases. The first phase was completed in July 1999 and resulted in two reports. The first of these, *Setting Priorities for Drinking Water Contaminants*, examines past approaches used by federal agencies, state and local governments, public water utilities, and other organizations for establishing priorities among drinking water contaminants and other environmental pollutants. It also recommends a phased decision process, associated time line, and related criteria to assist EPA efforts to set priorities and decide which contaminants already on a CCL should be subjected to regulation development, increased monitoring, or additional research. The NRC also convened a workshop on "emerging" drinking water contaminants and published the proceedings in a second report entitled *Identifying Future Drinking Water Contaminants*. Preceding a dozen papers presented by government, academic, and industry scientists at the workshop is a short committee report that outlines a conceptual approach to the creation of future CCLs. In that report, the committee strongly urged EPA to consider the benefits of a more carefully considered and detailed description of the requirements of a CCL development process, especially regarding the identification of critical drinking water contaminants for regulatory activities from among tens of thousands of potential candidates.

The second phase of the study focused on refining specific methods and processes to identify and narrow a very broad universe of potential contaminants into a smaller, more focused list for planning and action by interested parties. The specific tasks of the second phase are as follows:

1. Identify and evaluate a process to narrow, focus, and prioritize contaminants from a preliminary list for inclusion on a smaller, more manageable list of contaminants, including chemical and microbiological contaminants. The process and methods will include simple (semi) quantitative tools to cull the broad preliminary list of contaminants. The tools that are developed to narrow and focus future drinking water contaminant lists will be tested using validation case examples of currently regulated contaminants.

2. Explore the feasibility of developing virulence-activity relationships (VARs, now termed virulence-factor activity relationships or VFARs) for microbial contaminants. If a scientifically sound basis for developing VFARs is determined to be feasible, the committee will provide initial guidance and recommendations for interested parties on the steps necessary to construct and use VFARs.

3. Time and resources permitting, the committee will provide specific recommendations of methods for narrowing the broadest universe of contaminants to a smaller, preliminary contaminant list.

The Committee on Drinking Water Contaminants of the NRC addresses these three issues in the following report. We have recommended what may be considered a bold and innovative approach to selecting contaminants for inclusion on future CCLs. In our second report, we recommended that the CCL be developed in a two-step process. Initially, the "universe" of potential drinking water contaminants is identified by considering many possible categories and sources of contaminants. A preliminary CCL, or PCCL, is culled by a screening process and expert judgment from this universe. Then the CCL is selected from the PCCL using a more refined process in conjunction with expert judgment.

In this report, we provide initial guidance and several recommendations for how to accomplish the first step in this process. However, the bulk of the committee's effort for this final report was focused on providing a detailed paradigm for selection of the CCL from the PCCL. To this end, we have recommend that EPA develop and use a set of selected contaminant attributes to evaluate the likelihood that a contaminant or group of related contaminants would occur in drinking water at sufficient concentrations or prevalence to pose a public health risk. To make this determination, we recommend that the agency use a prototype classification algorithm in conjunction with expert judgment. Although this approach requires considerable initial investment by EPA, we feel that it represents a superior approach to relying exclusively on expert judgment or ranking schemes such as those reviewed in our first report. The committee has gone so far as to develop a demonstration algorithm to test the efficacy of this approach, and the results are compelling. Last but not least, the committee concludes that the construction and eventual use of VFARs within EPA's drinking water program is indeed feasible and merits careful consideration. We also provide some initial guidance and recommendations for their application herein.

The committee is grateful for the support of this project by Michael Osinski and his colleagues at EPA's Office of Ground Water and Drinking Water. In addition, we would not have been successful in our endeavors without the contributions of several experts who gave presentations to us during our first two meetings and aided in focusing our discussions. They include Fred Hauchman, EPA Office of Research and Development; Robert Clark, EPA Office of Research and Development; Kenneth Beattie, Oak Ridge National Laboratory; and Betty Olson, University of California at Irvine.

We have been highly fortunate as a committee to have the significant contributions and guidance of Mark Gibson, study director of this project and staff officer in the NRC's Water Science and Technology Board, and Carol Maczka, former program director for toxicology and risk assessment of the NRC's Board on Environmental Studies and Toxicology.

Ellen de Guzman, senior project assistant in the Water Science and Technology Board, provided excellent staff support throughout the second phase of this study. The commitment shown by the NRC staff helped keep the study on time and make it a success.

This report has been reviewed in draft form by individuals chosen for their diverse perspectives and technical expertise in accordance with procedures approved by the NRC's Report Review Committee. The purpose of this independent review is to provide candid and critical comments that will assist the institution in making its published report as sound as possible and to ensure that the report meets institutional standards for objectivity, evidence, and responsiveness to the study charge. The review comments and draft manuscript remain confidential to protect the integrity of the deliberative process. We wish to thank the following individuals for their review of this report: David Acheson, Tufts University; Caron Chess, Rutgers University; Gunther Craun, Gunther F. Craun and Associates; Joseph Delfino, University of Florida; Lynn Franklin, Pacific Northwest National Laboratory; Erik Olson, National Resources Defense Council; and, Fred Pontius, Pontius Water Consultants, Inc.

Although the reviewers listed above have provided many constructive comments and suggestions, they were not asked to endorse the conclusions or recommendations nor did they see the final draft of the report before its release. The review of this report was overseen by   Michael Kavanaugh, Malcolm Pirnie, Inc., and Frank Stillinger, Bell Laboratories, Lucent Technologies. Appointed by the National Research Council, they were responsible for making certain that an independent examination of this report was carried out in accordance with institutional procedures and that all review comments were carefully considered. Responsibility for the final content of this report rests entirely with the authoring committee and the institution.

I would also like to thank three former members of this committee for their past insights and contributions, many of which carried over into this report: Branden Johnson, New Jersey Department of Environmental Protection, Trenton; Michael McGuire, McGuire Environmental Consultants, Inc., Santa Monica, California; and, Warren Muir, NRC.

Finally, I thank the 13 members of this extraordinary committee. Each one brought a unique talent and exceptional degree of commitment to the tasks at hand. The diversity of perspectives made for enlivened and enlightening discussion throughout and ultimately led us to the forward-looking recommendations contained herein. I was honored to be part of it all.

DEBORAH L. SWACKHAMER
Chair, Committee on Drinking Water Contaminants

Contents

Executive Summary

Americans drink millions of gallons of tap water each day, usually with an unquestioning faith in its safety. Indeed, the provision and management of safe drinking water throughout the United States have been major triumphs of public health practice since the turn of the twentieth century. Despite advances in water treatment, source water protection efforts, and the presence of several layers of local, state, and federal regulatory protection, many sources of raw and finished public drinking water in the United States periodically contain chemical, microbiological, and other types of contaminants at detectable and sometimes harmful levels. Furthermore, the production and use of new chemicals that can reach water supplies and the discovery of emerging microbial pathogens that potentially can resist traditional water treatment practices and/or grow in distribution systems pose a regulatory dilemma: Where and how should the U.S. government focus its attention and limited resources to ensure safe drinking water supplies for the future? The availability of increasingly powerful analytical methods for the detection and identification of smaller amounts of chemicals and microorganisms in the environment, many of them never before detected, complicates these decisions.

To help address these difficult issues, one of the major requirements of the Safe Drinking Water Act (SDWA) Amendments of 1996 is that the U.S. Environmental Protection Agency (EPA) publish a list of unregulated chemical and microbial contaminants and contaminant groups every five years that are known or anticipated to occur in public water systems and that may pose risks in drinking water. The first such list, called the Drinking Water Contaminant Candidate List (CCL), was published in March 1998. The primary function of the CCL is to provide the basis for deciding whether to regulate at least five new contaminants from the CCL every five years. However, since additional research and monitoring need to be conducted for most of the contaminants on the 1998 CCL, the list is also used to prioritize these related activities.

This is the third report by the Committee on Drinking Water Contaminants (jointly overseen by the National Research Council's [NRC's] Water Science and Technology Board and Board on Environmental Studies and Toxicology). The committee was formed early in 1998 at the request of EPA's Office of Ground Water and Drinking Water to provide advice regarding the setting of priorities among drinking water contaminants in order to identify those contaminants that pose the greatest threats to public health. The committee is comprised of 14 volunteer experts in water treatment engineering, toxicology, public health, epidemiology, water and analytical chemistry, risk assessment, risk communication, public water system operations, and microbiology.

In its first report, *Setting Priorities for Drinking Water Contaminants*, the committee recommended a phased decision-making process, time line, and related criteria to assist EPA efforts to set priorities and decide which contaminants already on a CCL should be subjected to regulation development, increased monitoring, or additional health effects, treatment, and analytical methods research. That report also includes a review of several past approaches to setting priorities for drinking water contaminants and other environmental pollutants. The committee later organized and conducted an NRC workshop on emerging drinking water contaminants and subsequently published a second report entitled *Identifying Future Drinking Water Contaminants*. That report includes a dozen papers presented at the workshop by government, academic, and industry scientists on new and emerging microbiological and chemical drinking water contaminants, associated analytical and water treatment methods for their detection and removal, and existing and proposed environmental databases to assist in their proactive identification and potential regulatory consideration. Notably, the workshop papers are preceded by a short committee report that provides a conceptual approach to the creation of future CCLs. In this regard, the committee strongly urged EPA in its second report to consider the benefits of a more carefully considered and detailed description of the requirements of a CCL development process.

For this report, EPA asked the committee—which was partially reconstituted after the second report to include a new chair—to evaluate, expand, and revise as necessary the conceptual approach to the generation of future CCLs and any related conclusions and recommendations documented in the second report. In addition, EPA asked the committee to explore the feasibility of developing and using mechanisms for identifying emerging microbial pathogens (using what the committee now terms virulence-factor activity relationships, or VFARs) for research and regulatory activities—also as recommended in the second report. The contents, conclusions, and recommendations in this report are based on a review of relevant technical literature, information gathered at three committee meetings, and the expertise of committee members. As in its first two reports, the committee continues to emphasize the need for expert judgment throughout all CCL-related processes and for a conservative approach that errs on the side of public health protection.

The committee chose this perspective because public health is the basis for the SDWA and its amendments. Further, this report takes the position that scientific disagreements about the public health effects of contaminants and their relative severity are the norm and do not signal a deviation from sound science. For example, when data are sparse they may often appear consistent and coherent, but data gaps usually become evident as a problem is examined more fully by different methods and from different perspectives. The EPA faces a challenging task in assessing the available scientific information about contaminant risks and, based on that assessment, making decisions about which contaminants should be placed on a CCL for future regulatory and research consideration. Throughout this process, there is no replacement for policy judgments by EPA. As in its first report, the committee has purposely declined to define what constitutes "sufficient" or "adequate" data for making such decisions because this remains a matter of judgment that will vary with context.

RECOMMENDED APPROACH FOR THE DEVELOPMENT OF FUTURE CCLS

Because of the time constraints stipulated by the amended SDWA for publication of the first CCL, EPA was forced to rapidly develop and utilize a decision-making process for the creation of the 1998 CCL. The committee feels that the process used to develop the first CCL, although appropriate for the circumstances at the time, is not suitable as a long-term model. The process used in the future should be made more defensible and transparent, and its development should take place with increased opportunities for public input and comment. Similar comments can be made about policy decisions. These limitations are identified and discussed in Chapter 2 and provide a foundation for much of this report.

In its first report, the committee concluded that a ranking (rule-based) scheme that attempts to sort a relatively small number of drinking water contaminants already on a CCL in a specific order for regulation development, research, or monitoring is not appropriate. However, the committee subsequently concluded that such ranking schemes may be useful for sorting larger numbers of potential contaminants to determine which ones should be included on future CCLs. In its second report, the committee recommended that EPA develop a two-step process for the creation of future CCLs.

Two-Step Approach

Despite EPA's constrained resources, the lack of a comprehensive list of potential drinking water contaminants, and poor or nonexistent data on health effects, occurrence, and other attributes of the vast majority of potential contaminants, **the committee continues to recommend that EPA develop and use a two-step process for creating future CCLs as illustrated in Figure ES-1.** In summary, a broadly defined universe of potential drinking water contaminants is first identified, assessed, and culled to a preliminary CCL (PCCL) using simple screening criteria and expert judgment. All PCCL contaminants are then assessed individually using a "prototype" classification tool in conjunction with expert judgment to evaluate the likelihood that they could occur in drinking water at levels and frequencies that pose a public health risk to create the corresponding CCL. **The committee also continues to recommend that this two-step process be repeated for each CCL development cycle to account for new data and potential contaminants that inevitably arise over time. In addition, all contaminants that have not been regulated or removed from the existing CCL should automatically be retained on each subsequent CCL.**

It is important to note that although the basic concept for the CCL development approach has not changed, many of the associated guidelines and recommendations for its design and implementation have necessarily been revised and expanded in accordance with the most recent committee deliberations. The committee also notes that the amended SDWA specifically allows EPA to circumvent the CCL process and issue

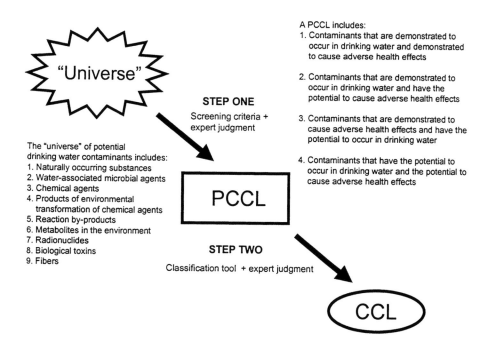

The "universe" of potential drinking water contaminants includes:
1. Naturally occurring substances
2. Water-associated microbial agents
3. Chemical agents
4. Products of environmental transformation of chemical agents
5. Reaction by-products
6. Metabolites in the environment
7. Radionuclides
8. Biological toxins
9. Fibers

STEP ONE
Screening criteria + expert judgment

STEP TWO
Classification tool + expert judgment

A PCCL includes:
1. Contaminants that are demonstrated to occur in drinking water and demonstrated to cause adverse health effects

2. Contaminants that are demonstrated to occur in drinking water and have the potential to cause adverse health effects

3. Contaminants that are demonstrated to cause adverse health effects and have the potential to occur in drinking water

4. Contaminants that have the potential to occur in drinking water and the potential to cause adverse health effects

FIGURE ES-1   Recommended two-step process for developing future CCLs.

interim regulations for any drinking water contaminant that is determined to pose an "urgent threat" to humans.

Sociopolitical Considerations

The committee recognizes that the development of a PCCL from the universe of potential drinking water contaminants, as well as the movement from a PCCL to the corresponding CCL, is a complex task requiring numerous difficult classification judgments in a context where data are often uncertain or missing. Due to data gaps and uncertainties, evaluating contaminants using widely varying data will often entail making assumptions. Because of this complexity, the committee believes that to be scientifically sound as well as publicly acceptable, the process for developing future CCLs must depart considerably from the process used to develop the first CCL. **The committee recommends that the process for selecting contaminants for future CCLs be systematic, scientifically sound, and transparent. The development and implementation of this process should involve sufficiently broad public participation.** Transparency should be incorporated into the design and development of the classification and decision-making process for future CCLs in addition to being an integral component in communicating the details of the process to the public. Otherwise, the public may perceive the process as subject to manipulation to achieve or support desired results. Therefore, sufficient information should be provided so that private citizens can place themselves in a similar position to decision-makers and arrive at their own reasonable and informed judgments. This may require making available to the public the software and databases used in the CCL development process. The central tenet that the public is, in principle, capable of making wise and prudent decisions should be recognized by EPA and reflected in the choice of a public participation procedure to help create future CCLs. A "decide-announce-defend" strategy that involves the public only after the deliberation process is over is not acceptable. Substantive a public involvement should occur throughout the design and implementation of the process. In this regard, EPA should strive to "get the right participation" (i.e., broad participation that includes the range of interested and affected parties) as well as to "get the participation right" (e.g., incorporating public values, viewpoints, and preferences into the process).

The ultimate goal of the contaminant selection process is the protection of public health by providing safe drinking water to all consumers. To meet this goal, the selection process must place high priority on the protection of vulnerable subpopulations as intended by the SDWA Amendments of 1996. **The committee recommends that not only should the definition of vulnerable subpopulations comply with the amended language of the SDWA, but it should also be sufficiently broad to protect public health;** in particular, EPA should consider including (in addition to those subgroups mentioned as examples in the amended SDWA) all women of childbearing age, fetuses, the immuno-compromised, people with an acquired or inherited genetic disposition that makes them more vulnerable to drinking water contaminants, people who are exceptionally sensitive to an array of chemical contaminants, people with specific medical conditions that make them more susceptible, people with poor nutrition, and people experiencing socioeconomic hardships and racial or ethnic discrimination.

Universe to PCCL

While the contaminants included on the first (1998) CCL certainly merit regulatory and research consideration, a broader approach to contaminant selection could potentially identify higher-risk contaminants. Although the committee was not able to deliberate extensively on the first step of the CCL development process (going from the universe of potential drinking water contaminants to a PCCL) due to time constraints, some initial guidance and several related recommendations can be provided, many of which reiterate and expand on those made in its second report:

• **EPA should begin by considering a broad universe of chemical, microbial, and other types of potential drinking water contaminants and contaminant groups** (see Table 3-1). The total number of contaminants in this universe is likely to be on the order of tens of thousands of substances and microorganisms, given that the Toxic Substances Control Act inventory of commercial chemicals alone includes about 72,000 substances. This represents a dramatically larger set of substances and microorganisms to be considered initially in terms of types and numbers of contaminants than that used for the creation of the 1998 CCL.

• **EPA should rely on databases and lists that are currently available and under development, along with other readily available information, to begin identifying the universe of potential contaminants that may be candidates for inclusion on the PCCL.** For example, EPA should consider using the Endocrine Disruptor Priority-Setting Database (EDPSD) to help develop future PCCLs (and perhaps CCLs). Although relevant databases and lists exist for many categories of potential drinking water contaminants, other categories have no lists or databases (e.g., products of environmental degradation). Thus, EPA should initiate work on a strategy for filling the gaps and updating the existing databases and lists of contaminants for future CCLs. This strategy should be developed with public, stakeholder, and scientific community input.

- As an integral part of the development process for future PCCLs and CCLs, all information used from existing or created databases or lists should be compiled in a consolidated database to provide a consistent mechanism for recording and retrieving information on the contaminants under consideration. Such a database could function as a "master list" that contains a detailed record of how the universe of potential contaminants was identified and how a particular PCCL and its corresponding CCL were subsequently created. It would also serve as a powerful analytical tool for the development of future PCCLs and CCLs. As a starting point, the committee recommends that EPA review its developing EDPSD to determine if it can be expanded and used as this consolidated database or whether it can serve as a model for subsequent development of such a database. The (re)design, creation, and implementation of such a database should be made in open cooperation with the public, stakeholders, and the scientific community.

- To assist generally in the identification of the universe of potential contaminants and a PCCL, the committee recommends that EPA consider substances based on their commercial use, environmental location, or physical characteristics (see Table 3-5). EPA should be as inclusive as possible in narrowing down the universe of potential drinking water contaminants for the PCCL. The committee envisions that a PCCL would contain on the order of a few thousand individual substances and groups of related substances, including microorganisms, for evaluation and prioritization to form a CCL. However, the preparation of a PCCL should not involve extensive analysis of data, nor should the PCCL itself directly drive EPA's research or monitoring activities.

- The committee recommends the use of a Venn diagram approach (Figure ES-2) to conceptually distinguish a PCCL from the broader universe of potential drinking water contaminants. Because of the extremely large size of the universe of potential drinking water contaminants, well-conceived screening criteria remain to be developed that can be applied rapidly and routinely by EPA in conjunction with expert judgment to cull that universe to a much smaller PCCL. Thus, the PCCL should include those contaminants that are demonstrated to occur or could potentially occur in drinking water *and* those that are demonstrated to cause or could potentially cause adverse health effects.

- Regarding the development of screening criteria for health effects, the committee recommends that human data and data on

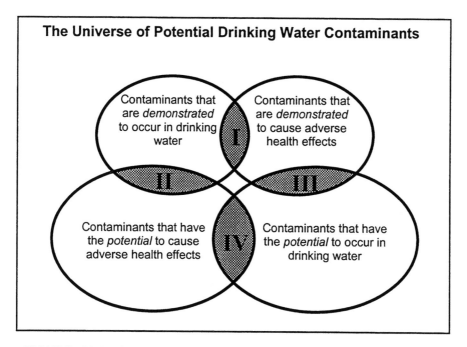

The Universe of Potential Drinking Water Contaminants

Contaminants that are *demonstrated* to occur in drinking water

Contaminants that are *demonstrated* to cause adverse health effects

I

II

III

Contaminants that have the *potential* to cause adverse health effects

Contaminants that have the *potential* to occur in drinking water

IV

FIGURE ES-2 Conceptual approach to identifying contaminants for inclusion on a PCCL through the intersection of their demonstrated and potential occurrence in drinking water and their ability to cause adverse health effects. Note, the sizes of the intersections and rings are not drawn to scale and do not represent an estimate of the relative numbers of contaminants in each area.

whole animals be used as indicators of demonstrated health effects and that other toxicological data and data from experimental models that predict biological activity be used as indicators of potential health effects.

• A variety of metrics could be used to develop screening criteria for the occurrence of contaminants in drinking water. These are identified in a hierarchical framework in the committee's first report and include (1) observations in tap water, (2) observations in distribution systems, (3) observations in finished water of water treatment plants, (4) observations in source water, (5) observations in watersheds and aquifers, (6) historical contaminant release data, and (7) chemical production data. **The committee recommends that the first four of these should be used as indicators of demonstrated occurrence and information that comes from items 5 to 7 should be used to determine potential occurrence.** For commercial chemicals, their potential for occurrence in drinking water may be estimated using a combination of production volume information and water solubility (see Figure 3-2). Most likely occurrence would involve high-production-volume chemicals with high water solubility.

- **Each PCCL should be published and thereby serve as a useful record of past PCCL and CCL development and as a starting point for the development of future PCCLs.**

- **Development of the first PCCL should begin as soon as possible to support development of the next (2003) CCL; each PCCL should be available for public and other stakeholder input (especially through the Internet) and should undergo scientific review.**

PCCL to CCL

The intrinsic difficulty of identifying potentially harmful substances or microorganisms for movement from a PCCL onto a CCL raises the question of what kind of process or method is best suited to this judgment. As previously noted, the sorting of perhaps thousands of PCCL contaminants into two discrete sets—one (the CCL) to probably undergo research or monitoring of some sort preparatory to an eventual regulatory decision and another much larger set that will not—is an exercise in *classification*. The committee considered three broad types of strategies for accomplishing this task: expert judgment, rule-based systems, and prototype classifiers (see Chapter 5 for further information).

Based on this review, the committee decided that a prototype classification approach using neural network or similar methods would seem to be an innovative and appropriate approach for EPA to consider. This strategy recognizes that in ordinary practice, one does not usually classify objects on the basis of a fixed algorithm (such as a rule-based scheme) but instead uses criteria based on prior classification of examples or prototypes. As such, prototype classifiers take advantage of the prototyping activity at which humans generally (and intuitively) excel. In simplest terms, a neural network is a mathematical representation of the complex network of biological neurons in higher organisms such as humans. Neural networks and similar methods start with prototypes (a "training set") that embody the kinds of outcomes one might wish to achieve. In this case, the training set would consist of chemicals, micro-organisms, and other types of potential drinking water contaminants that clearly belong on the CCL, such as currently regulated chemicals (if they were not already regulated), and those that clearly do not, such as some food additives generally recognized as safe by the U.S. Food and Drug Administration. For each contaminant in the training set, its "features" or attributes must be characterized. Using the training set, the neural network constructs the mode of combining and weighting the prototype attributes that best differentiate between the two categories. Thus, what has traditionally been accomplished a priori through the use of a ranking scheme that was most likely designed by experts and required the extensive use of expert judgment throughout would now be conducted on the basis of data that differentiate prototype examples. This a posteriori determination of weights on the basis of features sets prototype classification methods apart from such rule-based methods and expert judgment.

Contaminant Attributes

The committee recommends that EPA develop and use a set of attributes to evaluate the likelihood that any particular PCCL contaminant or group of related contaminants could occur in drinking water at levels and frequencies that pose a public health risk. These contaminant attributes should be used in a prototype classification approach, such as that described in Chapter 5, and in conjunction with expert judgment to help identify the highest-priority PCCL contaminants for inclusion on a CCL. A scoring system and related considerations for a total of five health effect and occurrence attributes are presented in Chapter 4, along with several "scored" examples of chemicals and microorganisms, to illustrate the utility of the recommended approach. For health effects, the committee identified severity and potency as key predictive attributes; prevalence, magnitude, and persistence-mobility comprise the occurrence attributes.

Although the committee spent a great deal of time deliberating on the number and type of contaminant attributes that should be used in the recommended CCL development approach, ultimately it decided that the five attributes listed above constitute a reasonable starting point for EPA consideration. Furthermore, the scoring metrics and related considerations for each attribute should be viewed in an illustrative manner. Thus, the committee does not explicitly or implicitly recommend these five (or that there necessarily should be five) attributes or that the related scoring metrics be directly adopted for use by EPA. **Should EPA choose to adopt a prototype classification approach to the development of future CCLs, the committee recommends that options for developing and scoring contaminant attributes should be made available for public and other stakeholder input and should undergo scientific review.** The committee also makes the following related recommendations:

- The assessment of severity should be based, when feasible, on plausible exposures via drinking water. The committee also recommends that EPA give consideration to different severity metrics such as a ranking through use of either quality adjusted or disability adjusted life-years lost from exposure to a contaminant.

- Regarding the assessment of contaminant prevalence, in some cases (particularly where contaminants have been included on a PCCL on the basis of potential rather than demonstrated occurrence), insufficient information will be available to directly assess temporal or spatial prevalence (or both). Thus, EPA should consider the possibility of including information on temporal and regional occurrence to help determine (score PCCL) contaminant prevalence. When prevalence cannot be assessed, this attribute must then go unscored and the attribute persistence-mobility used in its stead. The issue of changing (or incorporating) "thresholds" for contaminant detection, rather than relying on continually decreasing detection limits, is one that requires explicit attention and discussion by EPA and stakeholders.

- Because existing and readily available databases may not be sufficient to rapidly and consistently score health effect and occurrence attributes for individual PCCL contaminants, all information from existing or created databases or lists used in the development of a CCL and PCCL should be compiled in a consolidated database (as previously recommended).

- Contaminant databases used in support of the development of future CCLs should report summary statistics on all data collected, not only the quantifiable observations. In this regard, EPA should formalize a process for reporting means and/or medians from data with large numbers of "nondetect" observations. In addition, EPA may want to consider providing other measures of concentration in water supplies such as the 95th percentile of contaminant concentration.

Developing and Implementing a Prototype Classification Approach

Chapter 5 presents a framework for how existing contaminant data and past regulatory decisions could be used by EPA to develop a prototype classification algorithm to determine, in conjunction with expert judgment, whether or not a particular drinking water contaminant is of regulatory concern. More specifically, the committee demonstrates how a prototype classification approach—which must first be "trained" (calibrated) using a training data set containing both contaminants "presumed worthy of regulatory consideration" and those that are not—can be used in conjunction with expert judgment to predict whether a new (PCCL) contaminant should be placed on the CCL or not. The framework is intended to serve as a model of how EPA might develop its own prototype classification scheme for the creation of future CCLs. Use of the majority of currently regulated drinking water contaminants in the training data set to serve as contaminants presumed to be worthy of regulatory consideration can be simply described as "making decisions that are consistent with and build upon what has been done in the past."

The committee presents two alternative models for use in the scheme—a linear model and a neural network. Although the neural network performed better than the linear model (with respect to minimizing the number of misclassified contaminants), the committee cannot at this time make a firm recommendation as to which model EPA should use due to uncertainties in the training data set employed by the committee. **Thus, the committee recommends that EPA explore alternative model formulations and be cognizant of the dangers of overfitting and loss of generalization.** That is, EPA must be careful to avoid developing undue confidence in the precision of the training data sets ultimately used and being overzealous in finding an algorithm that produces no classification error in representing these data. The committee warns that this will impose "false structure" in the mapping and not truly capture the functional dependencies. Additionally, the danger of overfitting is especially present in neural network modeling because of the tremendous flexibility in the underlying mathematical relationships—resulting in a sacrifice of generalization (predictive) ability.

To adopt and implement the recommended approach to the creation of future CCLs, EPA will have to employ or work with persons knowledgeable of prototype classification methods and devote appreciable time and resources to develop and maintain a comprehensive training data set. In this regard, **the committee strongly recommends that EPA greatly increase the size of the training data set used illustratively in this report to improve predictive capacity.** One way in which EPA can expand the training data set and classification algorithm is to allow for the expected case of missing data. That is, purposefully include in the training data set drinking water contaminants for which the values of some attributes are unknown and develop a scheme that allows prediction of contaminants for which some attributes are unknown. EPA will also have to accurately and consistently assign attribute scores for all contaminants under consideration (i.e., contaminants in the training data set as well as contaminants to which the prototype classification algorithm will be applied for a classification determination). To do this, EPA will have to collect and organize available data and research for each PCCL contaminant and document the attribute scoring scheme used to help ensure a transparent and defensible process. As previously recommended, the creation of a consolidated database that would provide a consistent mechanism for recording and retrieving information on the contaminants under consideration would be of benefit. EPA will also have to withhold contaminants from inclusion in the training data set to serve as validation test cases that can assess the predictive accuracy of any classification algorithm developed for use in the creation of future CCLs.

If neural networks are ultimately used by EPA to establish a prototype classification approach for the creation of future CCLs, the transparency in understanding which contaminant attributes determine the contaminant category will be less than that of a linear model or more traditional rule-based scheme. However, if one acknowledges that the underlying process that maps attributes into categorical outcomes is very complex, there is little hope that an accurate rule-based classification scheme can be constructed. The fact that the nonlinear neural network performed better than the linear classifier is itself a strong indicator that the underlying mapping process is complex, and it would be a difficult task for a panel of experts (including this committee) to accurately specify the rules and conditions of such mapping. Furthermore, the decrease in transparency from using a neural network is not inherent or arbitrary, but rather derives from the difficulty in elucidating the mapping.

The committee notes that the underlying mapping in a neural network classifier can be examined just as one would conduct experiments to probe a physical system in a laboratory. Through numerical experimentation, one can probe a neural network to determine the sensitivity of the output to various changes in input data. Although a sensitivity analysis was not conducted due to time constraints, **the committee recommends that EPA should use several training data sets to gauge the sensitivity of the method as part of its analysis and documentation if a classification approach is ultimately adopted and used to help create future CCLs.**

Finally, the committee emphasizes that it is recommending a prototype classification approach to be used in conjunction with expert judgment for the selection of PCCL contaminants for inclusion on future CCLs. Thus, transparency is less crucial (though no less desired) at this juncture than when selecting contaminants from the CCL for regulatory activities as discussed in the committee's first report.

IDENTIFYING AND ASSESSING EMERGING WATERBORNE PATHOGENS

As noted in the committee's first report and discussed in greater detail in Chapter 6 of this report, the current approach to identifying and controlling waterborne disease is fundamentally limited in that the identification of pathogens is traditionally tied to the recognition of an outbreak. The committee feels strongly that this ongoing practice is not an effective or proactive means for protecting public health. Furthermore, current regulatory practice requires that methods to culture organisms of interest be developed before occurrence data can be gathered. Thus, a microorganism must ordinarily first be identified as a pathogen, and be capable of in vitro culture, before occurrence data are collected. This long-standing paradigm makes it very difficult or impossible to develop a database of potential or emerging pathogens. The committee feels that this constitutes a severe bottleneck to identifying and addressing potentially important emerging microbial contaminants in drinking water. Thus, a new approach to assessing pathogens could help overcome this serious and ongoing problem.

Virulence-Factor Activity Relationships

A virulence-factor activity relationship is the known or presumed linkage between the biological characteristics of a microorganism and its real or potential ability to cause harm (pathogenicity). The term is rooted in a recognition of the utility of using (quantitative) structure-activity relationships (QSARs or SARs) to compare the structure of new chemicals to known chemicals to enable prediction of their toxicity. Chapter 6 of this report responds to EPA's request that the committee explore the feasibility of developing VFARs for their construction and use in EPA's drinking water program. Furthermore, the committee provides a framework, initial guidance, and recommendations on the necessary steps for their construction and use to help identify emerging waterborne pathogens and predict their ability to cause disease in exposed humans.

For pathogenic microorganisms, besides the cell or organism itself, there are many levels of morphological components that can sometimes be used to identify pathogens. In addition to these large structures, there are smaller biochemical components including proteins, carbohydrates, and lipids that are related directly to the virulence of a particular microorganism. (In this report, virulence is defined broadly as the quality of being poisonous or injurious to life [i.e., virulent].) Some examples of these biochemical components include the outer coat of some bacteria (the lipid polysaccharide coat), attachment and invasion factors, and bacterial toxins. Together, these structures and compounds can generally be termed "virulence factors" and the blueprints for them are the genetic code of an organism. For this reason, a principal topic of Chapter 6 is the genetic structure of various microorganisms because of its direct relationship to virulence factors.

Owing to recent advances in molecular biology, the genetic structures of many thousands of microorganisms (especially bacteria and viruses) have been identified, reported, and stored in what are commonly called gene banks. Sophisticated computer programs allow for the sorting and matching of genetic structures and specific genes. The discipline that organizes and studies these genes is known as *bioinformatics*. Two other growing areas of related interest are *functional genomics* (i.e., understanding the specific role of genes in terms of the function of the organism) and *proteomics* (i.e., the science related to the study of the proteins made when the genomic blueprint is actually translated into functional molecules). The need and the ability to use these tools to address microbial contamination of drinking water are also reviewed in Chapter 6.

Framework

The central concept is to use microbial characteristics to predict virulence through VFARs. Microbial VFARs would function in much the same way as QSARs do—that is, to assist in the early identification of at least several potential elements of virulence. Research has increasingly shown certain common characteristics of virulent pathogens such as the production of specific toxins, specific surface proteins, and specific repair mechanisms that enhance their ability to infect and inflict damage in a host. Recently some of these "descriptors" (terminology often used in QSARs) have been tied to specific genes, and it has become evident that the same can be done for other descriptors as well. Identification of these descriptors, either directly or through analysis of genetic databases, could become a powerful tool for estimating the potential virulence of a microorganism. This is particularly true for two important aspects of virulence: potency and persistence in the environment. The committee conceives of VFAR as being the relationship that ties specific descriptors to outcomes of concern (see Figure ES-3).

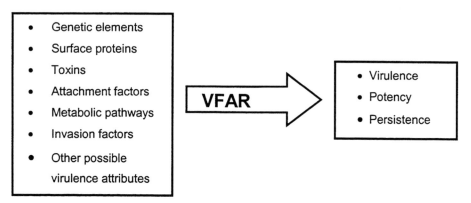

DESCRIPTORS   **OUTCOMES**

FIGURE ES-3 Schematic drawing of VFAR predicting outcomes of concern (virulence, potency, persistence) using the presence or quality of descriptor variables.

Feasibility

For the VFAR concept to be ultimately adopted and used by EPA in the agency's drinking water program, it must be feasible. This committee strongly believes this to be the case. Chapter 6 includes a review of several aspects concerning feasibility, including scientific validity and applicability; actual technological feasibility; the application of these technologies to studying disease in humans (validation); the degree to which these methodologies are being universally adopted within the scientific community; and the need for their development and use to adhere to the principles of transparency, public participation, and other sociopolitical considerations reviewed in Chapter 2. To one extent or another, each of these elements affects the ability of the VFAR concept to be developed, used, or validated. These elements either are present or can reasonably be expected to be available in the near future, so the committee concludes that the use of VFARs is indeed feasible.

While the technology, methodology, and even the genetic databanks exist, the application of a VFAR approach to assess waterborne pathogens would require considerable effort and expenditure of resources by EPA in conjunction with the Centers for Disease Control and Prevention, National Institutes of Health, and other federal and state health organizations. Such a "Waterborne Microbial Genomics" project would also require extensive expertise in bioinformatics, molecular microbiology, environmental microbiology, and infectious disease.

The committee fully recognizes that even the initial development of such a program (excluding its maintenance and expansion) is likely to require at least a five-year commitment and significant cooperation and expenditure of resources by EPA and other participating organizations. However, the opportunities for rapid identification of microbial hazards in water afforded by such a program would greatly improve the ability of EPA to quickly and successfully protect public health and improve water quality.

VFAR Conclusions and Recommendations

Despite the identification and discussion of some necessary caveats and limitations, the committee concludes that the construction and eventual use of VFARs in EPA's drinking water program is feasible and merits careful consideration. More specifically, the committee makes the following recommendations:

• **Establish a scientific VFAR Working Group on bioinformatics, genomics, and proteomics, with a charge to study these disciplines on an ongoing basis and periodically inform the agency as to how these disciplines can affect the identification and selection of drinking water contaminants for future regulatory, monitoring, and research activities.** The committee acknowledges the importance of several practical considerations related to the formation of such a working group within EPA, including how it should be administered and supported (e.g., logistically and financially) or where it could be located. However, the committee did not have sufficient time in its meetings to address these issues or make any related recommendations.

• **The findings of this report and those of the Biotechnology Research Working Group (BRWG, 2000:** *Interagency Report on the Federal Investment in Microbial Genomics***) should be made available to such a working group at its inception.** The committee views the activities of a VFAR Working Group as a continuing process in which developments in the fields of bioinformatics, genomics, and proteomics can rapidly be assessed and adopted for use in EPA's drinking water program.

• **The working group should be charged with the task of delineating specific steps and related issues and time lines needed to take VFARs beyond the conceptual framework of this report to actual development and implementation by EPA.** All such efforts should be made in open cooperation with the public, stakeholders, and the scientific community.

• **With the assistance of the VFAR Working Group, EPA should identify and fund pilot bioinformatic projects that use genomics and proteomics to gain practical experience that can be applied to the development of VFARs while it simultaneously dispatches the charges outlined in the two previous recommendations.**

• **EPA should employ and work with scientific personnel trained in the fields of bioinformatics, genomics, and proteomics to assist the agency in focusing efforts on identifying and addressing emerging waterborne microorganisms.**

• **EPA should participate fully in all ongoing and planned U.S. government efforts in bioinformatics, genomics, and proteomics as potentially related to the identification and selection of waterborne pathogens for regulatory consideration.**

1
Drinking Water Contaminant Candidate List: Past, Present, and Future

INTRODUCTION

The provision of safe drinking water throughout the United States has been a major triumph in U.S. public health practice since the turn of the twentieth century. The quality of this essential service is critical to community health because not only does it provide a life-giving substance to our communities, but it also has the potential to deliver harmful substances and microorganisms if not properly maintained. Maintenance of drinking water quality has been accomplished through several layers of federal, state, and local government laws, advisories, and regulations designed to protect public water supplies. Despite multiple levels of regulatory protection, however, many sources of raw and treated public drinking water in the United States contain chemical, microbiological, and even radiological contaminants at detectable and occasionally harmful levels (EPA, 1999a; Neal, 1985). The continuing presence of contaminants in water supplies, as well as documented outbreaks of waterborne disease and the many other outbreaks thought to go undetected, serve as a clear reminder that unprotected and contaminated drinking water can still pose health risks to the population (NRC, 1999a). Continuing public health vigilance is necessary to ensure that drinking water contaminants, especially newly identified ones, are appropriately addressed.

Perhaps the most important, comprehensive, and widely enforced law designed to protect the public from hazardous substances in drinking water is the Safe Drinking Water Act (SDWA). Enacted in 1974, it was significantly amended in 1986 and again most recently in 1996 and is administered by the U.S. Environmental Protection Agency (EPA). Prior to the passage of the original SDWA, the only enforceable federal drinking water standards were directed at waterborne pathogens in water supplies utilized by interstate carriers such as buses, trains, airplanes, and ships (NRC, 1997). The reader should refer to the 1997 National Research Council (NRC) report *Safe Water from Every Tap: Improving Water Service to Small Communities* (NRC, 1997) for an abbreviated review of the historical development of drinking water supply regulations in the United States. Alternatively, Pontius and Clark (1999) provide an extensive overview and discussion of this topic, especially as related to the SDWA and its subsequent amendments.

The purpose of the original SDWA was to ensure that public water systems (PWSs)[1] meet national primary drinking water regulations[2] for contaminants to protect public health. The SDWA also established a joint federal-state system to help administer the nationwide program and ensure compliance with federal standards. It is important to note that the SDWA does not regulate bottled water. Rather, bottled water is regulated at the federal level by the U.S. Food and Drug Administration under authority of the Federal Food, Drug, and Cosmetic Act. This report is concerned principally with requirements newly established in the SDWA Amendments of 1996.

Among other changes, the amended SDWA requires EPA to publish a list of unregulated contaminants and contaminant groups every five years that are known or anticipated to occur in public water systems and which may require regulation. This list, the Drinking Water Contaminant Candidate List—commonly referred to as the CCL—will provide the

---

[1] Public water systems subject to regulation under the amended SDWA are defined as distribution systems that provide water for human consumption through "constructed conveyances" (e.g., pipe networks, irrigation ditches) to at least 15 service connections or an average of 25 individuals daily for at least 60 days per year (EPA, 1998b).

[2] For chemical contaminants, a national primary drinking water regulation includes a nonenforceable criterion called the maximum contaminant level goal (MCLG) that is used to help set an enforceable standard called the maximum contaminant level (MCL) or treatment techniques (if contaminant monitoring is deemed not feasible). In general, MCLs are set as close to the MCLG as feasible, depending on risk management considerations such as an EPA determination that the cost of a setting an MCL at the MCLG is not justified by the benefits (EPA, 1996a). For microbiological contaminants, the original SDWA philosophically established a zero tolerance for disease-causing organisms as the health goal (i.e., the MCLG is set at zero). In practice, however, treatment performance techniques, rather than specific allowable concentrations of pathogens (such as MCLs), historically have served as the basis for regulating microbial contaminants in drinking water (NRC, 1999a).

basis for a mandated EPA decision to regulate (or not) at least five new contaminants every five years.[3]   EPA published the first draft CCL on October 6, 1997 (EPA, 1997a), and the first final CCL on March 2, 1998, hereafter referred to as the 1998 CCL (EPA, 1998a). The 1998 CCL is comprised entirely of chemical and microbial contaminants and contaminant groups. In addition to supporting the mandated development of drinking water regulations, each CCL is intended to be the source of priority contaminants for the agency's drinking water program as a whole, including research, monitoring, and guidance development.

The Committee on Drinking Water Contaminants (jointly overseen by the NRC's Water Science and Technology Board and Board on Environmental Studies and Toxicology) was formed in 1998 at the request of EPA's Office of Ground Water and Drinking Water to provide advice regarding the setting of priorities among drinking water contaminants in order to identify those contaminants that pose the greatest threats to public health. The original committee consisted of 14 volunteer experts in water treatment engineering, toxicology, public health, epidemiology, water and analytical chemistry, risk assessment, risk communication, public water system operations, and microbiology.

The committee's activities have been conducted in two discrete phases over a three-year period. During the first phase of the study (February 1998 through July 1999), the committee convened twice, leading to the development of its first report, *Setting Priorities for Drinking Water Contaminants* (NRC, 1999a). That report recommended a phased decision process, time line, and related criteria to assist EPA efforts to set priorities and decide which CCL contaminants should be subjected to regulation development, increased monitoring, or additional health effects, treatment, and analytical methods research. It also includes a review of several past approaches to setting priorities for drinking water contaminants and other environmental pollutants. First and foremost, the report emphasizes the need for expert judgment throughout this process

---

[3] It is important to note that Section 1412(b)(1)(d) of the amended SDWA allows EPA (after consultation with the U.S. Department of Health and Human Services) to issue interim regulations for any drinking water contaminant that is determined to pose an "urgent threat" to human health without adhering to the newly revised process for making regulatory decisions (i.e., the CCL process) or completing a cost-benefit analysis. However, a cost-benefit analysis and the required determination to regulate or not must be completed within three years after the interim rule, and the rule must be repromulgated or revised if necessary.

and for a conservative approach that errs on the side of public health protection.

During the first phase of study, the committee also organized and conducted an NRC workshop on emerging drinking water contaminants and subsequently published a second report entitled *Identifying Future Drinking Water Contaminants* (NRC, 1999b). That report includes a dozen papers presented at the workshop by government, academic, and industry scientists on new and emerging microbiological and chemical drinking water contaminants, associated analytical and water treatment methods for their detection and removal, and existing and proposed environmental databases to assist in their proactive identification and potential regulation. The workshop papers are preceded by a short committee report that provides a conceptual approach to the creation of future CCLs. The committee strongly urged EPA to consider the benefits of a more careful, detailed assessment of the CCL development process, especially regarding the identification of critical drinking water contaminants for regulatory activities from among tens of thousands of potential candidates.

For the second phase of the study (August 1999 through February 2001), EPA asked the committee—which was partially reconstituted, including a new chair—to evaluate, expand, and revise as necessary the conceptual approach for the generation of future CCLs and related conclusions and recommendations documented in the committee's second report. EPA also asked the committee to explore the feasibility of developing mechanisms for identifying emerging microbial pathogens (using what the committee now terms virulence-factor activity relationships, or VFARs; see Chapter 6 for further information) for research and regulatory activities as recommended in the committee's second report.

This chapter provides a brief summary of the purpose, development, and implementation status of the 1998 CCL, an overview of the recommended two-step process for the generation of future CCLs, and an overview of two closely related programs required by the amended SDWA. Chapter 2 describes important sociopolitical issues that EPA should consider when prioritizing contaminants for inclusion on future CCLs. Chapter 3 provides some initial recommendations for conducting the first step of the CCL development process. Chapter 4 describes in detail the second step of the recommended CCL development process and includes a general discussion of how EPA can implement the recommended approach. Chapter 5 builds on Chapter 4 and provides an overview and pros and cons of several classification approaches that EPA could use to help develop future CCLs. It also provides and discusses the results of the committee's attempt to demonstrate and validate the utility of the recommended approach. Lastly, Chapter 6 responds to EPA's request that the committee explore the feasibility of developing VFARs as a tool to help identify emerging waterborne pathogens and provides some initial guidance and recommendations on the necessary steps for their construction and use.

DEVELOPMENT OF THE 1998 CCL

Shortly after passage of the 1996 SDWA Amendments and prior to the development of the first CCL, EPA began work on a conceptual, risk-based approach to identifying and selecting unregulated chemical and microbiological drinking water contaminants as priorities for its drinking water program. This conceptual approach, called the contaminant identification method (CIM), was intended to identify and classify potential contaminants into several possible regulatory and nonregulatory categories for future activities (EPA, 1996b). These categories included contaminants to be placed on the CCL (for future regulatory determinations), those requiring further toxicological research, those recommended for monitoring, those needing health advisory development or other guidance, and those for which no action was required. The CIM was also intended to be used to reevaluate currently regulated drinking water contaminants as periodically required under the amended SDWA. However, extensive work on the CIM was suspended shortly after its inception due to the time constraints stipulated by the SDWA Amendments for publication of the first CCL. Instead, EPA relied primarily on the advice of the National Drinking Water Advisory Council[4] (NDWAC) Working Group on Occurrence and Contaminant Selection[5] for developing the

---

[4] NDWAC was chartered under the original SDWA and established in 1975 under the authority of the Federal Advisory Committee Act to provide independent advice and recommendations to EPA on drinking water issues and SDWA policies (EPA, 1999e). Its 15 members are appointed by the Office of Ground Water and Drinking Water, represent a broad base of interests and expertise, and serve staggered three-year terms. Several working groups were formed within NDWAC after the SDWA Amendments of 1996 to assist EPA in the implementation of many of its new and revised statutory requirements. Further information about NDWAC can be obtained at http://www.epa.gov/safewater/ndwac/council.html.

draft 1998 CCL.

At the first meeting of the working group, EPA proposed a total of 391 contaminants (including 25 microorganisms) taken from 10 lists of potential drinking water contaminants as a reasonable starting point for developing the draft CCL (EPA, 1997a). A total of eight lists—most originating from a variety of EPA programs (see Table 1-1)—and 262 chemicals and chemical groups were ultimately retained and evaluated by EPA. EPA also specifically deferred consideration of 21 contaminants for the draft CCL based solely on the possibility of their being endocrine disruptors and of 35 pesticides pending further evaluation of their potential to occur at levels of health concern (see Tables 4-2 and 4-3 of NRC, 1999a). At the recommendation of the working group, EPA first evaluated each chemical according to whether it had demonstrated or potential occurrence in drinking water (EPA, 1997a). Only those contaminants that met either of two criteria for occurrence were subsequently and similarly evaluated for evidence or suspicion that they cause adverse health effects via drinking water or other exposure routes.

Also at the recommendation of the working group, EPA sought external expertise in identifying and selecting potential waterborne pathogens for inclusion on the draft 1998 CCL (EPA, 1997a). For this purpose, EPA convened a workshop of microbiologists and public health specialists and provided an initial list of microorganisms for their immediate consideration (EPA, 1997b). The list included bacteria, viruses, protozoa, and algal toxins selected on the basis of disease outbreak data, published literature documenting the occurrence of known or suspected waterborne pathogens, and other related information. All of the microorganisms included on the initial list, as well as other potential microbiological contaminants that arose during deliberations, were evaluated individually against a set of baseline criteria related to an organism's (1) public health significance, (2) known waterborne transmission, (3) occurrence in source water, (4) effectiveness of current water treatment, and (5) adequacy of analytical methods as developed by the workshop participants. The evaluation also assessed the basic research and data needs for each microorganism. When published, the draft CCL included every microbiological contaminant recommended by the workshop participants and subsequently adopted by the full NDWAC.

---

[5] The NDWAC Working Group on Occurrence and Contaminant Selection consisted of engineers, microbiologists, toxicologists, and public health scientists from government agencies, water utilities, and other stakeholder groups.

TABLE 1-1 Chemical Lists Considered for Development of Draft 1998 CCL

List	Summary and Notes
1991 Drinking Water Priority List (DWPL)	Excluding disinfection by-products for which regulations were being developed under the Disinfectants and Disinfection Byproducts Rule
Health advisories (HAs)	All contaminants with HAs or HAs under development by EPA
Integrated Risk Information System (IRIS)	Contaminants adopted from IRIS based on a risk-based screen developed by EPA in anticipation of the 1994 DWPL
Contaminants identified by-public water systems	List of non-target contaminants identified in public water systems in anticipation of the 1994 DWPL
List of contaminants found at Comprehensive Environmental Response, Compensation, and Liability Act (CERCLA) sites	Top contaminants from a 1995 CERCLA list of prioritized hazardous substances
Stakeholder summary list	Contaminants proposed by participants in a December 2-3, 1997, stakeholder meeting on EPA's CIM
Toxic Release Inventory (TRI) list	Chemicals that met criteria for assessing the potential of a contaminant to occur in public water; derived from a 1994 TRI list of 343 chemicals
Office of Pesticide Programs (OPP) ranking	Pesticides and degradates taken from OPP ranking of pesticides from highest to lowest potential to reach groundwater

SOURCE: Adapted from EPA, 1997a; NRC, 1999a.

The draft 1998 CCL included 58 unregulated[6] chemical and 13 microbiological contaminants and contaminant groups (chemical contaminants were further divided into preliminary data need categories such as those requiring additional health effects data but not occurrence data) and was made publicly available for comments in the *Federal Register* (EPA, 1997a). EPA considered all comments, data, and other information provided by the public and several stakeholder groups in preparing the final CCL.

The 1998 final CCL (EPA, 1998a) comprises 60 contaminants and contaminant classes, including 10 microbial contaminants and groups of related microorganisms and 50 chemicals and chemical groups, as alphabetically listed in Table 1-2. A total of four microorganisms and eight chemicals and chemical groups were removed from the draft CCL. However, one chemical (perchlorate) and one broad group of microorganisms (cyanobacteria, other freshwater algae, and their toxins) were added based on public comments and the continued input of the working group. Modifications to the draft CCL were also reviewed and formally approved by the full NDWAC prior to publication of the final 1998 CCL.

With the exception of sulfate (see footnote 6), the CCL includes contaminants that are not currently subject to any proposed or promulgated primary drinking water regulation, but are known or anticipated to occur in public water systems and may require regulation under the SDWA (EPA, 1998a). Thus, the 1998 CCL is intended to be the primary source of priority contaminants for future regulatory actions by EPA's drinking water program until the next CCL is published in 2003. Figure 1-1 summarizes the current time line for the development, promulgation, and implementation of the 1998 CCL and future CCLs and two other related programs required under the amended SDWA that are described later in this chapter. For further information on the development of the 1998 CCL, please refer to Chapter 4 of the committee's first report, *Setting Priorities for Drinking Water Contaminants* (NRC, 1999a).

---

[6] In accordance with the SDWA Amendments of 1996, all contaminants on the 1998 CCL were not subject to any proposed or promulgated national primary drinking water regulation, with the exception of nickel, aldicarb and its degradates, and sulfate, which were included because of prior obligations to complete regulatory action for them (EPA, 1997a).

TABLE 1-2 1998 Drinking Water Contaminant Candidate List (CCL)

Microbiological Contaminants

Acanthamoeba (guidance)
Adenoviruses
Aeromonas hydrophila
Caliciviruses
Coxsackieviruses
Cyanobacteria (blue-green algae), other freshwater
  algae, and their toxins
Echoviruses
Helicobacter pylori
Microsporidia (Enterocytozoon and Septata)
Mycobacterium avium intracellulare

Chemical Contaminants	CASRN[a]
1,1,2,2-Tetrachloroethane	79-34-5
1,2,4-Trimethylbenzene	95-63-6
1,1-Dichloroethane	75-34-3
1,1-Dichloropropene	563-58-6
1,2-Diphenylhydrazine	122-66-7
1,3-Dichloropropane	142-28-9
1,3-Dichloropropene	542-75-6
2,4,6-Trichlorophenol	88-06-2
2,2-Dichloropropane	594-20-7
2,4-Dichlorophenol	120-83-2
2,4-Dinitrophenol	51-28-5
2,4-Dinitrotoluene	121-14-2
2,6-Dinitrotoluene	606-20-2
2-Methyl-phenol (*o*-cresol)	95-48-7
Acetochlor	34256-82-1
Alachlor ESA and other acetanilide pesticide degradation products	N/A
Aldrin	309-00-2
Aluminum	7429-90-5
Boron	7440-42-8
Bromobenzene	108-86-1
DCPA mono-acid degradate	887-54-7
DCPA di-acid degradate	2136-79-0
DDE	72-55-9
Diazinon	333-41-5
Dieldrin	60-57-1
Disulfoton	298-04-4
Diuron	330-54-1
EPTC	759-94-4
Fonofos	944-22-9
Hexachlorobutadiene	87-68-3
p-Isopropyltoluene (*p*-cymene)	99-87-6
Linuron	330-55-2
Manganese	7439-96-5
Methyl bromide	74-83-9

continues

TABLE 1-2 Continued

Chemical Contaminants	CASRN[a]
Metolachlor	51218-45-2
Metribuzin	21087-64-9
Molinate	2212-67-1
MTBE	1634-04-4
Naphthalene	91-20-3
Nitrobenzene	98-95-3
Organotins	N/A
Perchlorate	N/A
Prometon	1610-18-0
RDX (1,3,5-trinitrohexahydro-*s*-triazine)	121-82-4
Sodium	7440-23-5
Sulfate	14808-79-8
Terbacil	5902-51-2
Terbufos	13071-79-9
Triazines and degradation product of triazines (including, but not limited to Cyanizine [21725-46-2], and atrazine-desethyl [6190-65-4]	N/A
Vanadium	7440-62-2

NOTE: DCPA = (Dacthal) dimethyl-2,3,5,6-tetrachlorobenzene-1,4-dicarboxylate; DDE = 1,1-dichloro-2,2,-bis(*p*-diclorodiphenyl) ethylene; EPTC = *S*-ethyl dipropylthiocarbamate; MTBE = methyl-*t*-butyl ether; RDX = royal Dutch explosive.
[a]Chemical Abstracts Service Registry Number.
SOURCE: EPA, 1998a.

IMPLEMENTATION STATUS OF THE 1998 CCL

As noted by EPA, sufficient data are necessary to analyze the extent of exposure and risk to populations (particularly for vulnerable subpopulations such as infants and immuno-compromised persons as mandated by the amended SDWA) via drinking water in order to determine appropriate regulatory action (EPA, 1998a, 2000b). If sufficient data are not available, additional data must be obtained before any meaningful assessment can be made for a specific contaminant. In this regard, a table listing several categories of preliminary data needs for all chemicals on the draft 1998 CCL (EPA, 1997a) was expanded to include the microorganisms on the final CCL. These preliminary data need categories are now collectively called future action ("next-step") categories (EPA, 1998a). All 1998 CCL contaminants are currently divided into one or more of these categories (see Figure 1-2 and Table 1-3), which are used to help set priorities for EPA's drinking water program. It is important to note that there has been periodic reassignment of contaminants into and

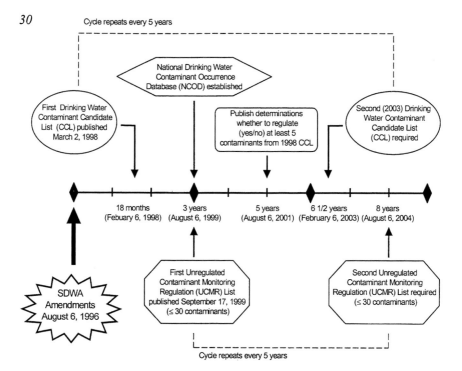

FIGURE 1-1 Current time line and interaction of selected major regulatory requirements of the SDWA Amendments of 1996. SOURCE: Adapted from EPA, 1997c; NRC, 1999a.

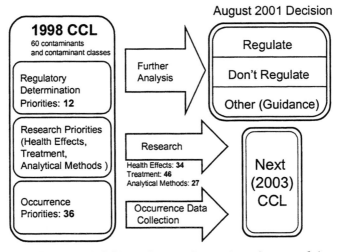

FIGURE 1-2 The 1998 CCL and next step categories as of June 2000. SOURCE: Adapted from EPA, 1999d, 2000b.

out of these categories since publication of the draft 1998 CCL as additional data have been obtained and evaluated. The current "regulatory determination priorities" category shown in Table 1-3 includes those contaminants considered to have sufficient data to evaluate both exposure and risk to public health and to support a regulatory decision (EPA, 2000b). Thus, the contaminants in this next-step category will be used to select five or more contaminants for which EPA will make a determination to regulate or not by August 2001. This category also includes those contaminants (sodium and *Acanthamoeba*) for which EPA intends to develop nonenforceable guidance rather than drinking water regulations. At present, only those contaminants in the regulation determination priorities category that ultimately receive a decision to be regulated, not regulated, or issued a health advisory will be removed entirely from the CCL process (i.e., not be retained on the 2003 CCL).

As noted previously by the committee (NRC, 1999a), the first CCL began as an essentially unranked list of research needs for drinking water contaminants. Additional research and monitoring must be conducted for many, if not most, of the contaminants on the current CCL as indicated in Table 1-3 (EPA, 2000b). Thus, EPA faces a daunting task in assessing the available scientific information about CCL contaminant risks and, based on that assessment, making a risk management decision about which contaminants should be moved off one of the research lists and into regulatory action.

Research Plan for 1998 CCL

Since its publication in March 1998, however, EPA has made progress in setting an overall CCL research strategy and schedule through its Office of Research and Development (ORD) which has the overall responsibility for shaping and guiding the agency's research agenda. The overall goal of ORD's CCL research process is to provide appropriate information for the Office of Water's (OW's) regulatory determinations concerning CCL contaminants. More specifically, this research is intended to identify the scientific and engineering data needed and to characterize the risks posed by 1998 CCL contaminants. It is beyond the scope of this report to describe the CCL research strategy in great detail. However, the committee notes that several elements from its first report (NRC, 1999a) for setting regulatory and research priorities for contaminants already on a CCL have been incorporated by EPA and an overview

TABLE 1-3 CCL Future Action Next-Step Categories[a]

Regulatory Determination Priorities (12)	Research Priorities			Occurrence Priorities (36)
	Health Effects (34)	Treatment (46)	Analytical Methods (27)	
Acanthamoeba (guidance)	Adenoviruses	Adenoviruses	Adenoviruses	Adenoviruses
Sodium (guidance)	*Aeromonas hydrophila*	*Aeromonas hydrophila*	*Aeromonas hydrophila*	*Aeromonas hydrophila*
1,3-Dichloropropene[b]	Caliciviruses	Caliciviruses	Caliciviruses	Caliciviruses[e]
Aldrin[b]	Coxsackieviruses	Coxsackieviruses	Coxsackieviruses	Coxsackieviruses[e]
Boron[b]	Cyanobacteria (blue-green algae)	Cyanobacteria (blue-green algae)	Cyanobacteria (blue-green algae)	Cyanobacteria (blue-green algae)[e]
Dieldrin[b]	Echoviruses	Echoviruses	Echoviruses	Echoviruses[e]
Hexachlorobutadiene	*Helicobacter pylori*	*Helicobacter pylori*	*Helicobacter pylori*	*Helicobacter pylori*[e]
Manganese	Microsporidia	Microsporidia	Microsporidia	Microsporidia[e]
Metolachlor[b]	*Mycobacterium avium intracellulare*	*Mycobacterium avium intracellulare*	*Mycobacterium avium intracellulare*	*Mycobacterium avium intracellulare*
Metribuzin[b]	1,1,2,2-Tetrachloroethane	1,1,2,2-Tetrachloroethane	1,2-Diphenyl-hydrazine	1,2-Diphenylhydrazine[e]
Naphthalene	1,2,4-Trimethylbenzene	1,2,4-Trimethylbenzene	2,4,6-Trichlorophenol	1,3-Dichloropropane
Sulfate	1,1-Dichloroethane	1,1-Dichloroethane	2,4-Dichlorophenol	2,4,6-Trichlorophenol[e]
	1,1-Dichloropropene	1,1-Dichloropropene	2,4-Dinitrophenol	2,4-Dichlorophenol[e]
	1,2-Diphenylhydrazine	1,2-Diphenylhydrazine	2-Methyl-phenol (o-cresol)	2,4-Dinitrophenol[e]
	1,3-Dichloropropane	1,3-Dichloropropane	Acetochlor	2-Methyl-phenol (o-cresol)[e]
	2,4,6-Trichlorophenol	2,4,6-Trichlorophenol	Alachlor ESA	Acetochlor[e]
	2,2-Dichloropropane	2,2-Dichloropropane	Diazinon	Alachlor ESA[e]
	2,4-Dinitrophenol	2,4-Dichlorophenol	Disulfoton	DCPA mono-acid degradate
	2,4-Dinitrotoluene	2,4-Dinitrophenol	Diuron	DCPA di-acid degradate
	2,6-Dinitrotoluene	2,4-Dinitrotoluene	Fonofos	DDE
	2-Methyl-phenol (o-cresol)	2,6-Dinitrotoluene	Linuron	Diazinon[e]
		2-Methyl-phenol	Organotins[c]	

Aluminum	(o-cresol)	Perchlorate	Disulfoton[e]
Bromobenzene	Acetochlor	Prometon	Diuron[e]
DCPA mono-acid degradate[b]	Alachlor ESA	RDX	EPTC
DCPA di-acid degradate[b]	Aluminum	Terbufos	Fonofos[e]
p-Isopropyltoluene (p-cymene)	Bromobenzene	Triazines and degradation products[d]	Linuron[e]
Methyl bromide[b]	DCPA mono-acid degradate		MTBE
MTBE	DCPA di-acid degradate		Molinate
Nitrobenzene	DDE		Nitrobenzene
Organotins[c]	Diazinon		Perchlorate[e]
Perchlorate	Disulfoton		Prometon[e]
RDX	Diuron		RDX[e]
Triazines & degradation products[b, d]	EPTC		Terbacil
Vanadium	Fonofos		Terbufos[e]
	p-Isopropyltoluene (p-cymene)		Organotins[c]
	Linuron		Triazines & degradation products[d,e]
	Methylbromide		
	Molinate		
	MTBE		
	Nitrobenzene		
	Organotins[c]		
	Perchlorate		
	Prometon		
	RDX		
	Terbacil		
	Terbufos		

NOTE: See Table 1-2 for definition of chemical acronyms.

[a]Table reflects some movement of contaminants between next-step categories since the CCL was published on March 2, 1998 (EPA, 1998a), the final Unregulated Contaminant Monitoring Regulation List was published on September 17, 1999 (EPA, 1999g), and publication of EPA's SAB review draft of the Research Plan for the Drinking Water Contaminant Candidate List (EPA, 2000b).

[b]These chemicals will be deferred to EPA's Office of Pesticide Programs for health effects research and assessment.

[c]Organotins include monobutyltin trichloride, dibutyltin dichloride, monomethyltin trichloride, and dimethyltin trichloride.

[d]Degradation products include, but are not limited to, Cyanazine and atrazine-desethyl.

[e]Suitable analytical methods must be developed prior to obtaining occurrence data.

SOURCE: EPA, 2000b.

of the development and current status of EPA's CCL Research Plan is provided below.

A draft version of the research plan (EPA, 2000b) was currently under review by EPA's Science Advisory Board (SAB) and available at the time this report was written. Notably, the CCL Research Plan (report) is expected to be revised significantly in response to the SAB review (Fred Hauchman, EPA, personal communication, 2000). The CCL Research Plan report addresses five major questions:

1.   What is EPA's plan for identifying and ranking research needs for the 1998 CCL contaminants?
2.   What analytical methods are needed to adequately address occurrence, exposure, health effects, and treatability issues?
3.   What are the occurrence and exposure issues associated with CCL contaminants in source water, finished water, and drinking water distribution systems?
4.   Are there significant health risks associated with exposure to CCL contaminants?
5.   How effective are candidate treatment technologies for controlling CCL contaminants?

EPA decided on a two-phased approach to form the basis for the 1998 CCL Research Plan (EPA, 2000b). Phase I is a screening level effort in which the CCL contaminants are evaluated with regard to available methods, health risk, and treatment information. This screening process involves the examination of minimum data sets that can be used to determine if a contaminant should be moved into the regulatory determination priorities category of the CCL or moved into Phase II. In Phase II, a more in-depth examination is conducted to determine whether the contaminant should be recommended for regulation, guidance should be developed, or a recommendation not to regulate should be made. In general, Phase II research involves the generation of a comprehensive database for each CCL contaminant on its health effects, analytical methods, occurrence, exposure, and treatment options. Because of the complexity of the CCL research process and the need to integrate ORD's efforts, an Implementation Team comprised of researchers and managers from ORD's laboratories and centers as well as representatives from OW will be established. The team will be responsible for providing oversight and coordinating the CCL research process while balancing the agency's resource commitments against the requirements of the CCL process.

The CCL Research Plan was developed by EPA in close consultation with outside stakeholders, including the American Water Works Association (AWWA), the AWWA Research Foundation (AWWARF), other government agencies,[7] universities, and other public and private sector groups (EPA, 2000b). In addition, several expert workshops that helped in developing the 1998 CCL itself were used to help identify research needs for specific contaminants. For example, EPA and AWWARF jointly sponsored a three-day conference in September 1999 that was intended to review all aspects of the proposed CCL Research Plan and make suggestions for future research activities (AWWARF, 2000). Representatives attended the meeting from the water utility industry, state and federal health and regulatory agencies, professional associations, academia, and public interest groups, and recommendations and results from the meeting were incorporated into the CCL Research Plan.

After the AWWARF-EPA workshop in September 1999, a special panel was convened by EPA to examine the risk assessment and risk characterization issues associated with the CCL Research Plan. Recommendations from that panel were utilized in developing the two-phased research approach outlined in the CCL Research Plan report. Implementation of the CCL Research Plan will require the coordinated efforts of both government and nongovernment entities, as did its creation (EPA, 2000b). In this regard, EPA intends to make all aspects of 1998 CCL research planning, implementation, and communication a collaborative process through a series of public workshops and stakeholder meetings held periodically over the next few years.

LIMITATIONS OF THE FIRST
CCL DEVELOPMENT PROCESS

EPA stated in the draft 1998 CCL that the "first CCL is largely based on knowledge acquired over the last few years and other readily available information, but an enhanced, more robust approach to data collection and evaluation will be developed for future CCLs" (EPA, 1997a). Several public commenters on the draft CCL also noted the need for a more systematic and scientifically defensible approach to selecting contaminants for future CCLs (EPA, 1998c). Chapter 4 of the committee's

---

[7]Centers for Disease Control and Prevention, National Institute of Environmental Health Sciences, and National Institute for Occupational Safety and Health.

first report (NRC, 1999a) summarizes the development of the first CCL in detail. The committee's second report (NRC, 1999b) briefly described some limitations of the first CCL development process before presenting its recommended conceptual approach to the development of future CCLs. Chapter 2 of this report more fully describes these and other limitations, especially as related to various sociopolitical issues surrounding the development of future CCLs.

Partly due to these limitations, the committee recommended in its second report (NRC, 1999b) that a new type of screening process be used to identify and evaluate a broader universe of microbiological, chemical, and other types of potential drinking water contaminants in order to provide a more objective list of contaminants of concern. In this regard, a conceptual two-step process for the creation of future CCLs was outlined and recommended to EPA.

RELATED SDWA PROGRAMS

In accordance with the SDWA Amendments of 1996 and as indicated in Figure 1-1, the development and use of future CCLs will be coordinated closely with two other drinking water programs: the National Drinking Water Contaminant Occurrence Database (NCOD) and the Unregulated Contaminant Monitoring Regulation (UCMR) (EPA, 1998a). Both of these programs, as well as the CCL, are the responsibility of EPA's Office of Ground Water and Drinking Water. EPA completed the first working release of the NCOD and the UCMR prior to its amended SDWA statutory deadline of August 1999.

National Drinking Water Contaminant Occurrence Database

The NCOD stores data on the occurrence of both regulated and unregulated drinking water contaminants. It is intended to support EPA efforts in the identification and selection of contaminants for placement on future CCLs; subsequent and related research, monitoring, and regulatory activities; and the periodic (six-year) review of existing drinking water regulations for possible modification as required under the amended SDWA (EPA, 2000g). An additional purpose is to inform the public about contaminants detected in drinking water and make available the data sets that help form the primary basis for EPA's drinking water-related regulatory and research actions. EPA requested input from the public, states, and the scientific community regarding the NCOD's design, structure, and use (AWWA, 1997; EPA, 1997c).

The first release of the NCOD became operational in August 1999 (as mandated) and included occurrence data on various physical, chemical, microbial, and radiological contaminants found in public water systems and ambient (source) water (EPA, 2000g). More specifically, it contained some summary statistics of PWS data stored in EPA's Safe Drinking Water Information System (SDWIS) and ambient water stored in the National Water Information System (NWIS) of the U.S. Geological Survey (USGS). The second release of NCOD became operational in late August 2000 and included several changes intended to increase its functionality. For example, the second release of NCOD completely refreshes summary PWS data every quarter (Lew Summers, EPA, personal communication, 2000) and is supported by an NCOD User's Guide (EPA, 2000h).

At present, four types of NCOD queries have been defined: (1) public right to know; (2) occurrence data survey for preliminary CCL[8]; (3) regulation determination/development; and (4) regulation revision (EPA, 2000g). In brief, the public right-to-know query allows a user to query the database for a specific contaminant in specific political jurisdictions (i.e., national, state, county, or city) grouped by population and source water type. The query on occurrence data survey for preliminary CCL presents information on unregulated contaminants in public drinking water from EPA's SDWIS and ambient source water from NWIS provided by USGS. A regulation determination/development query is still under construction but will allow users to view summary information and download PWS sample data that could be used to help select contaminants for future regulation or to develop new national primary drinking water regulations (NPDWRs). Last, the regulation revision query (also still under construction) will allow users to view summary data and to download a data set that could be used in the periodic revision of existing NPDWRs as required under the amended SDWA.

Despite these ongoing improvements, EPA has provided (EPA, 2000g) some self-assessed data limitations (and strengths) associated with the first and second releases of the NCOD, along with several cautions to NCOD users, including the following:

---

[8] Note, the term "preliminary CCL" as used for this NCOD query differs substantially from its use throughout this report.

- The NCOD does not contain occurrence data from every public water system or from every state. Only PWS occurrence data reported to the SDWIS are available using a public water system query in NCOD.
- The NCOD contains data both for currently unregulated contaminants required to be monitored by PWS under the UCMR (see more below) and for the occurrence of regulated contaminants with health-based drinking water MCLs. However, not all states and territories, or PWSs within states and territories, have reported data for either type of contaminant data as yet. Furthermore, the historical data goes back only to 1983.
- The NCOD contains occurrence monitoring data from sampling locations throughout a PWS. However, detections do not necessarily mean that the contaminant would be found at the tap.
- The NCOD contains ambient (source) water quality data from USGS for river basins from 1991 to 1998. Ambient occurrence data are provided to identify presence in a watershed; however, contaminant occurrence in the ambient data does not imply that the contaminant is also present in a nearby PWS.
- Although the NCOD data sets will be updated over time, they may still reflect a lag time of at least six months from data provided directly from a PWS. Thus, getting data that reflect the current conditions of a PWS is not possible from NCOD.
- Reports generated by the use of EPA's NCOD database are designed to provide coarse summaries of the underlying data. The amount of occurrence data already stored in the NCOD is quite large and is expected to increase by as much as 1 gigabyte (1,000 megabytes) each quarter. This could result in very large download files that could adversely affect the performance of EPA public information servers. For this reason, NCOD downloads are currently available only from reports generated by selecting single contaminants.

Interested readers are encouraged to visit EPA's Web site on the NCOD at http://www.epa.gov/ncod/ for further information.

Unregulated Contaminant Monitoring Regulation

Section 125 of the 1996 SDWA Amendments requires EPA to substantially revise the previous SDWA regulations for unregulated contaminant monitoring (UCM; Title 40, Code of Federal Regulations, Part 141) (EPA, 1999g). The new program includes (1) development of a new list of UCMR contaminants every five years; (2) a representative sample of small public water systems serving 10,000 persons or fewer to conduct the monitoring (in addition to all large systems); (3) placement of the monitoring data in the NCOD; and (4) notification of consumers that monitoring results are publicly available. The 1996 amendments also limit the number of unregulated contaminants to be monitored by a PWS in any given period to a maximum of 30 and specify that EPA pay the reasonable costs of analyzing the samples taken by those systems designated as "small." EPA plans to use data generated by the UCMR to (1) evaluate and rank contaminants on the 1998 CCL and help develop future CCLs; (2) support its determinations of whether to regulate a contaminant under the drinking water program; and (3) support the development of drinking water regulations. The final UCMR rule will replace almost all of the existing monitoring requirements of the existing UCM rule when it takes effect on January 1, 2001.

In accordance with recommendations from a previous report (EPA, 1997d) on options for developing the UCMR, EPA used the original occurrence priorities of the 1998 CCL (as published on March 2, 1998) as the primary basis for selecting contaminants for future monitoring under the UCMR (EPA, 1999f,g). These 26 chemical and 8 microbiological contaminants[9] were then evaluated primarily for the analytical methods and the level of information available for them at the time of development of the 1999 UCMR List (see Table 1-4 for a current alphabetical listing). Based on these evaluations, EPA developed a three-tier monitoring approach that allows assessment monitoring to start promptly for contaminants with approved analytical methods (UCMR List 1), while accommodating the need to delay implementation for contaminants requiring further refinement of analytical methods to initiate screening survey monitoring (UCMR List 2) and those that need method development for prescreen testing (UCMR List 3) (EPA, 1999c,f,g). Please refer to the final UCMR rule (EPA, 1999f) for further information on assessment monitoring for List 1 contaminants and the proposed rule for screening survey monitoring for List 2 contaminants (EPA, 2000j).

In summary, List 1 contains 12 chemical contaminants that require monitoring for one continuous year between 2001 and 2003 at all 2,744

---

[9] It is important to note that the most recent occurrence priorities category of the 1998 CCL (see Table 1-3) includes two contaminants (*Mycobacterim avium intercellulare* and 1,3-dichloropropane) that were not listed in that category at the time the CCL was first published and were thus not evaluated or listed on the 1999 UCMR List.

TABLE 1-4 1999 UCMR List

Contaminant	Analytical Method(s) Availability and Adequacy
List 1 Chemicals (No Microorganisms)	
2,4-Dinitrotoluene	Available and adequate for assessment monitoring
2,6-Dinitrotoluene	Available and adequate for assessment monitoring
Acetochlor	Available and adequate for assessment monitoring
DCPA mono-acid degradate	Available and adequate for assessment monitoring, but all approved methods identify total mono- and di-acid forms
DCPA di-acid degradate	Available and adequate for assessment monitoring, but all approved methods identify total mono- and di-acid forms
DDE	Available and adequate for assessment monitoring
EPTC	Available and adequate for assessment monitoring
Molinate	Available and adequate for assessment monitoring
MTBE	Available and adequate for assessment monitoring
Nitrobenzene[a]	Available and adequate for assessment monitoring
Perchlorate[b]	Available and adequate for assessment monitoring
Terbacil	Available and adequate for assessment monitoring
UCMR List 2 Microorganisms	
Aeromonas hydrophilia	Method proposed; ready for delayed screening survey monitoring
UCMR List 2 Chemicals	
1,2-Diphenylhydrazine	Method proposed; ready for screening survey monitoring
2,4-Dichlorophenol	Method proposed; ready for screening survey monitoring
2,4-Dinitrophenol	Method proposed; ready for screening survey monitoring
2,4,6-Trichlorophenol	Method proposed; ready for screening survey monitoring
2-Methyl-phenol (*o*-cresol)	Method proposed; ready for screening survey monitoring
Alachlor ESA[c]	Being refined
Diazinon	Method proposed; ready for screening survey monitoring
Disulfoton	Method proposed; ready for screening survey monitoring
Diuron	Method proposed; ready for screening survey monitoring
Fonofos	Method proposed; ready for screening survey monitoring
Linuron	Method proposed; ready for screening survey monitoring
Nitrobenzene[a]	Method proposed; ready for screening survey monitoring
Prometon	Method proposed; ready for screening survey monitoring
RDX[c]	Being refined
Terbufos	Method proposed; ready for screening survey monitoring
UCMR List 3 Microorganisms	
Adenoviruses	No method currently available
Caliciviruses	No method currently available
Coxsackieviruses	Methods available but not standardized
Cyanobacteria (blue-green algae)	Methods available but not standardized
Echoviruses	Methods available but not standardized

continues

TABLE 1-4 Continued

Contaminant	Analytical Method(s) Availability and Adequacy
Helicobacter pylori	No method currently available
Microsporidia	No method currently available
UCMR List 3 Chemicals	
Lead-210 (^{210}Pb)^d	No method currently available
Polonium-210 (^{210}Po)^e	No method currently available

NOTE: See Table 1-2 for definition of chemical acronyms.

[a] Originally included on List 1 (EPA, 1999c,f,g), EPA recently proposed (EPA, 2000j) to also add nitrobenzene to List 2 to allow for refinement of an analytical method that would permit detection at lower levels.

[b] To meet the reporting requirements of the UCMR, all participating laboratories must successfully complete EPA's Perchlorate Performance Testing Program (EPA, 2000k).

[c] If methods are developed in a timely fashion for these two contaminants, they may be added for monitoring in a separate action, probably in 2003, or during the next UCMR five-year monitoring cycle beginning in 2006 (EPA, 2000j).

[d] Originally proposed to be added to UCMR List 1 (EPA, 1999g), it was later added to List 3 because no suitable methods were available (EPA, 1999f).

[e] Originally proposed to be added to UCMR List 1 (EPA, 1999g), it was later added to List 2 for methods refinement (EPA, 1999f) and subsequently proposed to be moved to List 3 because ultimately no suitable methods were determined available (EPA, 2000j).

SOURCE: Adapted from EPA, 1999c,f,g, 2000j.

large PWSs serving more than 10,000 persons and at a representative national sample of 800 (out of 66,000) small systems serving 10,000 or fewer persons (EPA, 1999f,g). Monitoring for the contaminants on UCMR Lists 2 and 3 is not required until EPA promulgates revisions to the UCMR final rule that specifies analytical methods and related sampling requirements. However, EPA recently revised List 2 and published proposed analytical methods and monitoring requirements for 14 (13 chemicals and 1 microorganism) of its now 16 contaminants (see Table 1-4; EPA, 2000j). More specifically, EPA is proposing to require screening survey monitoring for these 13 chemical contaminants at 180 randomly selected small systems with the small systems doing the sampling and EPA conducting the testing and reporting beginning in January 2001. A total of 120 randomly selected large systems would begin List 2 chemical monitoring in January 2002. A second (delayed) screening survey for *Aeromonas* will be performed in 2003 by 180 other small systems and 120 other large systems. The delay is intended to allow laboratories to gain experience with the new method and develop the capacity for testing in large systems. More generally, evaluation of the newly proposed methods during screening survey monitoring for List 2 contaminants will include developing the data necessary to support the determination of practical quantitation levels, which are needed to support possible future regulations, as well as determining the occurrence of the analytes measured.

Notably, the addition of the majority of List 2 contaminants will not require any PWS to monitor for more than 30 total unregulated contaminants during the first five-year UCMR monitoring cycle, as specified in the amended SDWA. At this time, EPA does not expect to publish analytical methods for List 3 contaminants before the next UCMR is required in 2004 (Rachel Sakata, EPA, personal communication, 2000). Therefore, it is likely that these contaminants will be retained on the 2003 CCL (at least as occurrence priorities) and the 2004 UCMR and will be monitored accordingly. In this regard, the 2004 UCMR is expected to use the occurrence priorities from the next (2003) CCL as the primary basis for selecting contaminants for future monitoring under the UCMR (EPA, 1999d).

IDENTIFYING AND SELECTING CONTAMINANTS FOR FUTURE CCLS

As noted earlier, the committee produced this report at the request of EPA to build upon, expand, and revise as necessary the conceptual approach recommended in its second report (NRC, 1999b). In that report, the committee stated that if resources were unlimited and health effects and occurrence information were perfect, an ideal CCL development process would include the following features:

- It would meet all statutory requirements of the SDWA Amendments of 1996, such as requirements for consultation with the scientific community and opportunities for public comment.
- It would begin with identification of the entire universe of potential drinking water contaminants prior to any attempts to rank or sort them.
- It would address risks from all potential routes of exposure to water supplies, including dermal contact and inhalation as well as ingestion.
- It would use the same identification and selection process for chemical, microbial, and all other types of the potential drinking water contaminants.

- It would use mechanisms for identifying similarities among contaminants and contaminant classes to assess the potential risks of individual contaminants—especially emerging contaminants.
- It would result in CCLs containing only contaminants that when regulated would reduce disease, disability, and death, and excluding contaminants that have few or no adverse effects on human health (e.g., contaminants removed or detoxified through conventional drinking water treatment methods).

However, EPA's resources are still constrained; no comprehensive list of potential drinking water contaminants yet exists; and health effects, occurrence, and other related data for the vast majority of potential contaminants are poor or nonexistent (NRC, 1999b). Despite these limitations, the committee continues to recommend that EPA develop and use a two-step process for creating future CCLs as illustrated in Figure 1-3. In brief, a broad universe of potential drinking water contami-

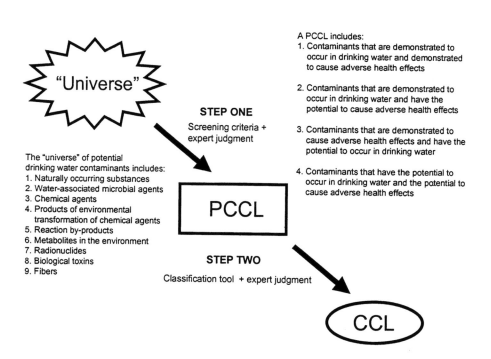

FIGURE 1-3 Recommended two-step process for developing future CCLs.

nants is examined and narrowed to a preliminary CCL using simple screening criteria and expert judgment. All PCCL contaminants are next individually assessed using a "prototype" classification tool in conjunction with expert judgment to create the corresponding (and much smaller) CCL.

The committee also continues to recommend that this two-step process be repeated for each CCL development cycle to account for new data and potential contaminants that inevitably arise over time. In addition, all contaminants that have not been regulated or removed from the existing CCL should be retained automatically on each subsequent CCL. Chapters 3 to 5 of this report provide detailed descriptions, examples, and recommendations for implementing the recommended two-step approach.

PERSPECTIVE OF THIS REPORT

As its previous reports, the promotion of public health remains the guiding principle of the committee's recommendations and conclusions in this report. As in those documents, the committee recognizes that questions of economic impact, required technological shifts, and political orientations and concerns are all related to how safe drinking water is provided and at what cost. However, the committee has adopted an explicitly public health orientation because section 1412(b)(1)(A)(i) of the amended SDWA specifically directs the EPA administrator to identify "contaminants for listing [that], first, may have an adverse effect on the health of persons." Further, section 1412(b)(1)(c) specifies that EPA must focus on contaminants that pose the "greatest health concern." Therefore, in framing this report the committee has chosen to adopt an explicit public health perspective, rather than any of a number of other possible perspectives (e.g., enterprise centered, economic development, legal). The report should be read with this qualification in mind.

2
Sociopolitical Considerations for Developing Future CCLs

INTRODUCTION

In its two previous reports (NRC, 1999a,b), the committee emphasized that the decisions related to the development of a Drinking Water Contaminant Candidate List (CCL), as well as in the prioritization of CCL contaminants for subsequent regulatory or research activities, must be scientifically defensible and transparent. In Chapter 1, the development and implementation status of the first CCL and two related programs are described briefly. This chapter discusses the nature of the perennial task facing the U.S. Environmental Protection Agency (EPA) in developing and implementing a decision-making process for the creation of future CCLs in conjunction with several important social and political issues. More specifically, the interrelated issues of sound science, risk perception, social equity, legal mandates to consider the risks for vulnerable populations, and the proper role of transparency and public participation are discussed. In addition, several potentially helpful conceptual frameworks for risk perception and public participation are described. In so doing, the committee seeks to provide a solid foundation and background support for a systematic, scientifically sound, transparent, and equitable approach to the development of future CCLs, which is fully described later in this report.

LIMITATIONS OF THE FIRST CCL DEVELOPMENT PROCESS

Because of the severe time constraints stipulated by the Safe Drinking Water Act (SDWA) Amendments of 1996 for publication of the first CCL, EPA was forced to develop and utilize a decision-making process for the creation of the 1998 CCL that the committee feels was not sufficiently defensible, transparent, or available for public comment. In particular, several major policy decisions were made during the process that lacked sufficient explanation and justification. By identifying and thoroughly discussing these limitations, the committee aims to illustrate how important it is to arrive at a more systematic CCL development mechanism that directly addresses these and other sociopolitical issues. The committee notes that its second report (NRC, 1999b) also describes (albeit summarily) some limitations of the first CCL development process.

A major policy decision made during the development of the first CCL was to use completely separate approaches to evaluate potential chemical and microbiological drinking water contaminants. The committee believes that the justification given by EPA (EPA, 1997a) for conducting two independent assessments was not adequate and perpetuates the long-established and often unnecessary regulatory practice of treating chemical and microbial drinking water contaminants separately and differently. As reviewed in the committee's first report (NRC, 1999a) and in more detail in Chapter 6 of this report, rather than regulating each type of microorganism to a specific concentration as done for chemicals, regulators historically have established a "zero-tolerance" goal for microbiological contaminants. Indicator organisms, particularly fecal coliforms, are then used to show the possible presence of microbial contamination resulting from human waste. While this approach has served well for indicating widespread sewage contamination of surface waters and for controlling diseases such as cholera and typhoid fever, several deficiencies in this approach have come to light in recent decades. For example, some bacteria and many viruses and protozoa show greater resistance to conventional treatment methods than do fecal coliforms. This approach has also led to a deficiency of occurrence databases for microbial contaminants. The committee continues to believe that the time is rapidly approaching when the same risk assessment principles should be applied to the management of microbial contaminants as are applied to chemical contaminants. Indeed, as described in Chapter 1 and elsewhere in this report, the committee recommends a two-step approach for the development of future CCLs that will similarly assess chemical, microbial, and other types of potential drinking water contaminants.

Second, all potential chemical drinking water contaminants that were considered initially for inclusion on the CCL were taken directly from existing databases and lists of chemicals produced by various regulatory programs within EPA and by stakeholder groups (see Table 1-1; EPA, 1997a). Although this was useful for developing a CCL in a short time period, EPA excluded from consideration several tens of thousands of chemicals that might pose a threat to safe drinking water but have not yet been identified or included on one of the selected lists (NRC, 1999b). For example, the first CCL development process did not evaluate radionuclides or pharmaceuticals. Moreover, reliance on databases created primarily for purposes other than supporting drinking water research and regulatory activities led to the inclusion of chemicals (e.g., acetone) on the draft 1998 CCL that were ultimately determined not to merit such attention and were subsequently dropped. In addition, reliance on these existing lists and databases implies a policy decision to focus the CCL solely on chemicals already identified by EPA programs, increasing the likelihood that a newly emerging chemical threat would be missed by the process unless it caused a major problem.

Although the chemical and microbial contaminants included on the 1998 CCL certainly merit regulatory and research attention, a broader approach to contaminant selection could potentially identify higher-risk contaminants. In short, the committee characterized this overall approach as "looking under the lamp post" for a relatively few types and numbers of drinking water contaminants compared to the universe of potential contaminants (NRC, 1999b; see Chapter 3 for further information).

A third major policy decision was the exclusion of contaminants from further consideration if their occurrence in drinking water was not first determined to be demonstrated or anticipated based on available information (EPA, 1997a). By evaluating occurrence before any evaluation of health effects data, drinking water contaminants with potential adverse health effects would be excluded from the 1998 CCL solely because of missing or inadequate data on occurrence.

Fourth, EPA decided to defer consideration of 23 chemicals and chemical groups for inclusion on the draft 1998 CCL based solely on the possibility of their being endocrine disruptors (EPA, 1997a). The rationale for this policy decision was that these types of chemicals were then under general review by EPA's Endocrine Disruptor Screening and Testing Advisory Committee and another NRC committee. Similarly, a list of 35 pesticides that indicated a high risk of leaching into groundwater but met no other criteria for inclusion on the draft 1998 CCL were also deferred pending further evaluation by EPA's Office of Pesticide Programs for their potential to occur at levels of health concern. Both of these policy decisions imply that research on the health effects of these important chemicals and their occurrence in drinking water could be delayed at least until the development of future CCLs.

Finally, the stipulated size of the CCL reflected an unstated policy decision on the general amount of resources EPA would devote to the regulation of drinking water contaminants. In this regard, a total of 262 chemicals and groups of related chemicals were identified initially for consideration during preparation of the 1998 draft CCL (EPA, 1997a). As noted in the committee's first report (NRC, 1999a) however, EPA made it clear that the total number of contaminants on the draft and final 1998 CCLs would have to be reduced from 262. Ultimately, the final 1998 CCL included a total of 60 individual chemicals, or groups of related chemicals, and microorganisms (EPA, 1998a). Thus, for planning and discussion purposes, the committee has always considered that future CCLs would similarly be limited to no more than 100 or so total contaminants as noted elsewhere in this report. Indeed, the committee feels that EPA's difficulty in developing a highly complex research plan for the 1998 CCL (reviewed in Chapter 1) supports this contention.

The committee also notes that the entire 1998 CCL development process allowed for only limited public participation. As noted in Chapter 1, EPA relied heavily on the advice of the National Drinking Water Advisory Council (NDWAC) Working Group on Occurrence and Contaminant Selection for the development of the approach used to create the draft 1998 CCL. Although NDWAC's meetings are open to the public and include experts from various stakeholder groups, it cannot be considered to represent the broad spectrum of public views on this issue. Thus, for the most part, public input into the development of the 1998 CCL was confined to the two-month public comment period for the draft 1998 CCL.

The committee, several public commenters, and EPA recognized the need for a more systematic, scientifically sound, and transparent process for selecting contaminants for future CCLs (EPA, 1998a,c; NRC 1999a,b). Specific comments indicative of the lack of transparency in the decision-making process for the draft 1998 CCL included calls for clarification of the process as a whole by EPA so that it could be more fully understood (EPA, 1998c). Requests were also made to EPA for explanations and justifications of the screening criteria used to narrow the field of candidate contaminants. Questions were raised as to how these specific criteria were selected, defined, operationalized, and weighted. Several other comments focused specifically on the health effects criteria (e.g., whether carcinogenic effects received priority over other health effects or whether priority was given to contaminants with more complete toxicological data). Some commenters complained of insufficient explanation and justification for the inclusion or exclusion of specific contaminants.

To a large extent, the widespread recognition of these limitations helped lead to the formation of this National Research Council (NRC) committee at the request of EPA to advise it on developing regulatory and research priorities for the 1998 CCL and the creation of subsequent CCLs. Thus, a detailed discussion of these issues provides a necessary and appropriate foundation for much of this report. The committee believes that any proposed CCL classification scheme must directly incorporate the principles of transparency, scientific defensibility, and equity if it is to be successful at the policy level.

USE OF SOUND SCIENCE IN FUTURE REGULATORY DECISIONS

The CCL is intended to be a central element in EPA's future regulatory strategy for its drinking water program. Section 1412(b)(3)(A)(i) of the amended SDWA requires EPA to use the "best available, peer-reviewed science and supporting studies conducted in accordance with sound and objective scientific practices. . .". The use of peer-reviewed science will not, however, guarantee agreement among all parties that might be affected by the listing of a chemical or microorganism on a CCL since scientists often weigh the different strands of evidence and supporting data differently. Indeed, the committee explicitly noted in its preceding report that expert judgment must play a substantial role in the process of developing a CCL (NRC, 1999b). Furthermore, disagreements on some CCL listings are to be expected and do not necessarily indicate that they are unsound. Rather, the soundness of the judgments will have to be decided in the more-or-less usual way of reasoned and supported argument among the contending and interested parties. This question was dealt with in greater detail in the first report of the committee, and its conclusions are repeated here (NRC, 1999a):

> [The committee] takes the position that scientific disagreements are the norm and do not signal a deviation from sound science. These disagreements may be based on values other than strictly scientific ones, however, this does not mean that the sides of the debate are not based on sound science. Indeed, it is not unusual for scientists to disagree on the application of sound science to public policy issues. Any scheme that

affects the provision of public water is likely to engender legitimate scientific disagreement. The report also recognizes that identifying and agreeing on what is sound science is itself a difficult and error-prone enterprise. It therefore makes no recommendations on what "soundness" entails, letting the accepted mechanisms of peer regard, peer review, and scientists' habits of critical thinking continue to serve as the ultimate arbiters.

NATURE OF THE TASK

The daunting task before the EPA and for which the committee is charged to provide advice is how to take a large, unordered set of chemicals, microorganisms, and other potential drinking water contaminants and separate it into two sets:[1] one (the CCL) to receive occurrence monitoring or research of some sort preparatory to an eventual decision to regulate or not and another set that will receive no regulatory or research attention aside from that otherwise dictated by the advancing interests of science and commerce. This sorting of contaminants into two discrete sets based upon available occurrence and health effects attributes gleaned from the scientific literature is a *classification* problem.

More specifically, the committee's objective is to recommend a scientifically sound, transparent, and equitable process that can be used to identify and cull from the universe of potential drinking water contaminants a list (CCL) that contains primarily contaminants for which EPA may justify expending considerable, albeit limited, resources to develop drinking water regulations or to pursue occurrence monitoring or health effects, treatment, or analytical methods research. This is the central idea behind the CCL as required under the SDWA Amendments of 1996. In effect, this means that EPA is probably limited to preparing a CCL that has perhaps up to 100 contaminants and groups of related contaminants on it. This represents a full two-order-of-magnitude reduction from a total universe of potential drinking water contaminants that may number

---

[1] A third set could be considered that includes those drinking water contaminants that are (or can be) determined to present an urgent threat to public health. As noted in Chapter 1, the amended SDWA specifically allows EPA to circumvent the CCL process and issue interim regulations for such contaminants. Thus, they are not included in this discussion and are not a major focus of this report.

in the tens of thousands given the number of chemicals currently in commercial use.[2] As noted in Chapter 1 (see Figure 1-3), the committee has previously suggested (NRC, 1999b) and continues to suggest a preliminary step that reduces the universe of potential contaminants to a smaller list of perhaps a few thousand (the preliminary CCL or PCCL). Before the problem of reducing this list to the CCL can be discussed; however, an overview of the difficulties of conducting even a coarse screen to get to the PCCL is in order.

If one were to assume, as seems plausible, that only a very small proportion of the universe of potential drinking water contaminants are likely to be high-risk contaminants (e.g., of sufficient toxicity and likelihood to become prevalent in drinking water), any screening of this list must be highly accurate with respect to correctly identifying those contaminants that are not a problem. Appendix A of the committee's first report (NRC, 1999a) included a quantitative analysis of this situation, many elements of which are summarized below.

The arithmetic of culling a list containing perhaps tens of thousands of potential drinking water contaminants to a much smaller, but still large, list of "high-risk" contaminants quickly reveals some inherent dilemmas. Assuming one could reduce such a list of contaminants down to a list of a few thousand (the PCCL) with some accuracy (e.g., it would include only chemicals with a genuine potential to occur in drinking water and cause adverse health effects in exposed persons), this judgment must be made with considerable accuracy. If one were to make an error in only one of a hundred contaminants, wrongly believing it has potential for contaminating drinking water or that it has more health significance than it actually does, almost a quarter of the contaminants on a smaller list of around 2,000 (the PCCL) will be "false positives" (one of a hundred contaminants on a list of about 50,000 produces 500 false positives). Thus, a very high level of specificity is necessary to avoid cluttering the PCCL with a high proportion of relatively harmless contaminants. (In this case, a specificity of 99 percent is the proportion of harmless contaminants that are correctly identified as harmless).

On the other hand, the requirement for a relatively high level of specificity runs counter to the usual public health emphasis of acting in a health-protective manner. As stated in both of its previous reports (NRC,

---

[2] The total number of contaminants in this universe could be quite large, based on the European experience (see Appendix A of this report) and given that the Toxic Substances Control Act inventory of commercial chemicals alone includes about 72,000 substances (NRC, 1999b).

1999a,b), the committee continues to recommend that EPA "err on the side of public health protection," opting for high sensitivity in the generation of future CCLs. However, the opposing requirement not to include false positives makes it more likely that certain contaminants that may truly pose a health risk will be passed over as well (i.e., false negatives are left behind while trying to avoid false positives).

Another approach would be to proceed "from the other direction" by starting at the final list (the CCL) and trying to populate it with contaminants already known or reasonably suspected to be problematic on other grounds (e.g., chemicals that already have health advisories or are included on some list of environmental concern). Using this strategy, one would be ignoring the huge bulk of contaminants for which little or no data have been accumulated. To a large extent, the draft 1998 CCL was developed using just such an approach. Yet the unwelcome "surprises" (e.g., methyl-*t*-butyl ether [MTBE]) invariably arise from the large group of contaminants with little or no data. Perhaps an argument could be made that this practice is acceptable since the high-risk characteristics described should receive priority in any regulatory scheme and EPA can circumvent the CCL process to develop interim regulations for any contaminants that are determined to represent an urgent threat to public health (EPA, 1998a). However, it is important to note that one of the goals of the CCL—to avoid such surprises—would be compromised to some extent.

The unpleasant arithmetic properties of screening large numbers of contaminants aside, one must also consider the difficulty of conducting any classification task where imperfect and incomplete data must be used to answer a sophisticated question: in this case, Does a chemical, microbiological, or other type of contaminant pose an existing or future threat to drinking water supplies?

Because of its general importance, the task of classification has been the subject of a great deal of research in recent years (see, for example, Bowker and Star, 1999). One need only consider commonplace examples to see how difficult and complex a task it can be. For example, applications to college are made on a relatively standard data collection format, including readily quantifiable scales such as SAT scores, grade point averages, and demographic data; have little or no missing data; and have sufficient history and numbers to make quantification and statistical investigations with adequate power possible. Despite these strengths, the level of public confidence in the accuracy of the classification procedure (i.e., admit-don't admit) is not high, with an understanding that many worthy applicants will be rejected and some relative failures will be admitted. Perhaps worse, suspicion exists that students are admitted or rejected in a nonrandom fashion although the underlying mechanisms are often hard to discern.

To summarize, the placement of a contaminant first on the PCCL and from there on the CCL involves not one, but several, difficult classification judgments. For example, does the chemical produce a health effect? ("Health effects" is a category.) What are the specific health effects? (Health effects are categorized into different types or diseases that change periodically.) What is the nature of the evidence? (Evidence is placed into several, often overlapping categories such as animal studies, epidemiological studies, and "reliable" studies.) What appears at first to be a "simple" classification exercise quickly reveals itself to be a complex task in which many choices are being made, some explicitly, some as a result of given prior classifications, and some implicitly or without conscious knowledge of the classifiers.

RISK PERCEPTION

The selection of microorganisms, chemicals, and other types of contaminants for inclusion on a CCL will be based on judgments of their potential health risks, including an evaluation of the severity of their effects, their potency, and the likelihood of their occurrence in drinking water. These risk judgments must be made in a context of considerable scientific uncertainty (e.g., due to data gaps and the use of models to estimate potency and environmental fate), complexity (e.g., variability in the vulnerability of subpopulations and the effects of contaminant mixtures), and controversy (e.g., issues concerning acceptable evidence, relevant data, and the fairness and acceptability of risks). Faced with this context, people rely on their assumptions, values, beliefs, and in general, their worldviews, as well as on the information available to them (which to some extent is also dependent on their worldviews) in order to make judgments about risks. Therefore it should not be surprising that people differ in their perceptions of risk and that these disagreements reflect differences in their worldviews.

A worldview can be defined as a deeply held "orienting disposition" toward the world and its social organization that guides a person's perceptions, interpretations, analyses, and responses in a wide variety of complex situations (Peters and Slovic, 1996). An individual's worldview develops from his or her life experiences, social interactions, and education. It includes perceptions of self-identity and local environment (e.g., local hazards, local socioeconomic conditions), political beliefs and moral values, and views and values held by the social groups with which an individual identifies and belongs. The prevailing views of one's discipline, or the values of the institution by which one is employed, may also be incorporated into one's worldview and influence how one perceives risks (see, for example, Barke and Jenkins-Smith, 1993; Kraus et al., 1992; Slovic et al., 1995). Another important aspect of an individual's worldview is the primary reasoning scheme a person uses in complex situations such as those involving the risk perception of an environmental hazard.

Research over the past 30 years has emphasized the differences in risk perception between scientists and "lay people" who are not professionally trained in science (e.g., Sowby, 1965; Starr, 1969). According to this research, scientists tend to adopt a quantitative approach to risk and emphasize considerations such as dose and exposure. On the other hand, lay people generally adopt a more qualitative approach, emphasizing the fairness and voluntary nature of the risk, its effects on future generations, and the characteristics of the risk such as whether it is known, uncontrollable, or capable of producing catastrophic effects (Tesh, 1999). At the aggregate level, surveys have found differences in average risk perception scores when scientists as a group were compared with lay people as a group (Barke and Jenkins-Smith, 1993; Kraus et al., 1992; Slovic et al., 1995). However, these surveys also found a wide spectrum of views on risk perception within each group indicating that at the individual level, the risk perceptions of many scientists and lay people may not differ substantially. For example, it is not unusual that when confronted by complex environmental hazards, lay people often become self-taught, scientific experts who work closely with professional scientists to evaluate the technical aspects of the risks (Brown, 1992, 1997; Tesh, 1999). On the other hand, many scientists have attempted to achieve a balance between quantitative and qualitative approaches to the evaluation of environmental risks. The wide spectrum of views on risk perception found at the individual level among scientists as well as among lay people reflects differences in worldviews within these two heterogeneous groups.

Three schemes of reasoning can be differentiated theoretically and are discussed below to aid understanding of risk perception (although an individual's primary reasoning scheme is likely to be some combination of these) as related to the classification of drinking water contaminants for regulatory consideration. In the "utilitarian" reasoning scheme, each person is assumed to be a self-interested "utility calculator," determining the optimum balance of personal satisfaction from among various options and the information available (Anderson, 1993). At the societal level, the goal is the efficient and optimum distribution of costs and benefits so as to maximize benefits for the majority of society's members. In this scheme, risks would be ranked on a common metric such as expected number of deaths per year, quality adjusted life-years (QALYs), or disability adjusted life-years (DALYs), and this metric would provide the basis for comparisons and cost-benefit trade-offs among risks. This reasoning scheme tends to juxtapose widely different forms of death (e.g., immediate death, death after a long and debilitating illness) as well as voluntary and involuntary risks (Bennett, 1999). It is also generally indifferent to issues of equity or social justice (Morrow and Bryant, 1995). In the context of risk perception, this reasoning scheme tends to assume that some level of risk is necessary for "growth" and therefore attempts to answer in a quantitative, cost-benefit fashion the question: How safe is safe enough? Policies associated with (but not necessarily logically entailed by) this reasoning scheme tend to emphasize managing risks over risk avoidance and avoiding false-positive errors (e.g., ameliorating a risk that later proves harmless) over false-negative errors (e.g., failing to detect an important health hazard).

A second reasoning scheme focuses on the interpretation, elaboration, and assertion of rights (or entitlements to rights) and has been called "liberal rationalism" (Anderson, 1993). Reciprocity (e.g., mutual tolerance, respect, trust, goodwill) is the key value, and social justice is the goal of this approach. In the context of environmental risk, this approach would be concerned with the fair distribution of hazards among social groups and would attempt to answer the following question: How fair is safe enough (Rayner and Cantor, 1987)? In this scheme of reasoning, the "average person" does not exist; instead risks are perceived as varying by social group. Policies addressing societal demands for environmental justice, the protection of vulnerable subpopulations, and the right to tap water that is safe to drink are based on this reasoning scheme.

A third reasoning scheme, called "critical reason," is concerned with "big-picture" issues such as a search for the common good, the essential purposes of policies and activities, and the characteristics of the ideal society (Anderson, 1993). It involves thinking self-consciously about big-picture goals and purposes and integrating the grounds for society's basic values, beliefs, practices, priorities, and institutions with one's own values, beliefs, interests, and activities. In this, ideals such as the goods one should seek, the "good life," social equality, "best practices," and the proper consideration and treatment of humans and the ecosystem are used as evaluative standards. Presupposed by this reasoning scheme is a notion of "deliberative democracy" in which members of an open-minded community of equals are willing to move beyond self-interest and attempt to reach consensus on the general interest and common good (Einsiedel and Eastlick, 2000).

In the context of environmental risk, critical reasoning might ask whether a risk is necessary or justifiable given the kind of society that is desired and whether the decision about the acceptability of the risk was reached through an open and democratic process. For example, regarding the development of drinking water regulations, critical reasoning might ask whether the setting of a maximum contaminant level protects the public from a risk or rather acts to legitimize the risk. Policies emphasizing risk avoidance, toxic chemical use reduction or elimination, concerns for future generations, and concerns for community cohesion and participatory decision-making would be based on this critical reasoning scheme.

As discussed in great detail in Chapter 4, future CCLs will entail the evaluation of contaminant attributes such as the severity of potential health effects, potency (dose-response relationship), occurrence in drinking water, and the likelihood of resulting exposures. Each of the three reasoning schemes would approach the evaluation of these attributes differently. For example, a utilitarian approach to the severity of a contaminant's potential health effects might focus on effects that are easily measurable such as deaths, injuries, or monetary damages in order to rank contaminants in a simple, direct fashion. Although such an approach has the appearance of "neutrality," hidden assumptions and values concerning which health effects are considered more or less severe are inherent in the choice of the metric. For example, embedded in the choice of metric might be a bias for ranking prevalent diseases over rare diseases, cancers over birth defects, chronic over acute diseases, and so forth. Because these values and biases are implicit, they are not likely to be discussed.

A liberal rationalism approach might address the issue of severity by comparing hazards in terms of the effects they have on the most susceptible groups. Alternatively, the potential health effects occurring in one vulnerable population (e.g., infants) might take precedence over the effects occurring in all other subpopulations. Here the values and biases would be out in the open and could be debated more easily.

A critical reasoning approach might explore what it is about certain health effects that makes them perceived to be more severe than others. For example, what is it about cancers that usually makes them appear more severe than other health effects such as mood changes, depression, infertility, and developmental disorders? The goals would be to facilitate deliberation on the hidden, taken-for-granted values embedded in society's concept of severity and to reach consensus on a concept of severity that would lead to improvements in disease prevention, protection of future generations, and protection of the ecosystem. The critical reasoning approach might also explore how the severity of an effect changes when one moves from an individual to a societal perspective. Finally, such an approach might eschew the ranking of effects by severity altogether and take the position that any hazard that is known or suspected to cause an adverse effect in humans should be minimized or eliminated.

PROTECTION OF VULNERABLE SUBPOPULATIONS

Section 1412(b)(1)(c) of the SDWA Amendments of 1996 specifically requires EPA to give priority to selecting contaminants for inclusion on future CCLs that present the greatest public health concern, taking into consideration ". . . the effect of such contaminants upon subgroups that comprise a meaningful portion of the general population (such as infants, children, pregnant women, the elderly, individuals with a history of serious illness, or other subpopulations) that are identifiable as being at greater risk of adverse health effects due to exposure to contaminants in drinking water than the general population." In short, EPA must act protectively to ensure that vulnerable subpopulations receive safe drinking water. In this way, the goal of providing safe drinking water to all consumers can be achieved.

The committee recommends that the list of vulnerable subpopulations described in the amended SDWA should not be seen as a minimum list, but rather as several examples of possible vulnerable subpopulations. A minimum list must go much further than this. In this regard, EPA should consider including other subpopulations that are potentially vulnerable, such as all women of childbearing age, fetuses, the immunocompromised, people whose genetic disposition makes them more vulnerable to drinking water contaminants, people who are exceptionally sensitive to an array of chemical contaminants, people with specific medical conditions that make them more susceptible, and people with poor nutrition. As scientific knowledge about the determinants of susceptibility expands, our ability to identify vulnerable subpopulations will improve.

It should also be recognized that all people experience changes in susceptibility and risk over time. For example, fetuses and the elderly are recognized as exceptionally susceptible to a variety of chemicals and microorganisms. All people experience hormonal changes during puberty that may lead to increased susceptibility to certain chemicals (Golub, 2000). Most women bear children at some point in their lives, and pregnancy is a time of exceptional sensitivity to a wide variety of environmental contaminants (Selevan et al., 2000). As our population ages and medical science becomes increasingly more able to treat diseases that were once fatal, the proportion of people who are especially susceptible to chemical and microbial exposures continues to grow. For example, the most rapidly growing demographic group in the United States is individuals over age 85 (FIFARS, 2000). Individuals with AIDS, diabetes, and severe heart disease are now living many years longer than in the past. Formerly incurable malignancies are now treatable, although with medical approaches that often suppress immunity and thus render individuals more susceptible to environmental contaminants. For these and similar reasons, it should be understood that the legal mandate to protect vulnerable subpopulations is not a mandate to provide special protection to specific groups, but rather a directive to provide the broadest public health protection to society as a whole.

The need to protect vulnerable subpopulations is not only legally mandated by the amended SDWA, but also justified on equity and environmental justice grounds. Subpopulations experiencing socioeconomic hardships and racial or ethnic discrimination tend in general to have poorer health and poor access to adequate health care—factors that can make them more susceptible to drinking water contaminants (Brown et al., 2000; IOM, 1999). In addition, conditions that can make a person more susceptible to drinking water contaminants, such as HIV infection, are also more prevalent in these subpopulations. Finally, many of these subpopulations live in areas that might be at higher risk of exposure to toxic chemicals through air, soil, and drinking water. For example, in the southern portion of the United States, a large proportion of the populations experiencing socioeconomic hardships and racial or ethnic discrimination lives in rural areas served by small water utilities. In general, small water utilities tend to violate the provisions of the SDWA more often than large systems and are less stringently regulated than the large systems (EPA, 1999b). In addition, many of the toxic waste sites in the South are located in rural areas and could pose a threat to the groundwater supplies used by small water utilities (Bullard, 1994).

The mandate to protect vulnerable subpopulations has implications for the evaluation of chemical and microbial contaminant attributes such as the severity of their potential health effects and their occurrence in drinking water (see Chapter 4). For example, severity would not be assessed solely by its prevalence in the general population or by its effect on the "average person," but would also be judged by its prevalence in vulnerable subpopulations. In the evaluation of occurrence, the frequency of detection in space and time may be less important than the locations at which a contaminant is detected (e.g., rural areas, American Indian reservations).

At a recent expert workshop focused on susceptibility in microbial pathogen risk assessment (Balbus et al., 2000), consensus was achieved on the need to better define the agents and health outcomes associated with "susceptibility." Some particularly relevant questions raised and discussed included the following:

• Are there specific characteristics of a pathogen that make it more or less hazardous?

• What health effects should be considered as outcomes? Should only adverse health effects be considered?

• Should a change in an individual's immune state always be considered a positive outcome or should it also be viewed as "adverse" if it places people at risk for later, more serious and/or chronic health effects? When microbial pathogens are the concern, should immunity be considered a lifelong or a temporary state?

• Should susceptibility be treated as a dichotomous or a continuous variable (e.g., susceptible or not versus an individual's probability of response)? Should susceptibility be framed as the population's distribution of individual probabilities of a specific response to a specific agent?

• Should a "susceptible subpopulation" be considered to include people at the upper end of the population's probability distribution (e.g., 95th or 99th percentile) of response to pathogens or all people above the population's average response (i.e., greater than 50 percent likelihood of response)?

Workshop participants concluded that these and other issues must be addressed on a pathogen-specific basis.

Therefore, the concepts and values that underlie the meaning of "susceptibility" have to be clarified before such groups can be appropriately identified and protected (Parkin et al., 2000). As noted above, susceptibility can be defined either on the individual or the population scale. Thus, an updated working consensus of "susceptible" will be needed to identify and protect vulnerable subpopulations in accordance with the amended SDWA and in the creation of future CCLs. Without this clarification, different stakeholders are likely to approach the term with different conceptual frameworks regarding their perceptions of risk. As a consequence, they may have conflicting but unrecognized differences about what persons and groups should be considered eligible for inclusion in such subpopulations. For example, are susceptible people those who are at elevated risk because of exposure or because of an inherent, nonmodifiable trait? Are risk and susceptibility conceived as related primarily to a contaminant's inherent characteristics (e.g., chemical structure or virulence of a waterborne pathogen), the host's immune status, or some characteristic of the subpopulation itself? Until such issues are resolved, any one definition of susceptible is likely to have important public policy consequences because it may not necessarily address all people who need to be protected from the adverse health events associated with all contaminants.

However, the committee emphasizes that none of these questions or the important issue of what "meaningful portion of the general population" actually means under the amended SDWA can be answered based solely on scientific findings. Rather, the answers will depend in part on societal values and on viable, democratic means of resolution. In this regard, the resulting deliberative process may require several iterations before a working consensus emerges (Franz and Jin, 1995; Malone, 1994). Strong and widespread social support will be important in implementing effective programs to ensure safe drinking water for vulnerable subpopulations.

TRANSPARENCY AND PUBLIC PARTICIPATION

Increasing public concern and activism on environmental issues have resulted in demands that federal, state, and local regulatory and enforcement policies be made more transparent and incorporate public participation. For example, one of the key demands of environmental justice advocates is "the right to participate as equal partners at every level of decision-making including needs assessment, planning, implementation, enforcement and evaluation." (Gibbs and CCHW, 1995) To respond adequately to such legitimate demands, the decision-making process for developing future CCLs should include an oversight mechanism to allow public participation in all aspects of its design, development, and implementation. The process would also have to be transparent (i.e., ". . . easily understood, where information about the policy is available, where accountability is clear, and where citizens know what role they play in the implementation of the policy"; Finkelstein, 2000)

Transparency

Fundamental to the notion of transparency are the principles of equity, fairness, and democracy. The transparency of a decision-making process may help to ensure that resulting decisions are not perceived as having been made capriciously or "behind closed doors." Yet how can the transparency of a policy or decision-making process be evaluated when there is no consensus standard to measure it? To this end, the committee recommends a recently proposed information communication standard for risk assessment that could have broader applicability as a general standard for transparency in decision-making. This standard can be summarized as providing sufficient information on the decision-making process such that citizens are allowed ". . . the opportunity to place themselves in a similar position as the [decision-maker]. . . to make as informed a choice . . . as if they themselves had gone through the [decision-making] process . . ." (Hattis and Anderson, 1999). In other words, one of EPA's major goals in developing future CCLs should be to explain the process sufficiently so that with the information supplied an informed citizen could arrive at their own reasonable and informed judgments. To meet such a standard would require that transparency be incorporated into the design and development of the decision-making process (and any models used in the process) in addition to being an integral component in communicating the details of the decision-making process to the public.

The issue and importance of transparency were raised at a November 1999 stakeholder meeting to discuss the implementation status of the 1998 CCL. Notably, EPA pledged that it would produce as part of the forthcoming CCL regulatory determination process a detailed support document that would describe comprehensively the rationale for all decisions to regulate (or not) CCL contaminants and provide a review of all the data used to support such decisions (Michael Osinski, EPA, personal communication, 2000).

EPA has previously attempted to address the issue of transparency in its *Guidance for Risk Characterization* (EPA, 1995). In an accompanying memo, the former EPA administrator noted that stakeholders in environmental issues desire sufficient information to allow independent assessments and judgments about the significance of environmental risks and the reasonableness of EPA's corresponding risk reduction actions. The administrator stated that "we must adopt as values transparency in our decision-making process and clarity in communication with each other and the public regarding environmental risk and the uncertainties associated with our assessments of environmental risk." This entails a full and open characterization of risks. The EPA administrator added that by doing so, EPA would have to disclose the key scientific analyses and policy choices, uncertainties, and core assumptions that underlie its decisions.

Furthermore, the guidelines state that achieving transparency in risk characterization would require a frank and open discussion of the uncertainty associated with an assessment as a whole and its components along with the impacts of key factors or variables on the overall decision-making process (EPA, 1995). They acknowledge that information from different sources carries different kinds of uncertainty and that understanding these differences is important when uncertainties are combined. The guidelines reassure risk assessors and managers that a frank and comprehensive discussion of uncertainties and their impacts on the decision-making process would not necessarily reduce the public's perceived validity of the process, but instead would likely enhance public trust and serve as a useful indicator of the confidence decision-makers had in the process itself and in resulting decisions. Although not mentioned in the guidelines, an added benefit of such a discussion of uncertainties is that "it helps the [decision-maker] function more honestly in a context that may often exert pressures for more unambiguous answers than can readily be produced" (Hattis and Anderson, 1999).

A recent evaluation of the use of models in an environmental assessment effort called the "ULYSSES Project" in Europe has similarly reported that a full discussion of uncertainties could promote public trust and enhance the credibility of the assessment (Dahinden et al., 1999). However, the authors warned that a full discussion of uncertainties could also produce public doubts and skepticism about the results of the assessment. In this regard, Yearley (1999) and Lopez and Gonzalez (1996) found that how the public receives a presentation of uncertainties is most influenced by its existing "lay knowledge" of a particular issue, its history of experience and participation with a related regulatory agency, and the resulting accumulation (or deterioration) of trust and credibility concerning the agency's agenda, policies, and decisions.

An important question for EPA in developing future CCLs is, How much information should be provided to the public in order to effectively characterize the uncertainties in the decision-making process? The 1996 NRC report *Understanding Risk: Informing Decisions in a Democratic Society* warns that "simple characterizations are likely to give an erroneous impression of the extent of uncertainty, but more careful and elaborate characterizations may be incomprehensible to nonspecialists . . . ". Thus, the goal would be to characterize the uncertainties in such a way that citizens would understand the level of uncertainty in the process and ". . . appreciate where scientists agree and where they disagree." In this regard, the committee again maintains that such disagreements are normal and expected and do not necessarily signal a deviation from the application of sound science.

As discussed later in greater detail (Chapters 3 to 5), this report recommends and outlines a type of triage approach to move forward from a universe of potential drinking water contaminants to arrive ultimately at a much shorter list (the CCL) that will largely form the basis of EPA's future drinking water program. A major aspect of this triage approach will involve the development and use of a "prototype" classification tool that may have a similar degree of complexity and uncertainty as models that have previously been utilized for the purposes of environmental risk assessment (e.g., those employed in the ULYSSES Project). Therefore, the committee believes that in the implementation of this recommended approach, EPA will have to deal with the same issues of transparency and the full discussion of uncertainties that have emerged from the use of these environmental risk assessment models.

The proposed classification tool is similar in concept to those already used in medicine for clinical diagnoses of a wide variety of illnesses from appendicitis to myocardial infarction (Baxt, 1995). Classification models have also been used successfully in marketing and financial contexts to sort people into various consumer niches or credit risk groups; in security contexts for fingerprint, speech, and face recognition; and in weather forecasting. Although the recommended classification model approach is innovative and indicates a willingness to adopt techniques successfully employed elsewhere, the committee cautions that it may run the risk of being viewed by the public in a "conspiratorial" fashion. For example, the public may wonder whether such a modeling approach is merely "a vehicle to prove what we think we already know" or whether it represents "an honest attempt to find answers that are not predetermined" (Oreskes, 1998). In addition, the public could perceive the process as subject to manipulation to achieve or support results wanted in the first place. Finally, the process could be perceived as simply a means to remove accountability from decision-makers by placing it on an "objective" modeling process (Yearley, 1999).

As noted previously, to gain widespread credibility and acceptance, the CCL decision-making process must be transparent. It is important to note, however, that transparency is not necessarily synonymous with simplicity. A process that appears on the surface to be simple and easy to understand may in fact be riddled with hidden assumptions. In contrast, it is possible for a CCL decision-making process that involves complex classification modeling to be made relatively transparent. This will require that transparency be integral to its design, and EPA must be ready and able to support each step in the process as if the process itself were on trial.

First, the use of a classification tool needs justification. The successful experience of using such tools in other contexts and applications would help make the case for its use in sorting various potential drinking water contaminants. In addition, referring to the use of the tool in contexts that are familiar in the day-to-day experience of the public (e.g., marketing and credit profiling) could enhance public understanding of the process (Dahinden et al., 1999).

Second, the methodology for designing and calibrating the decision-making process must be defended. This important issue and related considerations are discussed in depth in Chapter 5. To this end, the committee recommends that EPA make clear that the design of the process was in part based on a "retrospective" approach whereby EPA starts with a scenario it wants to end up with (e.g., a scenario that builds on past correct EPA decisions to regulate or not to regulate certain chemicals) and then calibrates the model based on this scenario. The results of citizen focus groups conducted in Europe (for the ULYSSES Project) indicated that this retrospective type of approach to model development would be acceptable to the public (Dahinden et al., 1999). However, the choice of a scenario upon which to calibrate the model may not be a trivial, noncontroversial one and therefore may have to be vigorously defended. In addition, disputes may occur (e.g., among decision-makers and between decision-makers and the public) regarding the issue of what minimum levels of sensitivity and specificity the model must have in order to be judged "adequate." Some justification must also be made for the selection of the key parameters of the model (i.e., measures or attributes of potential health effects and occurrence), as well as a discussion of the magnitude of the effect each chosen parameter has on the model's results and the quality of data for each parameter (e.g., uncertainties, data gaps, timeliness of the data). The choice of parameters must not be based simply on the fact that quantitative data are available for them, in other words: "There is a human tendency to count what is easy to count, and then, as a kind of 'doublethink,' to mistake what is counted for what counts" (Hattis and Anderson, 1999).

Third, if decision-making for including or excluding certain contaminants on future CCLs will ultimately depend on a combination of EPA judgment and the results of a classification tool (as recommended in this report), then this relationship must be fully articulated along with the background assumptions underlying agency judgments. Furthermore, EPA will have to justify how the consistency and explicitness of its decisions can be maintained in these situations. Other related issues, such as to what extent political (including budgetary) contingencies will affect EPA's decisions in conjunction with scientific and efficiency considerations (e.g., regarding the size of future CCLs), will also have to be fully aired.

Fourth, it can be expected that some decisions to include or exclude specific contaminants from the CCL will be controversial. For example, EPA received and responded on a contaminant-by-contaminant basis to public comments that opposed the inclusion of several contaminants and groups of related contaminants (e.g., aluminum, organotins) on the draft 1998 CCL (EPA, 1998a,c). Thus, to help ensure transparency and legitimacy in the development of future CCLs, any key criteria, data, or assumptions that ultimately made the difference between inclusion or exclusion in such cases must be clearly identified and carefully justified.

Although a classification model approach is recommended for the creation of future CCLs, the committee notes it may also be worthwhile to use the tool to aid thinking on the issue of contaminant selection for regulation and research. For example, if the use of the tool produces unexpected results, it will force decision-makers to review the assumptions, parameter choices, and uncertainties incorporated in the model as well as how the tool works (Ravetz, 1999). Conducting a review of this kind might advance knowledge on the science of decision-making as well as the science involved in the regulation of drinking water contaminants. In addition, if such a review were discussed fully in a public forum, the transparency of the model would also be enhanced (i.e., it would look less like a "black box" mysteriously churning out results).

Two additional ways to enhance the transparency of the classification model would be (1) to remove or add parameters to determine how the selection of contaminants changes (a discussion of such results would also serve to improve the transparency of the process) and (2) to make the software and databases used to design, develop, and implement the model available to the public so that citizens can attempt to go through or recreate the process themselves. However, the committee realizes that the latter may be impractical.

To conclude this discussion, Hattis and Anderson (1999) provide an appropriate quote summarizing the importance of transparency in decision-making:

> . . . We quantifiers will only succeed in being helpful to democratic decision-making if our work is designed and presented in such a way that it helps affirm, rather than supplant, the decision-making autonomy of our audience.

Public Participation

"Public participation encompasses a group of procedures designed to consult, involve, and inform the public to allow those affected by a decision to have an input into that decision" (Rowe and Frewer, 2000). Furthermore, Renn and colleagues (1993) noted that the central tenet of public participation is that the public is, in principle, capable of making wise and prudent decisions.

The 1996 NRC report *Understanding Risk: Informing Decisions in a Democratic Society* adopts this central tenet and is critical of agencies that rely on a "decide-announce-defend" strategy that involves the public only after the deliberation process is over (NRC, 1996). However, the report uses the term "deliberation" rather than "participation" to emphasize the need for substantive public involvement throughout the decision-making process (Chess, 2000; NRC 1996). The report discusses at length the importance of "getting the right participation" (i.e., sufficiently broad participation that includes the range of interested and affected parties) and "getting the participation right" (e.g., incorporating public values, viewpoints, and preferences into the process).

Public participation procedures vary from one-way flows of information (e.g., surveys, focus groups, public comment), where the aim is to elicit public opinions, to collaborative forms of decision-making such as negotiated rule making (Fiorino, 1990; Laird, 1993), consensus conferences (Einsiedel and Eastlick, 2000), citizen juries (Lenaghan et al., 1996), and citizen panels (Renn et al., 1993), where the aim is to elicit decisions and judgments that will form the basis for actual policies (Beierle, 1998). A brief description of several public participation procedures and evaluative criteria to assess their strengths and weaknesses has been proposed by Rowe and Frewer (2000). Not surprisingly, there is no procedure that is preferred in all situations (NRC, 1996). However, an effective public participation procedure might entail a hybrid or combination of procedures such as the three-step procedure proposed by Renn et al. (1993). This approach attempts to integrate (1) technical expertise, (2) values and concerns of stakeholders, and (3) common sense and personal experience of the general public to balance the legitimate demand for public participation with the needs for a scientifically sound policy and agency accountability.

In a given situation, the most effective procedure will depend, among other factors, on the aims and rationale for participation. Regarding the development of future CCLs, at least three rationales can be used to justify increased public participation: political, normative, and epistemic (Perhac, 1998). Each rationale leads to a different definition of who should participate on behalf of the "public," and this in turn affects the choice of participation procedure.

The political rationale is that public participation enhances the political viability, legitimacy, and transparency of the process as well as the credibility of the regulators. It is the recognition that even the most scientifically sound process will be difficult to implement if it is perceived by the public as unfair or biased. Using this rationale, the "public" would be defined as those people whose acceptance is crucial for the viability and legitimacy of the process, such as representatives of specific stakeholder groups. For example, negotiated rule making is a public participation procedure that corresponds to this definition of public.

The normative rationale appeals to democratic principles and holds that the public has a right of involvement since it is the "owner" of publicly funded regulatory policies and the most appropriate source of the value judgments that are necessary in any decision-making process. This rationale assumes that all are affected by regulatory policies and therefore all have the right to participate, not just representatives of stakeholder groups. Under this rationale, a public participation procedure should ensure that all citizens' values and preferences are fairly represented—regardless of whether these citizens are organized—and that the output of the procedure (e.g., decisions or recommendations) has a genuine impact on policy. Public participation procedures that follow from this rationale would include referenda, public opinion surveys, focus groups, consensus conferences, and citizen juries.

Lastly, the epistemic rationale recognizes that the public possesses important factual knowledge (e.g., local knowledge) as well as special insight on societal values and therefore public participation will result in better decisions. Under this rationale, the "public" might be defined as those people who possess special insight on values or unique factual knowledge that is relevant to a given decision-making process. A procedure that follows from this definition of the public would be citizen advisory committees.

General recommendations to facilitate public participation in environmental programs are provided in *The Model Plan for Public Participation,* developed for the EPA by the Public Participation and Accountability Subcommittee of the National Environmental Justice Advisory Council (EPA, 1996c). Hampton (1999) provides recommendations to ensure that public participation procedures satisfy the criteria of equity, fairness, and justice. Among these are the following:

- The public should be involved in defining the process of participation.
- Public involvement should start early in the process (e.g., at the time of agenda setting or when value judgments become important to the process).
- Participants should have access to appropriate resources such as the information necessary to participate fully in the process, access to scientists, technical assistance, and sufficient time to prepare for the deliberations.
- Prior agreement should be reached with the participants as to how the output of the procedure (e.g., recommendations, decisions) will be used and how it will affect agency policy decisions.

The NRC Committee on Risk Characterization concluded in its 1996 report, *Understanding Risk: Informing Decisions in a Democratic Society*, that it was not possible to predict which public participation procedure would work most effectively in any given situation, and this committee concurs. Each procedure has its advantages and limitations, but a successful outcome will usually depend less on the inherent aspects of a procedure and more on other factors such as the history of an issue, the level of conflict, the level of public trust in the agency, the agency's intentions and expectations for the selected procedure, and how well the agency implements the procedure (Chess, 2000; NRC, 1996).

SUMMARY: CONCLUSIONS AND RECOMMENDATIONS

The committee recognizes that the development of a PCCL from the universe of potential drinking water contaminants, as well as a contaminant's movement from a PCCL to the corresponding CCL, is a complex task requiring numerous difficult classification judgments in a context where data are often uncertain or missing. The evaluation of contaminant attributes, such as severity of health effects, potency, and occurrence in drinking water (see Chapter 4), will often entail making assumptions because of data gaps and uncertainties. Moreover, evaluation of the severity of health effect and making comparisons of severity among different health effects (e.g., cancers versus impotence) will depend on explicit and implicit value judgments as well as on the choice of reasoning scheme (e.g., utilitarian, quantitative). Because of this complexity, the committee believes that to be scientifically sound as well as publicly acceptable, the process for developing future CCLs must depart considerably from the process used to develop the first (1998) CCL. The committee recommends that the process for selecting contaminants for future CCLs be systematic, scientifically sound, and transparent. The development and implementation of the process should involve sufficiently broad public participation. The ultimate goal of the contaminant selection process is the protection of public health through the provision of safe drinking water to all consumers. To meet this goal, the selection process must place high priority on the protection of vulnerable subpopulations.

More specifically, the committee makes the following recommendations:

• The definition of vulnerable subpopulations not only should comply with the amended language of the SDWA, but also should be sufficiently broad to protect public health; in particular, EPA should consider including (in addition to those subgroups mentioned as examples in the amended SDWA) all women of childbearing age, fetuses, the immuno-compromised, people with an acquired or inherited genetic disposition that makes them more vulnerable to drinking water contaminants, people who are exceptionally sensitive to an array of chemical contaminants, people with specific medical conditions that make them more susceptible, people with poor nutrition, and people experiencing socioeconomic hardships and racial or ethnic discrimination.

- Transparency should be incorporated into the design and development of the classification and decision-making process for future CCLs in addition to being an integral component in communicating the details of the process to the public. Otherwise, the public may perceive the process as subject to manipulation to achieve or support desired results. Therefore, sufficient information should be provided such that citizens can place themselves in a position similar to decision-makers and arrive at their own reasonable and informed judgments. This may require making available to the public the software and databases used in the process.

- The central tenet that the public is, in principle, capable of making wise and prudent decisions should be recognized and reflected in the choice of public participation procedures used to help create future CCLs. A "decide-announce-defend" strategy that involves the public only after the deliberation process is over is not acceptable. Substantive public involvement should occur throughout the design and implementation of the process. EPA should strive to "get the right participation" (i.e., sufficiently broad participation that includes the range of interested and affected parties) as well as to "get the participation right" (e.g., incorporating public values, viewpoints, and preferences into the process).

3

The Universe of Potential Contaminants to the Preliminary CCL

INTRODUCTION

As noted in Chapter 1, the Safe Drinking Water Act (SDWA) Amendments of 1996 require the U.S. Environmental Protection Agency (EPA) to periodically publish a list (the Drinking Water Contaminant Candidate List [CCL]) of unregulated contaminants and contaminant groups that are known or anticipated to occur in public water systems and which may require regulation (EPA, 1998b). The CCL is intended primarily to provide the basis for a mandated EPA decision whether to regulate or not at least five new (CCL) contaminants every five years (see Figure 1-1). More generally, each successive CCL is intended to be the source of priority contaminants for the agency's drinking water program as a whole, including research, monitoring, and guidance development. The first CCL, published in March 1998, was created under very pressing time restraints by EPA with significant input from the National Drinking Water Advisory Council (NDWAC) Working Group on Occurrence and Contaminant Selection. The limitations associated with its rapid development were summarized in the committee's second report (NRC, 1999b) and are described more fully in Chapter 2 of this report. To a large extent, it was the internal and external recognition of these limitations and the corresponding call for a more systematic, scientifically defensible, and transparent approach to the creation of future CCLs that led EPA to request the formation of this National Research Council (NRC) committee.

TWO-STEP APPROACH

In its second report (NRC, 1999b), the committee proposed a conceptual two-step process (see Figure 1-3) for the creation of future CCLs that would take a much broader approach to contaminant selection than that used to create the 1998 CCL and, thus, would have a better potential to identify high-risk contaminants. At EPA's request, the committee evaluated, expanded, and revised as necessary the conceptual approach and related conclusions and recommendations from its second report to form the majority of this report. Therefore, it is important to note that although the basic concept for the CCL development approach has not changed, many of the associated guidelines and recommendations for its design and implementation have necessarily been revised and expanded in accordance with this second phase of committee deliberations. The committee continues to recognize, however, that the need for policy judgments by EPA cannot and should not be removed from any CCL development process. Furthermore, in making decisions regarding the placement of a contaminant on a preliminary CCL (PCCL) or CCL, EPA should use common sense as a guide and err on the side of public health protection.

This chapter provides some initial guidance and recommendations for conducting the first step of the CCL development process. Consistent with the inclusive nature of the recommended process, the first step is to consider a broad universe of chemical, microbial, and other types of potential drinking water contaminants and contaminant groups. The total number of contaminants in this universe is likely to be on the order of tens of thousands of substances and microorganisms, given that the Toxic Substances Control Act inventory of commercial chemicals alone includes about 72,000 substances (NRC, 1999b). It is from this universe that contaminants will be selected first for inclusion on a PCCL—which may include a few thousand contaminants—and then on a corresponding CCL. Thus, the creation of a PCCL from the universe would entail an almost two-order-of-magnitude reduction of potential drinking water contaminants. The inherent difficulties associated with such a task are discussed in Chapter 2.

As noted earlier, the recommendation that EPA begin by identifying and assessing the universe of potential drinking water contaminants to arrive at a PCCL represents a dramatically larger set of substances to be considered initially in terms of types and numbers of contaminants than that used for creation of the 1998 CCL. Because of the proposed size of this universe, well-conceived screening criteria must be developed that can be rapidly and routinely applied in conjunction with expert judgment to cull the universe of contaminants to a much smaller PCCL. Thus, the PCCL may be thought of as a much more manageable and less conceptual list than the universe of potential contaminants. As such, a PCCL should contain individual substances and groups of related substances, including microorganisms, that merit further consideration for inclusion on the CCL. However, the committee continues to recommend that the preparation of a PCCL should not involve extensive analysis of data, nor should it directly drive EPA's research or monitoring activities (NRC, 1999b).

THE UNIVERSE OF POTENTIAL
DRINKING WATER CONTAMINANTS

Recognizing that no single comprehensive list of potential drinking water contaminants exists, the committee previously identified nine major categories (with twelve subcategories) of individual and related groups of substances and microorganisms that comprise the universe of potential drinking water contaminants (NRC, 1999b).[1] These are listed in Table 3-1, along with examples of each category or subcategory. It is important to recognize that many contaminants (including the examples provided) could belong to more than one of these categories.

The committee continues to recommend that EPA begin identifying the universe of potential contaminants by considering the categories and subcategories of potentialcontaminants listed in Table 3-1. Furthermore, EPA should start this task by relying on databases and lists that are currently available (see Tables 3-2 and 3-3 for chemicals and Table 3-4 for microorganisms) and under development along with readily available information to supplement them. However, while relevant databases and lists exist for many of these categories of potential drinking water contaminants, many have no lists or databases (e.g., products of environmental degradation). Thus, EPA should develop a strategy for filling the gaps and updating the existing databases and lists of contaminants (e.g., through involvement of the NDWAC or panels of experts) for future CCLs. This strategy should be developed with public, stakeholder, and scientific community input. In addition, to generally assist in identifying

---

[1]According to SDWA Section 1401(6), "The term 'contaminant' refers to any physical, chemical, biological, or radiological substance in water." This definition has not been revised since the inception of the SDWA in 1974 and, thus, includes nontoxic and potentially beneficial "contaminants."

TABLE 3-1 Universe of Potential Drinking Water Contaminants

Category	Examples[a]
Naturally occurring substances	Nitrates, humic acid, terpines, arsenic, lead, radon
Microbial agents	
Naturally occurring agents in water	*Legionella*, toxic algae
Agents associated with human feces	Enteric viruses, coxsackie B viruses, rotavirus
Agents associated with human and animal feces	Enteric protozoa and bacteria, *Cryptosporidium*, *Salmonella*
Agents associated with human and animal urine	Nanobacteria, microsporidia
Agents associated with water treatment and distribution systems	Biofilms, *Mycobacterium*
Chemical agents	
Commercial chemicals	Gasoline and additives, chlorinated solvents, trichloroethylene, 1,4-dioxane, cumene
Pesticides	Atrazine, malathion
Pharmaceuticals	Diclofenac (anti-inflammatory), acetaminophen (analgesic), ethynllestradiol (estrogen)
Cosmetics	Stearates, glycols
Food additives	Butylated hydroxyanisole, propylene glycol, dyes
Water additives, including impurities	Aluminum
Water treatment and distribution system leachates and degradates	Vinyl chloride, chloroform
Products of environmental transformation of chemical agents	Dichlorodiphenyldichloroethylene, trichloroacetic acid
Reaction and combustion byproducts	Anthracene, benzopyrene, 2,3,7,8-tetrachlorodibenzodioxin,
Metabolites in the environment	Methylmercury, dimethylarsenic, dibutyltin,
Radionuclides	Radon, iodine-131, strontium-90
Biological toxins	Endotoxin, aflatoxin
Fibers	Asbestos

[a] Some examples can belong to more than one category of contaminants (e.g., enteric viruses might also be associated with animal feces).
SOURCE: Adapted from NRC, 1999b.

TABLE 3-2 Examples of Existing and Planned Information Sources for Chemicals Demonstrated or Having the Potential to Cause Adverse Health Effects[a]

Name	Responsible Agency or Organization	Notes
Endocrine Disruptor Priority-Setting Database	EPA	Health effects data on endocrine disruption collected from a variety of databases
Everything added to Food in the United States Database	U.S. Food and Drug Administration (FDA)	Toxicologic information on 2,000 substances added to food
Hazardous Substances Data Base	National Library of Medicine (NLM)	Summary of peer-reviewed health effect studies (about 2,000)
Integrated Risk Information System	EPA	Official EPA summary of health effects information and reference doses or concentrations for approximately 600 compounds
International Agency for Research on Cancer (IARC)	IARC	Expert group summaries of carcinogenic properties for a wide variety of substances and mixtures
MEDLINE	NLM	Abstracts of peer-reviewed studies in medical literature
National Research Council	NRC	Expert group publications summarizing health effects information, critical end points, and doses (e.g., arsenic, radon)
Peer-reviewed published literature		Individual studies about health effects and related information (e.g., metabolism)
Registry of Toxic Effects of Chemical Substances	National Institute for Occupational Safety and Health	Tabulation of effect levels for many substances reported in scientific literature

continues

TABLE 3-2 Continued

Name	Responsible Agency or Organization	Notes
Toxic Substances Control Act Test Submissions— Health Effects	EPA	Information on unpublished health effects data for industrial chemicals
TOXLINE	NLM	Abstracts of peer-reviewed toxicology-related studies

[a] Includes acute and chronic health effects, such as genotoxicity, developmental toxicity, reproductive toxicity, immunotoxicity, and carcinogenicity.
SOURCE: Adapted from EDSTAC, 1999; NRC, 1999b.

the universe of potential contaminants and a PCCL, the committee recommends that EPA consider adding substances based on their commercial use, environmental location, or chemical characteristics as listed in Table 3-5.

As an integral part of the developing future CCLs, the committee continues to recommend (NRC, 1999b) that the information used from any such lists be combined in a consolidated database to provide a consistent mechanism for recording and retrieving information on the contaminants under consideration. The database should be designed to accommodate a wide variety of chemicals, microorganisms, mixtures of agents, and other types of potential contaminants that are not necessarily defined by a unique chemical formula.

Thus, the database could function as a "master list" that contains a detailed record of how the universe of potential contaminants was identified and how a particular PCCL and its corresponding CCL were subsequently selected. The design, creation, and implementation of such a database should be made in open cooperation with the public, stakeholders, and the scientific community, the importance of which is discussed in Chapter 2.

Notably, this recommendation is similar to a recommendation from EPA's Endocrine Disruptor Screening and Testing Advisory Committee (EDSTAC) for the development of a database for setting priorities for screening and testing various substances for endocrine disruption (EDSTAC, 1999). After its report was published, EPA began development of the Endocrine Disruptor Priority-Setting Database (EDPSD) in response to that recommendation (ERG-EPA, 2000). This database, now

TABLE 3-3 Examples of Existing and Planned Information Sources for Identifying Chemicals with Demonstrated or Potential Occurrence in Drinking Water Supplies

Name	Responsible Agency or Organization	Notes
Chemicals in Consumer and Cosmetic Products	FDA	Information on chemicals that have been registered voluntarily by manufacturers
Comprehensive Environmental Response, Compensation, and Liability Act Information System	EPA	Contaminant data for Superfund sites
Endocrine Disruptor Priority-Setting Database	EPA	Health effects on endocrine disruption collected from a variety of databases.
Environmental Monitoring and Assessment Program	EPA	Monitoring information for air, groundwater, surface water, biota, and soil contaminants
Food Quality Protection Act (FQPA) "Cumulative to Pesticides" List	FDA	List of chemicals satisfying FQPA statutory requirements of being cumulative to pesticides
Generally Regarded as Safe Substances	FDA	Ingredients that can be added to food
National Drinking Water Contaminant Occurrence Database	EPA	First release online in August 1999; superceded by current second release, which became operational in August 2000; see Chapter 1 for further information
National Human Exposure Assessment Survey	EPA	Surveys designed to assess human exposure via multiple pathways (food, water, air, dust)

continues

TABLE 3-3 Continued

Name	Responsible Agency or Organization	Notes
National Stream Quality Accounting Network	U.S. Geological Survey (USGS)	Water quality data for large subbasins of rivers
National Water-Quality Assessment Program	USGS	Contaminant monitoring data for surface and ground water, some data available on-line
Permit Compliance System	EPA	Information on municipal and industrial wastewater discharge
Priority-Based Assessment of Food Additives (PAFA) Database	EPA	Contains administrative, chemical, and toxicological information on more than 2,000 substances added directly to food
Toxic Substances Control Act Inventory and Updates	EPA	Production volumes and sites for industrial chemicals
Toxics Release Inventory	EPA	Information about a select number of chemicals
Unregulated Contaminant Monitoring Rule (UCMR)	EPA	First UCMR List published September 17, 1999; see Chapter 1 for further information

SOURCE: Adapted from EDSTAC, 1999; NRC, 1999b.

TABLE 3-4 Examples of Existing and Planned Information Sources for Occurrence and Health Effects of Water-Associated Microbial Agents

Name	Responsible Agency or Organization	Notes
FoodNet	Centers for Disease Control and Prevention (CDC)	Provides data on incidence of diseases associated with key enteric bacteria
GenBank	National Institutes of Health-National Library of Medicine	Internet-based database with information on gene sequences for key microorganisms (see Chapter 6 for further information)
Land use data and mapping (e.g., sewage discharge, number of farms or heads of livestock)	USGS, states	
National Ambulatory Medical Care Survey	National Center for Health Statistics (NCHS) of the CDC	Conducted in 1990, the survey provided data from office-based physicians through examination of patient records and gave an indication of the number of persons who seek a physician and are diagnosed
National Animal Health Reporting System	U.S. Department of Agriculture Animal and Plant Health Inspection Service, Veterinary Service, and Centers for Epidemiology and Animal Health	Pilot project begun in March 1998, it will include all 50 states reporting on disease cases in commercial livestock (cattle, sheep, swine, poultry, fish)
National Hospital Discharge Survey	NCHS	Begun in 1988, the survey assesses the number of patients treated in hospitals
National Mortality Followback Survey	NCHS	Represents about 1% of U.S. resident deaths

continues

TABLE 3-4 Continued

Name	Responsible Agency or Organization	Notes
National Notifiable Diseases Surveillance System	NCHS	Compiles U.S. statistics on diseases. Reported cases are summarized by type of disease, reported month, state, age, and race in some cases. The data represent only clinically identified cases and case ratios (cases to total population) or incidence rates that are most often reported annually
National Waterborne Disease Outbreak Database	CDC, EPA	Catalogs reporting waterborne disease outbreaks since 1920
State department of health data	By state	Generally, state health departments report cases of disease by county

SOURCE: Adapted from NRC, 1999b.

operational and undergoing advanced development and refinement, could serve as a starting point for EPA in the selection of chemicals for the PCCL (and CCL), or EPA could create a new database that might be used for multiple purposes. Indeed, in a demonstration of its recommended process for going from a PCCL to a CCL, the committee relied extensively on the EDPSD to help score several occurrence attributes for a wide variety of chemicals (see Chapters 4 and 5).

In its present form, the EDPSD could be used to help provide EPA with information about chemical occurrence or potential occurrence in drinking water since most readily available data sources that would be useful for occurrence screening are already included in the database. However, obtaining information about health effects is somewhat more problematic. The EDSTAC database understandably focuses on obtaining information on health end points that are related to endocrine disruption rather than on the complete spectrum of health effects that drinking water contaminants may elicit. While expanding the EDPSD to include all types of potential drinking water contaminants and their health effects would require considerable effort and expenditure of resources, this may

TABLE 3-5 Additional Considerations for Identification of the Universe of Potential Drinking Water Contaminants

Potential to Occur in Drinking Water	Potential to Cause Adverse Health Effects
Any gasoline additive, constituent, or contaminants of a petroleum product	Any substance purposely intended to "affect" living systems
Any substance "routinely" stored in an underground storage tank	Any carcinogen, mutagen, or teratogen
Any halogenated hydrocarbon	Any compound on the Centers for Disease Control and Prevention's "Biosafety List"
Any constituent found in a landfill leachate	Any substance identified in an epidemiological study that is associated with an elevated measure of health risk
Any soluble component of "normal" soil (e.g., arsenic)	
Any disinfectant by-product	Any hormonally active compounds
Any constituent of wastewater treatment or septage	Any enzyme inhibitor or inducer
Any chemical produced in "high volume" (use a cutoff)	Any behavioral modifier
Any compound found in sludge leachate	Anything that perturbs gene function
Any compound widely applied to land	Anything "flagged" by structure-activity relationship, quantitative structure-activity relationship or virulence-factor activity relationship[a] analysis
Any pharmaceutical excreted in urine or feces	
Any chemical routinely reported in a major biomonitoring program or study	
Any military munitions	

[a] The feasibility of developing and applying virulence-factor activity relationships, or VFARs, for use in identifying potential waterborne pathogens for regulatory consideration is the subject of Chapter 6 of this report.

prove less costly and more timely than creating an entirely new PCCL-CCL comprehensive database.

DISTINGUISHING THE PCCL FROM THE UNIVERSE

In the committee's second report (NRC 1999b), contaminants from the universe are included on the PCCL if they (1) are *known* to have adverse health effects and the potential to occur in drinking water, (2) are *known* to occur in drinking water (unless known not to pose a significant health risk), or (3) are *believed* to pose potential drinking water risks as identified through occurrence criteria (e.g., release data, production data, fecal loading) and health criteria (e.g., toxicity data, structure-activity relationships [SARs], clinical data). However, additional conceptualization and refinement of the PCCL have occurred since it was first introduced as a major step in the process of generating future CCLs.

The committee now recommends the Venn diagram in Figure 3-1 as a useful way to view the PCCL as a subset of the universe of potential drinking water contaminants. The four shaded, intersection areas labeled I-IV represent the confluence of two major characteristics of a contaminant necessary for indicating whether it may cause a public health risk through exposure via drinking water.

These two characteristics are a contaminant's demonstrated or potential occurrence in drinking water and its intrinsic ability to produce adverse health effects in exposed persons. It is important to note that to

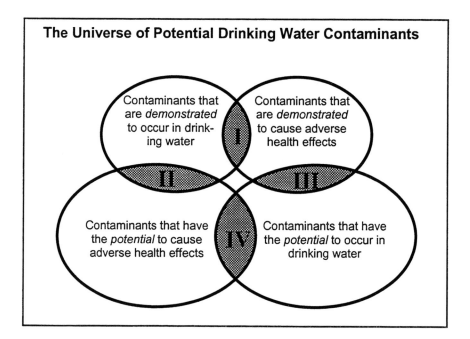

The Universe of Potential Drinking Water Contaminants

Contaminants that are *demonstrated* to occur in drinking water

Contaminants that are *demonstrated* to cause adverse health effects

I

II

III

Contaminants that have the *potential* to cause adverse health effects

Contaminants that have the *potential* to occur in drinking water

IV

FIGURE 3-1 Conceptual approach to identifying contaminants for inclusion on a PCCL through the intersection of their demonstrated and potential occurrence in drinking water and ability to cause adverse health effects. Note, the sizes of the intersections and rings in this Venn diagram are not drawn to scale and do not represent an estimate of the relative numbers of contaminants in each area.

effectively delineate the four "rings" for health effects and occurrence (and their intersections) from the universe of potential drinking water contaminants requires the development and use of screening criteria that define "demonstrated" versus "potential" for each characteristic (see more below). Otherwise, the use of a Venn diagram concept for the PCCL is meaningless. However, this conceptualization recognizes the importance of contaminants for which health effects or occurrence have not been demonstrated (but are possible), thus allowing for inclusion of emerging contaminants with limited data.

The contaminants that fall in intersection I are the highest priorities for placement on a PCCL because they have demonstrated occurrence in drinking water and are demonstrated to cause adverse health effects. Contaminants that fall in intersections II and III are of equivalent importance and have medium priorities for inclusion on a PCCL since they have either demonstrated occurrence in drinking water or demonstrated adverse health effects in conjunction with a potential to cause adverse health effects or a potential to occur in drinking water, respectively. Lastly, contaminants that have the potential to occur in drinking water and the potential to cause adverse health effects fall into intersection IV and have the lowest priority for inclusion on a PCCL. The committee expects that the drinking water contaminants of intersection I will comprise the smallest assemblage of contaminants, while intersection IV will comprise the largest group. For examples of Venn diagram contaminants see Table 3-6.

A significant remaining challenge lies in defining criteria that are to be used by EPA in conjunction with expert judgment to cull the universe of potential drinking water contaminants to a few thousand on the PCCL. Unfortunately, the committee was not able to deliberate extensively on the development of such criteria because sufficient time was not available to do so. The committee notes that this outcome was not unexpected, as reflected in the committee's statement of task for this second phase of work (see preface to this report). Thus, the PCCL is still treated on a largely conceptual basis as it was in the committee's second report (NRC, 1999b). The committee cautions that the Venn diagram in Figure 3-1 should not be interpreted to imply that a contaminant with limited or no data could not be included on a PCCL. Theoretically, a contaminant that is in the universe of potential drinking water contaminants and lying outside of all the intersections or even the rings in the diagram could be placed on a PCCL solely through the use of expert judgment. In this regard, the committee again notes that in formulating a PCCL, EPA should

TABLE 3-6 Examples of Venn Diagram Contaminants

Area of Venn Diagram	Chemical	Microbial
Area I	Aldicarb Diethylhexyl phthalate Lead Vinyl chloride	*Campylobacter jejuni* *Cryptosporidium parvum* *Escherichia coli* O157:H7
Area II	*n*-Hexane Salicylate	*Cyclospora* *Helicobacter pylori* Microsporidia
Area III	Dacthal degradates (DCPA)	*Pseudomonas aeruginosa*
Area IV	Pyrethrin Triethylene glycol	Cyanobacteria Nanobacteria
Demonstrated occurrence ring	Citric acid Phosphate Potassium ion	Coliphage
Potential occurrence ring	Acetic acid Glucose Glycine	*Stachybotrys*
Demonstrated health effects ring	Sodium pentothal	Ebola virus *Haemophilus influenzae* *Streptococcus pneumo- niae* West Nile virus
Potential health effects ring	Bilirubin	Cyanophage (viruses for blue-green algae)
In universe but not in any ring	Inert gases (argon, helium)	*Methanobacter* spp.

NOTE: DCPA = (Dacthal) dimethyl-2,3,5,6-tetrachlorobenzene-1,4-dicarboxylate.

use common sense as a guide and err on the side of public health protection.

GUIDELINES FOR DEVELOPING SCREENING CRITERIA

Criteria for Potential and Demonstrated Health Effects

The information that can be used to identify contaminants with potential and demonstrated health effects includes human data from epidemiological studies, clinical studies, and case reports; toxicological laboratory animal studies or field studies; and predictive biological activity or effects models (e.g., SARs). The feasibility of developing and using virulence-factor activity relationships, or VFARs, to identify emerging waterborne pathogens is discussed in Chapter 6. The term toxicological laboratory animal studies includes many types of studies such as whole studies, metabolic studies, and so forth. The committee recommends that human data and data on whole animals be used as indicators of demonstrated health effects and that other toxicological data and data from experimental models that predict biological activity be used as indicators of potential health effects. The committee has already provided general guidelines to evaluate and assess health effects data and prioritize the importance of their findings for deciding how to address contaminants already on a CCL (NRC, 1999a). However, these principles continue to apply and may be used to assist in evaluating potential drinking water contaminants for inclusion on a PCCL.

Potency is an important characteristic of a substance's ability to cause health effects. Of course, every substance can have some health effect, given a sufficiently high dose. However, the dose at which it causes adverse health effects, especially compared to the concentrations that may occur in drinking water, is an important consideration when selecting a substance for the PCCL. As the exposure to a substance from drinking water nears the dose that may cause health effects, it becomes more important to consider including that substance on the PCCL. Furthermore, substances can have a variety of health effects that range from minor and reversible to irreversible, and life threatening. In general, greater consideration should be given to including substances on the PCCL that cause serious, irreversible effects as opposed to those that cause less serious effects. The committee is not suggesting that less serious effects such as cholinesterase inhibition should be ignored; however, it recognizes that health effects such as cancer or birth defects may be given greater weight. The issues of a contaminant's potency and the severity of its health effects are discussed in greater detail in Chapter 4 for going from a PCCL to a CCL.

Criteria for Potential and Demonstrated Occurrence

A variety of metrics could be used to define occurrence of contaminants in drinking water. These are identified in a hierarchical framework in the committee's first report (NRC, 1999a) and include (1) observations in tap water, (2) observations in distribution systems, (3) observations in finished water of water treatment plants, (4) observations in source water, (5) observations in watersheds and aquifers, (6) historical contaminant release data, and (7) chemical production data. The committee recommends that the first four of these should be used as indicators of demonstrated occurrence and information from items 5 through 7 should be used to determine potential occurrence.

Recorded observations of contaminants in tap water, distribution water, finished water, or source water can be defined in terms of concentration, frequency of occurrence over time, and prevalence with respect to the number of facilities showing detects or people exposed. The committee believes that, generally, contaminant concentration alone should not be used as a relevant metric for culling from the universe of contaminants to those that will appear on the PCCL, although the committee recognizes that some consideration of concentration may be necessary as analytical procedures continue to reduce detection limits. EPA may want to consider binary data, such as found or not found in public water systems, for selecting chemicals for the PCCL from the universe. Also, the committee believes that frequency over time should not be used as the sole relevant metric for this step because it may place undue emphasis on contaminants that are found repeatedly and eliminate those that may have a significant impact but occur infrequently. The committee believes that prevalence at a large number of public water systems or prevalence at systems that serve large numbers of people is an important metric to determine inclusion into the demonstrated occurrence category. The appropriate threshold, in terms of number of facilities or number of people exposed, will have to be decided by EPA, which will also have to consider the manageability of the size of the resulting PCCL.

Of the metrics that serve as indicators of potential occurrence, the committee recommends that EPA use production or release data, combined with physical properties, to serve as useful indicators of the potential for chemical occurrence in watersheds and aquifers. These properties include persistence and mobility in aquatic systems. For chemical contaminants, these may include aqueous solubility, octanol-water partition coefficient, Henry's law constant, and recalcitrance. To screen initially for inclusion on the PCCL, which is appropriate at this stage, aqueous solubility could be used as the sole metric. For microbial contaminants, viability in ambient waters and particle charge or hydrophobicity are appropriate. The use of such properties reduces the reliance on recorded observations in watersheds or aquifers, data that are typically sparse. If necessary and in the absence of these data, contaminant properties could potentially be estimated using SARs and QSARs (quantitative structure-activity relationships) for chemicals or using VFARS in the future (see Chapter 6) for microorganisms.

For chemicals, a binary approach would serve to categorize the universe of chemicals being produced commercially (i.e., it would not include by-products or chemicals formed in the environment) into four bins for potential occurrence as illustrated in Figure 3-2. The committee recommends that if such an approach were used for commercial chemicals, all chemicals except those with those with both low production volume and low water solubility should be considered for inclusion on a PCCL. Furthermore, as indicated by the number of "Xs," such a categorization could also be used to roughly prioritize commercial chemicals for PCCL consideration. An example of a chemical in the high-water-solubility and high-production or release bin is MTBE (methyl-*t*-butyl ether). The aromatic hydrocarbon cumene is a good example of a chemical in the low-water-solubility and high-production or release bin. An example of a chemical in the high- water-solubility and low-production or release bin is the perchlorate ion. Finally, the steroid anti-inflammatory drug dexamethasone is an example of a low-production, low-water-solubility chemical that would not be expected to occur in high concentration in

Production Volume	Water Solubility	
	Low	High
Low	–	X
High	XX	XXX

FIGURE 3-2 Categories for relative potential of chemicals to occur in drinking water based upon consideration of production volume and water solubility.

drinking water. (However, expert judgment in considering the potent biological effects of this compound might well place it on a PCCL.) In this case, the challenge for EPA is to determine scientifically defensible and transparent thresholds for defining "high" and "low" for the two metrics. Again, these thresholds should be chosen considering the manageability of the size of the resulting PCCL.

It is important to note that several potential categories of drinking water contaminants would be missing after this initial screening exercise (see Tables 3-1 and 3-5). For example, EPA should review contaminants already included in the potential occurrence category ("ring") to determine if they have any important environmental degradation products, production or reaction by-products, or metabolites in the environment that should also be considered for inclusion on the potential occurrence list. EPA should also review naturally occurring substances and fibers to determine whether any of them should be included on the potential occurrence list. EPA may also want to review data for specific watersheds and aquifers to determine if any other contaminants should be included on the potential occurrence list. The committee again notes that its recommendation for the development and use of a well-designed, comprehensive database would greatly support the task of developing future PCCLs.

FATE OF THE PCCL

As noted earlier, the committee recommends that an entirely new PCCL be created every five years as a precursor to the development of the corresponding CCL. This should encourage a more thorough and timely consideration of the contaminants that comprise the PCCL than may occur if new substances were simply added to the previous PCCL (excluding those reaching the CCL). Thus, current and past PCCLs would be retained and used in conjunction with (or in lieu of and acting as) a comprehensive relational database useful for recording and understanding the process used to select the PCCL and ultimately the CCL. The committee notes that it is entirely reasonable to expect that prior PCCLs will be reviewed and thereby utilized as an obvious starting point for the creation of subsequent PCCLs. However, a former constituent of a PCCL may not appear on a new PCCL for a variety of reasons, such as the availability of new data that indicate it does not occur in drinking water or does not cause adverse health effects. In keeping with its inclusive nature, the PCCL should not be expected to maintain a more or less fixed number of potential drinking water contaminants.

SUMMARY: CONCLUSIONS AND RECOMMENDATIONS

The first CCL, published in March 1998, was prepared in a short time period by EPA with the assistance of NDWAC to meet the statutory requirements and mandated time line of the SDWA Amendments of 1996. The limitations associated with its necessarily rapid development have been summarized in the committee's second report (NRC, 1999b) and are fully described in Chapter 2 of this report. While the contaminants included on the first CCL certainly merit regulatory and research consideration, a broader approach to contaminant selection could potentially identify higher-risk contaminants. As previously noted, the NRC Committee on Drinking Water Contaminants continues to recommend that EPA develop and use a two-step process for the creation of future CCLs along with several related recommendations (listed below), many of which were originally described in the committee's second report (NRC, 1999b). However, several other associated guidelines and recommendations for CCL design and implementation have been revised and expanded as a result of the committee's second phase of deliberations and are also listed below. The committee continues to recognize that the need for policy judgments by EPA cannot and should not be removed from any CCL (or PCCL) development process. In making these decisions, EPA should use common sense as a guide and err on the side of public health protection.

Regarding the first step of this process (going from the universe of potential drinking water contaminants to a PCCL), the committee makes the following recommendations:

• EPA should begin by considering a broad universe of chemical, microbial, and other types of potential drinking water contaminants and contaminant groups (see Table 3-1). The total number of contaminants in this universe is likely to be on the order of tens of thousands of substances and microorganisms, given that the Toxic Substances Control Act inventory of commercial chemicals alone includes about 72,000 substances (NRC, 1999b). This represents a dramatically larger set of substances to be considered initially in terms of types and numbers of contaminants than that used for the creation of the 1998 CCL.

- EPA should rely on databases and lists that are currently available (see Tables 3-2 and 3-3 for chemicals and Table 3-4 for microorganisms) and under development, along with other readily available information to begin identifying the universe of potential contaminants that may be candidates for inclusion on the PCCL. For example, EPA should consider using the EDPSD to help develop future PCCLs (and perhaps CCLs).

- While relevant databases and lists exist for many "universe categories" of potential drinking water contaminants, others have no lists or databases (e.g., products of environmental degradation). Thus, EPA should initiate work on a strategy for filling the gaps and updating the existing databases and lists of contaminants (e.g., through involvement of the NDWAC or panels of experts) for future CCLs. This strategy should be developed with public, stakeholder, and scientific community input.

- As an integral part of the development process for future PCCLs and CCLs, all information from existing or created databases or lists used should be compiled in a consolidated database that would provide a consistent mechanism for recording and retrieving information on the contaminants under consideration. Such a database could function as a "master list" that contains a detailed record of how the universe of potential contaminants was identified and how a particular PCCL and its corresponding CCL were subsequently created. It would also serve as a powerful analytical tool for the development of future PCCLs and CCLs. As a starting point, the committee recommends that EPA review its developing EDPSD database to determine if it can be expanded and used as this consolidated database or can serve as a model for the subsequent development of such a database. Regardless, the (re)design, creation, and implementation of such a database should be made in open cooperation with the public, stakeholders, and the scientific community.

- To assist generally in the identification of the universe of potential contaminants and a PCCL, the committee recommends EPA consider substances based on their commercial use, environmental location, or physical characteristics as listed in Table 3-5.

- EPA should be as inclusive as possible in narrowing the universe of potential drinking water contaminants down to a PCCL. The committee envisions that a PCCL would contain on the order of a few thousand individual substances and groups of related substances, including microorganisms, for evaluation and prioritization to form a CCL. However, preparation of a PCCL should not involve extensive analysis of data, nor should it directly drive EPA's research or monitoring activities.

- The committee recommends the use of a Venn diagram approach (see Figure 3-1) to conceptually distinguish a PCCL from the universe of potential drinking water contaminants. However, because of the extremely large size of the universe of potential drinking water contaminants, well-conceived screening criteria remain to be developed that can be rapidly and routinely applied by EPA in conjunction with expert judgment to cull the universe to a much smaller PCCL. Thus, the PCCL should include those contaminants that have a combination of characteristics indicating that they are likely to pose a public health risk through their occurrence in drinking water. These characteristics are demonstrated or potential occurrence in drinking water and demonstrated or potential ability to cause adverse health effects.

- Regarding the development of screening criteria for health effects, the committee recommends that human data and data on whole animals be used as indicators of demonstrated health effects and that other toxicological data and data from experimental models that predict biological activity be used as indicators of potential health effects.

- A variety of metrics could be used to develop screening criteria for the occurrence of contaminants in drinking water. These are identified in a hierarchical framework in the committee's first report (NRC, 1999a) and include (1) observations in tap water, (2) observations in distribution systems, (3) observations in finished water of water treatment plants, (4) observations in source water, (5) observations in watersheds and aquifers, (6) historical contaminant release data, and (7) chemical production data. The committee recommends that the first four of these should be used as indicators of demonstrated occurrence and information from items 5 through 7 should be used to determine potential occurrence.

- For commercial chemicals, their potential to occur in drinking water may be estimated using a combination of production volume information and water solubility (see Figure 3-2). Most likely occurrence would involve high-production-volume chemicals with high-water-solubility.

- A new PCCL should be generated for each CCL development cycle to account for new data and emerging contaminants.

- Each PCCL should be published and thereby serve as a useful record of past PCCL and CCL development and as a starting point for the development of future PCCLs.

- Development of the first PCCL should begin as soon as possible to support the development of the next (2003) CCL; each PCCL should be available for public and other stakeholder input (especially through the Internet) and should undergo scientific review.

4
PCCL to CCL: Attributes of Contaminants

INTRODUCTION

As described earlier in this report, the committee continues to recommend a two-step process for the creation of future Drinking Water Contaminant Candidate Lists (CCLs) (see Figure 1-3). This chapter provides some guidance and recommendations for conducting the second step of the CCL development process: selecting preliminary CCL (PCCL) contaminants for inclusion on the corresponding CCL through use of a prioritization tool in conjunction with expert judgment. In general, the preliminary CCL (PCCL) may be thought of as a much more manageable and less conceptual list than the universe of potential contaminants. As such, the PCCL is anticipated to contain up to a few thousand individual substances and groups of related substances, including microorganisms, that merit further consideration for inclusion on the CCL. However, it is anticipated that nearly all of the contaminants on a PCCL will have incomplete information on their potential occurrence and health effects. Thus, any process for selecting PCCL contaminants for inclusion on a CCL must recognize and overcome such limitations. Furthermore, the absence of information for a particular PCCL contaminant should not necessarily be an obstacle to its inclusion on the CCL, as recommended in the committee's second report (NRC, 1999b). In all cases, some amount of expert judgment will be required for the assessment and promotion of each PCCL contaminant to its corresponding CCL.

OVERVIEW OF CONTAMINANT ATTRIBUTES

The committee's recommended approach to this daunting problem was to develop and use five attributes that contribute to the likelihood that a particular PCCL contaminant or group of related contaminants could occur in drinking water at levels and frequencies that pose a public health risk. In this regard, the committee devised a scoring system for each of these five attributes whereby the highest-priority PCCL contaminants are selected in conjunction with expert judgment for inclusion on a CCL. The five attributes are divided into health effect and occurrence categories. For health effects, the committee identified severity and potency as key predictive attributes. Prevalence, magnitude, and persistence-mobility comprise the occurrence attributes.

It is important to note that the committee spent a great deal of time deliberating on the number and type of contaminant attributes that should be used in the prototype classification algorithm approach recommended for use (in conjunction with expert judgment) in the development of future CCLs. Ultimately, the committee decided that these five contaminant attributes constitute a reasonable starting point for the U.S. Environmental Protection Agency (EPA) to consider, especially since they were subsequently found to aptly demonstrate the utility of the recommended CCL development approach (see Chapter 5). Furthermore, the metrics and related considerations presented in this chapter for scoring each attribute should similarly be viewed as illustrative. Thus, the committee does not explicitly or implicitly recommend these five (or necessarily a total of five) attributes or the related scoring metrics as being ideally suited for direct adoption and use by EPA. Rather, should EPA choose to adopt a classification approach for the development of future CCLs, the committee recommends that options for developing and scoring contaminant attributes should be made available for public and other stakeholder input and undergo scientific review.

Severity

The question of severity may be stated simply as, How bad is the health effect? In terms of this report, severity can be scored using the most sensitive health end point for a particular contaminant (e.g., the health effect that occurs at the lowest dose compared to other health effects reportedly caused by the contaminant) and considering vulnerable subpopulations (see Chapter 2). In other words, for the most sensitive health end point, what is the anticipated clinical magnitude in affected individuals? The committee recommends that the assessment of severity should be based, when feasible, on plausible exposures via drinking water.

This information can be ascertained from clinical reports, from animal bioassay results, or by inference from effects of similar compounds. Information from epidemiological studies, structure-activity relationships, or future virulence-factors activity relationships (see Chapter 6) may also prove useful. For illustrative purposes, a 10-level hierarchy for scoring the severity of health effects may be defined as in Table 4-1. It should be noted that in developing this table, it was necessary to consider the chronicity of the health effect.

An alternative approach to evaluating severity would be to perform a ranking using either quality adjusted or disability adjusted life-years (QALYs or DALYs), lost respectively, due to exposure to a contaminant. In this regard, various weighting scales can be used, each of which to some degree incorporates economic and social considerations of disease impact (Bowie et al., 1997; Havelaar et al., 2000; Hyder et al., 1998; Mauskopf and French, 1991). However, as noted in Chapter 2, the committee cautions that the use of approaches such as QALYs and DALYs may not adequately protect vulnerable subpopulations (Arneson and Nord, 1999). Thus, the committee recommends that EPA give consideration to different severity metrics.

Potency

Potency may be expressed simply as, How much of a contaminant does it take to cause illness? This is a relative scaling of the dose-response relationship. For carcinogens, an obvious metric for scaling is the cancer slope factor (q1), which is defined as the incremental risk divided by incremental dose in the low-dose region (EPA, 1999h). Databases of these potencies are available, such as EPA's Integrated Risk Information System (see Table 3-2; EPA, 2000f). A method for scaling carcinogenic contaminants would be to use the percentile of the contaminant's potency relative to the potencies of all contaminants being considered, including those drinking water contaminants with enforceable maximum contaminant levels (MCLs). The percentile (0-100) scale could then easily be converted to a 1 through 10 (decile) scale. For mutagens, a similar percentile ranking can be derived using bioassays results such as the Ames test.

For noncarcinogenic contaminants, a logical basis of comparison is the benchmark dose (BMD_{10}), which can be defined simply as the dose

TABLE 4-1 Scoring of Severity Attribute

Severity Score	Characteristic
0	No effect
1	Changes in organ weights with minimal clinical significance
2	Biochemical changes with minimal clinical significance
3	Pathology of minimum clinical importance (e.g., fluorosis, warts, common cold)
4	Cellular changes that could lead to disease; minimum functional change
5	Significant functional changes that are reversible (e.g., diarrhea)
6	Irreversible changes; treatable disease
7	Single organ system pathology and function loss
8	Multiple organ system pathology and function loss
9	Disease likely leading to death
10	Death

corresponding to a 10 percent excess risk above background levels (Crump, 1995). These can be computed for continuous (Crump, 1995), quantal (Gaylor et al., 1998), and to a lesser extent, graded responses (Gibson et al., 1997). BMDs for a contaminant can then be scaled by percentile BMD for that contaminant relative to the BMDs of all contaminants being considered, including contaminants with MCLs; the percentile scale can similarly be converted to a 1 through 10 scale. Alternatively, the lowest observed adverse effect level (LOAEL) or the no observed adverse effect level (NOAEL) dose[1] can be used.

For infectious agents, a logical basis of comparison is the median infectious dose (N_{50}), defined as the dose from a single exposure leading to infection of 50 percent of a population (Haas et al., 1999). This may be defined with reference to current MCLs.[2]

---

[1] The lowest dose that results in a statistically or biologically significant increase in the frequency or severity of adverse health effects between an exposed group and an appropriate control group and the lowest dose that does not, respectively.

[2] At the time of this writing, there are no MCLs for individual microbial pathogens—only treatment requirements. Thus, it may be appropriate to define the percentile with reference to pathogens for which treatment techniques have been set. At present, this would include *Giardia lamblia* and human enterovirus (both of which are regulated under the Surface Water Treatment Rule), *Legionella pneumophila* (which is regulated by implication under the Surface Water Treatment Rule), and *Cryptosporidium parvum* (which is to be regulated under the Enhanced Surface Water Treatment Rule).

If contaminants act via diverse health effect end points (e.g., a carcinogen that also has noncarcinogenic effects), then an appropriate potency score would be the worst (i.e., the highest) score of all of the relevant effects in order to err on the side of public health protection. When no experimental data are available to infer the potency of a chemical contaminant, the use of a (quantitative) structure-activity relationship should be considered. In the case of microbial agents, quantitative virulence-factor activity relationships (see Chapter 6) may become available in the future.

Prevalence

The attribute of prevalence may be defined as, How commonly does or would a contaminant occur in drinking water? Ideally, prevalence should be assessed based first on measurements in tap water, followed by measurements in distribution systems, finished water of water treatment plants, and source waters used for drinking water supply as discussed in the committee's first report (NRC, 1999a) and earlier in this report (see Chapter 3). If such data are not available, inferences may have to be made from general watershed or aquifer measurements, historical contaminant release data, or even chemical production data. The focus of this attribute is the geographical and temporal range (i.e., sporadic or episodic versus frequent) of occurrence or anticipated occurrence. Thus, prevalence has both spatial and temporal aspects.

For illustrative purposes, spatial and temporal prevalence can be consolidated into a single prevalence index using an approach such as that summarized in Table 4-2. Temporal prevalence represents the average fraction of time that a contaminant is found at a given locale (if multiple locations are sampled, the percentage of occurrence times at each site should be averaged among sites). Spatial (or geographical) prevalence represents the proportion of locales in which the contaminant would be found, such as all communities with public water systems for which contaminant data are available. For the purpose of assessing geographical prevalence, sites in the same watershed should be regarded as the same site. For example, if the temporal prevalence averaged 66 percent and the spatial prevalence averaged 80 percent, a score of 9 would be the result.

There are two important questions to be resolved with respect to assessing prevalence. First, in the absence of data either on temporal prevalence (e.g., many sites each examined only at a single point) or on

TABLE 4-2   Overall Prevalence Score Related to Temporal and Spatial Prevalence

Spatial Prevalence (%)	Temporal Prevalence (%)				
	<25	25-50	50-75	75-90	90-100
<25	1	2	3	4	6
25-50	2	4	5	7	8
50-75	3	5	8	9	9
75-90	4	7	9	10	10
90-100	6	8	9	10	10

spatial prevalence (e.g., one site examined many times), what score should be assigned? Second, prevalence may have to be defined with respect not to an absolute detection value (e.g., above the detection limit) but to a prevalence above some level likely to be of concern. If the latter is not done, the percentage prevalence on either a temporal or a spatial basis is anticipated to increase as analytical methods advance, since samples that would previously have scored as "nondetects" would be scored as "detects."

With respect to the first issue, if only temporal or only spatial prevalence information is available, then it may be appropriate to determine and use a default assumption in which the spatial prevalence and the temporal prevalence (in the absence of information on both factors) are assumed to be equal. In the second case, the committee believes that further consideration regarding the issue of decreasing detection limits is in order.

Furthermore, the committee notes that in many cases (particularly where contaminants have been included on a PCCL on the basis of potential rather than demonstrated occurrence), insufficient information will be available to assess temporal or spatial prevalence (or both) directly. In such circumstances, this attribute must then go unscored. However, the absence of prevalence information, as described below, will not necessarily preclude PCCL contaminants from being included on the corresponding CCL.

Magnitude

Magnitude can be defined as the concentration or expected concentration (e.g., based on chemical production) of a contaminant relative to a level that causes a perceived health effect. In lay terms, this might be stated, Is the level high enough to cause harm? However, the issue is not simply the absolute magnitude of a contaminant, but rather magnitude relative to potency.

As in the case of prevalence, if a substance has been included on a PCCL on the basis of potential rather than demonstrated occurrence, then data would not generally be available to evaluate (even on a 10-point scale) the magnitude of expected concentration in drinking water.

With substances for which at least some concentration measurements exist, a suitable metric for evaluating the magnitude would relate the median (as opposed to the mean) water concentrations to the potency. To score this attribute, the median water concentration and a measure of potency have to be combined in a simple and consistent manner to yield a numerical measure of scale. As noted previously, the committee recognizes that the available information with which to go from a PCCL to a CCL will almost always be imperfect and will often be poor. Thus, the following approach to scoring magnitude is suggested for illustrative purposes.

First, the median water concentration for the contaminant under evaluation is ranked relative to the numerical values for median occurrence of contaminants with MCLs,[3] on a decile basis (1-10 ranking, with 10 being compounds present at highest magnitude relative to the MCL medians[4]). This percentile is next multiplied by the converted decile score for potency and the square root is taken (e.g., if a compound is in the 9th decile for occurrence and its potency is given a score of 3, then

---

[3] Because of obvious differences in measurement approaches, chemical contaminants and microbial contaminants should be ranked separately with respect to chemical and microbial MCL values. Due to the current lack of specific MCLs for microorganisms (except coliform organisms and heterotrophic plate count organisms), it may be appropriate to develop "apparent MCLs" for each of the microorganisms regulated under a treatment technique option (i.e., *Giardia lamblia*, human viruses, *Legionella pneumophila*, *Cryptosporidium parvum*).

[4] Under the authority of the Safe Drinking Water Act Amendments of 1996, EPA has recently assembled expansive data on the concentrations of regulated compounds in public water supplies (EPA, 1999a).

the magnitude score is $5.2 = \sqrt{9 \cdot 3}$). It is important to note that this calculation gives greater weight to contaminants with many large-magnitude occurrences and high relative potencies than to contaminants that have fewer but higher-magnitude occurrences but are of low relative potency. In addition, contaminants that have many low-magnitude occurrences but high relative potencies will also receive less weight.

Persistence-Mobility

The persistence-mobility attribute of a contaminant is intended to describe the likelihood that the contaminant would be found in the aquatic environment based solely on its physical properties. For PCCL contaminants that have demonstrated occurrence in water, the occurrence attributes of prevalence and magnitude should be scored and take precedence over their persistence-mobility scores. However, in the absence of data on occurrence, persistence and mobility should be used to assess the potential for significant occurrence of PCCL contaminants in drinking water.

There are many chemical fate and persistence models that could be adapted for the current purpose. Recent examples include Bennett et al. (2000) and Gouin et al. (2000); however, most models require data on too many contaminant properties to be practical for screening perhaps thousands of chemicals on the PCCL. In addition, there appears to have been little prior effort to develop persistence-mobility metrics that are suitable for ranking chemicals and microorganisms together. To overcome these limitations, the committee recommends consideration of three general characteristics of contaminants that would foster their persistence and/or mobility in water systems:

1. high potential for amplification by growth under ambient conditions (applies to microbial contaminants and not to chemicals);
2. high solubility in water (applies primarily to chemicals), although the transportability of microorganisms may be assessed through sedimentation velocities and size and adsorption capabilities; and
3. stability in water (i.e., resistance to degradation via mechanisms such as hydrolysis, photolysis, or biodegradation in the case of chemicals; death or the ability to produce nonculturable or resistant states [e.g., spores and cysts] in the case of microorganisms).

It should be possible to assess these characteristics for a large number of contaminants (both chemical and microbial) by applying a simple, semiquantitative scoring scheme such as that illustrated in Tables 4-3 to 4-5. In this system, a score of 1 represents a characteristic that is relatively unfavorable persistence-mobility in water (low amplification, solubility, or persistence), while a score of 3 represents a characteristic that is relatively favorable persistence in water (high amplification, solubility, or persistence). More specifically, any given chemical or group of related chemicals would be scored using Tables 4-4 and 4-5, whereas microorganisms would be scored primarily using Tables 4-3 and 4-5. If the individual characteristics are scored according to this scheme, an overall score for persistence-mobility can be obtained on a scale of 1 to 10 by taking the arithmetic average of the scores and multiplying by 10/3.

TABLE 4-3 Scoring Contaminants for Microbial Amplification

Subscore	Doubling Time Under Environmental Conditions
Low (1)	>1 week
Medium (2)	1 day–1 week
High (3)	<1 day

TABLE 4-4 Scoring Contaminants for Solubility

Subscore	Solubility (mg/L)
Low (1)	<0.1
Medium (2)	0.1–10
High (3)	>10

TABLE 4-5 Scoring Contaminants for Stability

Subscore	Half-Life (Combined, All Mechanisms)
Low (1)	<1 day
Medium (2)	Days to weeks
High (3)	>Weeks

LESSONS LEARNED IN APPLYING THESE CRITERIA

The contaminant attributes and associated scoring criteria outlined in this chapter were applied to a panel of chemical and microbial validation test contaminants. The details of this demonstration are given in Chapter 5 to illustrate the utility of using such a classification approach for the creation of future CCLs. During the course of this demonstration, a number of procedural issues were discovered with respect to implementation of the approach. The following material summarizes the major factors identified during the scoring of various health effect and occurrence attributes.

Monitoring Data

Monitoring data are important in the scoring scheme, for both the prevalence and the magnitude attributes. For convenience in conducting this exercise, the committee relied extensively on EPA's developing Endocrine Disruptor Priority-Setting Database (EDPSD) to obtain usable monitoring data for chemicals (ERG-EPA, 2000). The committee commends EPA for beginning to obtain and compile environmental monitoring data as exemplified by the creation and ongoing development of the EDPSD in addition to the Unregulated Contaminant Monitoring Regulation List and the National Drinking Water Contaminant Occurrence Database (NCOD) described in Chapter 1. It is important to note, however, that monitoring data in the EDPSD from water supplies are limited, both in the number of chemicals for which monitoring data exist and in the amount of sampling. Without additional monitoring data compiled in a comprehensive database that facilitates priority setting (as recommended in Chapter 3), EPA will be hampered in terms of the quality of its priority-setting exercise and the ease of completing that exercise.

As noted earlier, some of the most relevant monitoring data for priority-setting activities in going from a PCCL to a CCL are data from water supplies. In keeping with this assertion, the committee relied, whenever possible, on drinking water monitoring data from the recently established NCOD as maintained in EDPSD. Earlier in this chapter, the committee described scoring criteria that use information on temporal and geographic occurrence. Because such data are not available in this particular database, however, the committee instead used information on population exposed and number of analyses with detects for prevalence. Expanding on the recommendation in Chapter 3 that EPA review the EDPSD database to determine whether it can be used to help develop a PCCL and perhaps help select PCCL contaminants for inclusion on a CCL, the committee also recommends that EPA consider the possibility of including information on temporal and regional occurrence. However, the committee notes that the EDPSD does contain exposure information from the U.S. Geological Survey's National Stream Quality Accounting Network and National Water-Quality Assessment Program, both of which include regional water quality information. Additionally, although information on the number of analyses with detects is included in the EDPSD and NCOD, information on the total number of analyses is not. Without denominator data, the usefulness of information on the number of detects is limited.

The magnitude score uses information on potency and the average concentration. Although some information on median concentration is included in the occurrence data in EDPSD, the median concentration is calculated using only the detected concentrations; nondetected values are not included. The median thus does not provide a true picture of the median concentration of a chemical in drinking water if nondetected values are not included and especially if the majority of observations are nondetects. EPA should develop a method of expressing an "average concentration" value that uses as much of the data, including nondetects, as possible. The literature suggests several approaches to this issue (Gilliom and Helsel, 1986; Haas and Scheff, 1990; Helsel and Cohn, 1988). In addition, EPA may want to consider providing other measures of concentration in water supplies, such as the 95th percentile of contaminant concentration. The committee can envision other scoring schemes that might use monitoring data rather than relying on median values. For example, a chemical may occur in a relatively limited geographic area of the United States at high concentrations and not be found to a great extent in other areas of the country; under this circumstance, the chemical may still warrant inclusion on the CCL.

Potency Compared to Monitoring Data

The potency score for chemicals was calculated using LOAELs,

NOAELs, and RfDs[5] from readily available health effects-related databases such as EPA's Integrated Risk Information System (IRIS) (EPA, 2000f). Although the number of chemicals for which these data exist is limited, the quality of the data for scoring this attribute was often high. This contrasts to information contained in the monitoring database that was used extensively (EDPSD). The difference in the quality of these databases is not unexpected, however, given that IRIS has existed for more than a decade, while monitoring databases are in much earlier stages of development.

Severity

In this demonstration, severity was scored for chemicals based on the health effect associated with the LOAEL. In some cases, this could result in a fairly low severity score because the health effect associated with the LOAEL was relatively minor such as a decrease in body weight gain. It is important to note, however, that such a chemical could cause health effects associated with significantly higher severity scores (e.g., birth defects) at only a slightly higher dose.

Severity and Potency

For chemicals that caused both cancer and noncancer health effects, potency was scored for both types of effects and the higher one was used in the model. The severity score was then based on the corresponding health end point used (e.g., LOAEL or cancer). In a few cases, the potency score was higher for the noncancer end point, and the health end point associated with the LOAEL had a low severity score. Thus, potency was scored first and severity was based on the end point on which potency was based. Alternatively, severity could have been scored first and then potency based on the end point associated with the severity score. Another approach could have scored potency and severity independently of each other. If the scoring had been done differently, the modeling results are likely to have been different. This decision to score

---

[5]An oral reference dose (or RfD) is an estimate of the concentration of a substance that is unlikely to cause appreciable risk of adverse health effects over a lifetime of exposure, including sensitive subgroups (Barnes and Dourson, 1988).

potency and then severity also affected the magnitude score since the potency score is used in calculating the magnitude score.

Vulnerable subpopulations were considered, when readily feasible, in the scoring. For example, the health end point ultimately used for scoring the potency of nitrate (see Box 5-1) was methemoglobinemia in infants (i.e., an excess of methemoglobin—the oxidized form of hemoglobin—resulting in cyanosis). In this case, the severity and potency scores were based on the effect in this population, rather than for adults, and the committee considered this reasonable. Consistent with the recommendation in Chapter 2 that EPA consider expanding the current working definition of vulnerable subpopulations in the amended Safe Drinking Water Act, the committee deems it appropriate for EPA to consider using health end point data based on vulnerable subpopulations, especially those that comprise a "meaningful portion of the general population."

SUMMARY: CONCLUSIONS AND RECOMMENDATIONS

The committee recommends that EPA develop and use a set of attributes to evaluate the likelihood that any particular PCCL contaminant or group of related contaminants could occur in drinking water at levels and frequencies that pose a public health risk. More specifically, these contaminant attributes should be used in a prototype classification algorithm approach, such as that described in Chapter 5, and in conjunction with expert judgment to help identify the highest-priority PCCL contaminants for inclusion on a CCL. In this chapter, the committee has presented a scoring system and related considerations for a total of five health effect and occurrence attributes. For health effects, the committee identified severity and potency as key predictive attributes; prevalence, magnitude, and persistence-mobility comprise the occurrence attributes.

Although the committee spent a great deal of time deliberating on the number and type of contaminant attributes that should be used in the recommended CCL development approach, ultimately, it decided that these five attributes constitute a reasonable starting point for EPA to consider. Furthermore, the scoring metrics and related considerations for each attribute should be viewed as illustrative. Thus, the committee does not explicitly or implicitly recommend that these five (or that there should be five) attributes the related scoring metrics be adopted directly for use by EPA. If EPA chooses to adopt a prototype classification approach for the development of future CCLs, the committee recommends that options for developing and scoring contaminant attributes should be made available for public and other stakeholder input and undergo scientific review. The committee also makes the following related recommendations:

• The assessment of severity should be based, when feasible, on plausible exposures via drinking water. The committee also recommends that EPA give consideration to different severity metrics such as a ranking through use of either quality adjusted or disability adjusted life-years lost due to exposure to a contaminant.

• Regarding the assessment of contaminant prevalence, in some cases (particularly where contaminants have been included on a PCCL on the basis of potential rather than demonstrated occurrence), information will often be insufficient to directly assess temporal or spatial prevalence (or both). Thus, EPA should consider the possibility of including information on temporal and regional occurrence to help determine (score PCCL) contaminant prevalence. When prevalence cannot be assessed, this attribute must then go unscored and the attribute of persistence-mobility used in its stead. The issue of changing (or incorporating) "thresholds" for contaminant detection, rather than relying on continually decreasing detection limits, is one that needs explicit attention and discussion by EPA and stakeholders.

• Existing and readily available databases may not be sufficient to rapidly and consistently score health effect and occurrence attributes for individual PCCL contaminants for promotion to a CCL. As recommended in Chapter 3, all information from existing or created databases or lists used in the development of a CCL and PCCL, should be compiled in a consolidated database that would provide a consistent mechanism for recording and retrieving information on the PCCL contaminants under consideration. As a starting point and as recommended in Chapter 3, EPA should review its developing EDPSD database to determine if it can be expanded and used (or serve as a model for the development of) such a consolidated database and to help develop future PCCLs and CCLs.

• Contaminant databases used in support of the development of future CCLs should report summary statistics on all data collected, not only the quantifiable observations. In this regard, EPA should formalize a process for reporting means and/or medians from data with large numbers of nondetect observations. In addition, EPA may want to consider providing other measures of concentration in water supplies such as the 95th percentile of contaminant concentration.

5

PCCL to CCL: Classification Algorithm

INTRODUCTION

The intrinsic difficulty of identifying potentially harmful agents for resource-intensive scrutiny such as the selection of a drinking water contaminant from a preliminary Drinking Water Contaminant Candidate List (PCCL) for inclusion onto a CCL raises the question of what kind of process or method is best suited to this judgment. As discussed in Chapter 2, the sorting of perhaps thousands of PCCL contaminants into two discrete sets, one (the CCL) that probably will undergo research or monitoring of some sort preparatory to an eventual regulatory decision and another much larger set that will not, is an exercise in *classification*.

The committee considered three broad types of strategies for accomplishing this task: expert judgment, rule-based systems, and prototype classifiers. It is important to note at the outset that there are no sharp boundaries between these three classification strategies since all are based on data to some extent and expert judgments factor into all to some degree. The main differences are the specific mix of data and expert judgment and the extent to which explicit or implicit judgments come together to produce predictable results. This chapter begins with a general overview of classification schemes. It is followed by an example application, framework, and related recommendations for how the U.S. Environmental Protection Agency (EPA) might develop its own prototype classification scheme for use in the creation of future CCLs.

OVERVIEW OF CLASSIFICATION SCHEMES

Expert Judgments

Many decisions (and their associated classifications) are made on the basis of the collective experience of experts. EPA has made extensive and regular use of expert committees (including this National Research Council [NRC] committee), advisory panels, peer review committees, and the like to help its staff (another assemblage of experts) make important policy decisions.

Clearly the composition of any expert group is critical to the outcome, and in recent years there has been a concerted effort within EPA to include a wide spectrum of "stakeholder" opinion in the expertise solicited (e.g., the September 1999 workshop to discuss EPA's draft CCL Research Plan; AWWARF, 2000). This is a recognition that where a particular expert stands on the issue is often influenced by where he or she sits in the real world (e.g., organizational affiliations). Of course, the outcome of any expert panel may be influenced equally, though to a largely unknown extent, by the absence of persons who could not participate in such meetings. Often the reasons for the absence of a particular perspective are random or accidental, as when schedules or timing do not permit participation at the last minute or result in a substitution for similar reasons.

Yet even when matters external to the question at hand are set aside, the dynamics of expert committees often influences the outcome in crucial ways. Thus, when a particular subject comes up (e.g., at the beginning of a meeting versus the end of a long day), who advocates for or against a position (involving questions of articulateness, seniority, and status) or the juxtaposition or context of agenda items can lead to very different outcomes for reasons unconnected with the content of the issues at hand. The presence or absence of EPA experts and the relative forcefulness of their participation can frequently alter the direction of a discussion in important ways, for example, directing it toward or away from regulatory and policy concerns that may not be apparent or uppermost in the minds of non-agency experts. For the same reasons, discussions of committees comprised solely of EPA staff and consultants are likely to have a different character than those with significant or predominant participation from experts outside the agency.

One strategy to neutralize these adventitious effects is to use a formal

Delphi procedure. The Delphi technique was introduced more than 30 years ago to limit interaction among participants and thereby optimize the quality of decisions (Dalkey, 1969; Linstone and Turoff, 1975). It is one of the formal group judgment methods used to obtain consensus and define disagreements on a specific question (Webler et al., 1991). The method assists in identifying important issues and needs (NRC, 1996, 1999c), integrating data and judgments (NRC, 1988, 1992), informing policy processes (NRC, 1996), structuring deliberations, modifying classification schemes, and ranking priorities (IOM, 1988; NRC, 1992). It may be used to obtain consensus on a time-limited issue or to facilitate longer-term building of common ground on issues. For example, the technique has been used by committees of the Institute of Medicine (IOM, 1992) and is being used at the U.S. Army's Tooele Chemical Agent Disposal Facility to identify current issues to be included in a stakeholder survey (NRC, 1999c).

Briefly, the Delphi process includes the solicitation and compilation of responses to a specific question. The answers are summarized (typically displayed with the range and mean of all responses) and provided to the participants, with each person invited to reconsider his or her position in light of the compilation. The answers received from this second request are again compiled. This process is repeated until group consensus is obtained (IOM, 1995; NRC, 1988). The technique is traditionally conducted with participants responding remotely and independently of each other. The Delphi method has been implemented with mailed or faxed surveys, e-mail instruments, face-to-face meetings or workshops, and iterations of closed computer networks and group dialogues. The means selected to implement the Delphi process involve trade-offs of cost, time, and commitment of the participants; the impact of influential individuals; confidentiality; duration and intensity of the process; response rate; and clarity of the responses (IOM, 1995).

The Delphi technique may be implemented alone or as part of a multistep process such as Renn and colleague's three-step procedure discussed in Chapter 2 (Renn et al., 1993), or it may be conducted for separate, dissimilar groups, commonly referred to as a double-Delphi system (NRC, 1992). For example, the same question could be asked of experts and nonexperts convened in two separate but simultaneous panels. The double-Delphi approach may be employed in workshops where the groups use separate computer networks in separate rooms and then share their consensus in reporting-out sessions with all groups present.

Although there has been relatively little evaluation of the effectiveness of the Delphi process, there are indications that it may not result in decisions much improved over those obtained through less structured processes (IOM, 1992). Its use for selecting candidates for the CCL, therefore, is questionable, but it remains a technique that potentially avoids some of the traditional pitfalls of expert opinion methods of classification.

Rule-Based Methods

Rule-based schemes take as inputs various features or parameters of an object and weigh and combine these features according to an algorithm that is decided upon in advance—usually as a result of some expert judgment. One characteristic of rule-based and expert systems is that their classification strategy is what is often called "Aristotelian," that is, objects (in this case potential drinking water contaminants) are assigned attributes (e.g., toxicity or solubility), and a set of rules is used to determine which class they are in (Bowker and Star, 1999). They are, thus, expert opinion strategies, in which the opinions are embedded into a fairly rigid algorithm. Their rigidity can be considered both their strength (they are objective and consistent, and they allow for high throughput) and their weakness (they do not easily allow for additional nuanced judgment). The weights and modes of combination used in a rule-based scheme are presumably determined using some preexisting idea or objective of what the scheme intends to capture; however, this is often not done in any systematic or explicit fashion.

The committee's first report reviewed 10 rule-based ranking schemes whose objective was to use data about chemicals to establish a priority for regulation or attention (NRC, 1999a). As noted in that report, there are no formal schemes that might be considered for prioritizing microbial contaminants. However, EPA and the American Water Works Association Research Foundation have jointly sponsored a series of expert workshops beginning in 1996 to develop a decision process for prioritizing emerging waterborne pathogens. Although the final report of these workshops is nearing completion, it was not available for review at the time this report was written. At the request of EPA, the rule-based systems were evaluated for their potential to help select contaminants (including microorganisms) that are already on a CCL for future action. All of the systems reviewed had at least one shortcoming, but of special concern was the extent to which (often) arbitrary and nonexplicit expert judgments were intrinsically embodied in what appeared to be objective ranking schemes. For example, various kinds of information (such as chemical persistence, solubility, and toxicity) had to be weighted and combined to produce a single number that allowed an ordinal ranking at the end of the process. The methods of combination (e.g., additive or multiplicative) and the weights given the various factors were all matters of judgment that were in place prior to the input of any data to the ranking system.

In short, the committee concluded that a ranking process that attempts to sort contaminants in a specific order is not appropriate for the selection of drinking water contaminants already on a CCL for regulation, research, or monitoring activities (NRC, 1999a). In the absence of complete information, the output of the prioritization schemes was found to be so uncertain (though this uncertainty is generally not stated) that they are of limited use in making more than preliminary risk management decisions about drinking water contaminants. The committee concluded, however, that they may provide a (semi)quantitative means for preliminarily screening and sorting large numbers of contaminants. Even with this limited use, however, the aforementioned considerations can still become serious issues.

Based on its collective experience, the committee emphasizes that there are some common and often troublesome problems that occur in developing new ranking systems and revising existing ranking systems to suit specific purposes. Many of these problems are similar to those noted earlier as related to the formation and deliberations of expert panels. For example, sometimes an expert group contains individuals who interpret the charge or understand the client's intended purpose differently, because they bring different disciplines, experiences, and/or motives to the process. A perhaps surprisingly common problem is that many such groups think they have a consensus about the purpose of the system on which they are working, but in fact do not. Even when a goal is clearly stated and mutually understood, group members may envision different types of ranking processes and final products as appropriately meeting the goal. Some group members may believe a simple ranking process is adequate, whereas others believe the process should be somewhat to very complex. The final product may be conceived as quantitative, semiquantitative, or qualitative, with a whole range of outputs from a few to many and from categorical to specific. Some groups have had long debates about what process and form will best fit the purpose, and some have come to near deadlock over how much scoring or ranking is enough or too much. Others have worked for months before they realized that they were trying to achieve different visions.

Another situation in which groups that are trying to develop ranking schemes have encountered difficulties is where science and policy issues meet. When there is a lack of clarity about which decisions are within the group's charge and which are better left to policy settings, groups have often gotten focused on narrow scientific issues, either not recognizing that there is a policy issue in the matter or inadvertently believing that there is a scientific "solution" to a policy problem. Groups have also gotten bogged down in specific scientific issues when it has been too difficult to address broader points of disagreement. A report sponsored by the Society of Environmental Toxicology and Chemistry is available that might help reduce such problems because it provides an expert panel consensus framework along with principles and guidelines to promote consistency in the development and use of chemical ranking and scoring systems (Swanson and Socha, 1997).

Prototype Classification Methods

An alternative classification strategy is sometimes referred to as "prototype classification" (Bowker and Star, 1999). This strategy recognizes that in ordinary practice and discourse one does not usually classify objects on the basis of a fixed algorithm, but instead uses criteria based on prior classification of examples or prototypes. The classic example is character recognition of an individual letter in handwriting, most commonly recognized by its similarity to an idealized example rather than by any fixed features such as height-to-width ratios. Prototype classifiers take advantage of the prototyping activity at which humans generally (and intuitively) excel.

Prototype classification schemes usually take the form of neural networks, clustering algorithms, machine learning classifiers, and their hybrids. These methods start with a known classification of prototypes (a "training set") that embody the kinds of outcomes one might wish to achieve. These prototypes are used to discern an algorithm that maps prototype features or attributes into classification outcomes. The prototype-based algorithm can then be used for classification of new objects. The neural network paradigm is discussed more fully later in this chapter.

Application of a prototype scheme for constructing the CCL would consist of a training set of chemicals, microorganisms, and other types of (potential) drinking water contaminants that would clearly belong on the CCL, such as currently regulated chemicals (if they were not already regulated), and those that clearly do not, such as food additives generally recognized as safe by the U.S. Food and Drug Administration. Each contaminant's "features" or "attributes" must be extracted and characterized. In this case, these would include parameters such as solubility, various measures of toxicity (quantitative or categorical), and occurrence data, if any. Using this as a training set, the neural network constructs both the mode of combination and the weighting factors that seem best to differentiate between the two categories.

It is important to note that the distinction between Aristotelian and prototype classification strategies is not sharp but is more a matter of emphasis. What in the ranking scheme was done a priori by experts is done instead on the basis of the data that differentiated prototype examples. This a posteriori determination of weights on the basis of features sets these methods apart from rule-based methods, but it should be clear that rule-based methods also depend on the data in a fundamental way. Conversely, prototype schemes emphasize past classification decisions in the construction of a classification algorithm but necessarily involve some expert judgment in determining which features should be used to characterize the prototypes.

The committee notes that prototype strategies have found use in commerce and other sciences, although their use for constructing something like the CCL would be innovative. Keller et al. (1995) have compiled papers describing studies of neural network applications in hazardous waste disposal, environmental monitoring, and reliability analysis. The Federal Aviation Administration has used a neural network for analysis of radiation directed at travelers' luggage at security checkpoints; numerous financial analysts have found neural networks to be useful in predicting stock performance and foreign exchange rates; and neural networks have been successful in the prediction of educational performance. These examples are well described by Garson (1998) and the references cited therein.

Which Strategy to Use?

To date, EPA has relied extensively on use of expert judgment and to a lessor extent on rule-based prioritization schemes to identify and rank drinking water contaminants for regulatory and research activities. It is clear that contaminant-by-contaminant consideration by panels of experts as to whether something should be placed on a CCL is not possible if the entire universe of potential drinking water contaminants is to be considered, as recommended in the committee's second report (NRC, 1999b) and again in this one. Some efficient screening method is required. Until now, this has usually meant the use of an a priori ranking or classifying system. However, none of the existing schemes for ranking chemicals that the committee previously reviewed (NRC, 1999a) seem able to fulfil this function readily, so one would have to be significantly modified or an entirely new one created. As discussed above, the difficulties are formidable, and there is no obvious reason why a new attempt will solve the problems of previous ones.

Use of a prototype classification strategy and neural network technology would seem to be an innovative new approach. Furthermore, since the objective is one of identification, not regulation per se, the method does not have to withstand regulatory challenge. The PCCL contaminants that it helps identify for inclusion on a CCL can be evaluated in conventional ways by EPA staff and external experts for further justification of why they do or do not belong on the CCL. The recommended system merely identifies and offers likely candidates in a systematic way.

The committee notes that a potentially serious drawback of using this technology is its perceived lack of "transparency" in that the neural network can easily appear as a black box, with little obvious indication of how it is "working." The importance of transparency in decision-making is discussed extensively in Chapter 2. However, the committee reiterates that transparency is not necessarily synonymous with simplicity. A CCL decision-making process that uses complex classification modeling can be made relatively transparent by emphasizing that the classification is based on prototypes of past regulatory decisions and should, thus, be readily defensible. The difference in this regard from more conventional methods is perhaps misleading. The committee emphasizes that there is little that is "transparent" or easily reproducible about expert judgment, for example. The "black box" in this case is the human brain. Such expert judgments still must be justified for regulatory purposes, but this is no different than what will be required as output from a neural network approach. Ranking systems are only superficially transparent, in that the weights and modes of combination are explicit and open for all to see, but how the weights are arrived at and the consequences of the modes of combination usually are not. As for the neural network approach, its outputs must also be justified for regulatory purposes.

The committee recommends, therefore, that EPA give careful consideration to and actively experiment with developing a prototype classification approach using neural network or similar methods (in conjunction with expert judgment) for identifying appropriate PCCL candidates for inclusion on the CCL. Further, EPA should use several training sets to gauge the sensitivity of the adopted method. As discussed in Chapter 2, the committee cautions that disputes may occur (e.g., among decision-makers and between decision-makers and the public) regarding the issue of what minimum levels of sensitivity and specificity the approach must have in order to be deemed "adequate." A robust result over different training sets would clearly lend support for this approach. Additional details of the recommended approach to the development of future CCLs are presented later in this chapter.

ILLUSTRATIVE EXAMPLE OF A PROTOTYPE CLASSIFICATION SCHEME FOR CCL CONTAMINANTS

The remainder of this chapter presents a demonstration of prototype schemes for classifying drinking water contaminants. As previously noted, prototype classification methods require a training data set. For illustrative purposes, the committee constructed a training data set based on contaminants that are presumed worthy of regulatory consideration and contaminants for which the committee can presume regulatory consideration is not necessary. The contaminants included in the training data set were then assigned values for the five health effect and occurrence attributes discussed in Chapter 4. For purposes of mathematical modeling, the report uses the following notation to represent the values of the five attributes for each contaminant: X_1 is severity, X_2 is potency, X_3 is prevalence, X_4 is magnitude, and X_5 is persistence-mobility. Depending on the category of the contaminant, each contaminant is assigned a value of the binary classification variable, the target (T). The committee uses $T = 1$ for contaminants that are "presumed worthy of regulatory consideration" and $T = 0$ for contaminants "presumed not worthy of regulatory consideration."

The prototype classification approach does not require that the contaminant attributes be those specified by the committee. One could use more attributes or fewer. They can be different attributes entirely. Redundant attributes can be integrated prior to processing. For example, in the absence of complete occurrence information one might use Boolean logic to combine prevalence *and* magnitude *or* persistence-mobility. Multidimensional attributes could be expanded. For example, the Henry's law constant and aqueous solubility for chemicals could be used directly rather than combined in a single persistence-mobility score. Also, the attributes can be ordinal or categorical. The objective is to come up with contaminant features that comprehensively encompass the information that determines a regulatory action decision.

The overall objective is to mathematically represent the mapping between the contaminant attributes (the values of X_is) and the target value. This is expressed mathematically as

$$Y = f(\{X_i\}; \theta), \tag{5-1}$$

where Y is the predicted value of the classification variable and θ collectively describes the parameters of the mapping function $f(\ )$. The most commonly used metric to evaluate the function's ability to capture the training data set is the mean squared error (*mse*):

$$mse = \frac{\sum_{j=1}^{N}(Y_j - T_j)^2}{N}, \tag{5-2}$$

where N is the total number of contaminants in the training data set and the subscript j denotes contaminant j. There is a great deal of choice in selection of the mapping function $f(\ )$. In this report, the committee presents two alternatives. One is based on a linear function, and the other derives from a neural network architecture. The training data set is used to "calibrate" the mapping function (i.e., to estimate the optimal values of the parameters).

The final step is to use an appropriate criterion to determine the optimal threshold value for Y that separates data into the two classes. One possible criterion is to set the threshold at that value of Y that minimizes the number of objects in the training data set that are misclassified. The resulting mapping can then be used to predict the classification for new contaminants to which values of X_i have been assigned. A predicted value of Y greater than the threshold would indicate that the contaminant belongs in the $T = 1$ category, and a predicted value of Y less than the threshold would indicate that the contaminant belongs in the $T = 0$ category.

The following sections of this chapter present the details of such an analysis. The committee emphasizes that the classification analysis presented here is not intended to lead to definitive conclusions about specific contaminants. The committee was limited in time and resources; hence the training data set used for this analysis was smaller than ideal and the attribute values are far from certain. Nonetheless, the committee believes that this analysis provides a valid demonstration of the methodology and could serve as a framework for a similar analysis that EPA might conduct to help classify PCCL contaminants for inclusion on the corresponding CCL.

The Training Data Set

The committee constructed a training data set consisting of 80 chemical and microbial contaminants, 63 of which were assigned to the "presumed worthy of regulatory action" category ($T = 1$) and 17 of which were assigned to the "presumed not worthy of regulatory action" category ($T = 0$). The contaminants included in the training data set are listed in Table 5-1. Those in the $T = 1$ category were selected from among currently regulated drinking water contaminants that have enforceable maximum contaminant levels (MCLs; see Chapter 1 for further information). Those in the $T = 0$ category are considered to be safe for human ingestion. Some of these were taken from the list of substances generally recognized as safe (GRAS) by the U.S. Food and Drug Administration. In discussing this illustrative example, the committee reiterates that it was constrained by time and data resources, so the list of contaminants in the $T = 0$ category is relatively small and includes only inorganic and organic chemicals. If the EPA conducts a similar analysis, the committee strongly recommends that it increase the size and types of drinking water contaminants (e.g., radionuclides) included in the training data set to improve predictive capacity.

TABLE 5-1 Contaminants Included in the Training Data Set

Presumed Worthy of Regulatory Consideration (T = 1)		Presumed Not Worthy of Regulatory Consideration (T = 0)
Inorganic Chemicals	**Organic Chemicals (continued)**	**Inorganic Chemicals**
Antimony	Diquat	Calcium
Barium	Endothall	Chloride
Beryllium	Endrin	Iron
Cadmium	Epichlorohydrin	
Chromium (total)	Ethylbenzene	**Organic Chemicals**
Cyanide	Ethylene dibromide	Ascorbic acid
Fluoride	Glyphosate	Benzoic acid
Mercury (total inorganic)	Heptachlor	Citric acid
Nitrite	Heptachlor epoxide	Ethanol
Selenium	Hexachlorobenzene	Folic acid
Thallium	Hexachlorocyclopentadiene	Glucose
	Lindane	Glycerin
Organic Chemicals	Methoxychlor	Glycine
Acrylamide	Oxamyl (Vydate)	Olestra
Alachlor	Pentachlorophenol	p-Aminobenzoic acid
Benzene	Polychlorinated biphenyls	(PABA)
Benzo[a]pyrene	(PCBs)	Phosphate
Carbofuran	Simazine	Propylene glycol
Carbon tetrachloride	Styrene	Saccharin
Chlordane	Toluene	Vanillin
Chlorobenzene	Toxaphene	
2,4-D	2,4,5-TP (Silvex)	
Dalapon	1,2,4-Trichlorobenzene	
o-Dichlorobenzene	1,1,1-Trichloroethane	
p-Dichlorobenzene	1,1,2-Trichloroethane	
1,2-Dichloroethane	Trichloroethylene	
1,1-Dichloroethylene	Vinyl chloride	
cis-1,2-Dichloroethylene	Xylenes (total)	
trans-1,2-Dichloroethylene		
Dichloromethane	**Microorganisms**	
1,2-Dichloropropane	Legionella	
Di(2-ethylhexyl) phthalate	Heterotrophic plate count	
Dinoseb	(HPC)	
Dioxin (2,3,7,8-TCDD)	Total coliforms	
	Viruses	

NOTE: 2,4-D = 2,4-dichlorophenoxyacetic acid; TCDD = 2,3,7,8-tetrachloro-dihenzo-p-dioxin; 2,4,5-TP = 2 (2,4,5-trichlorophenoxy) propionic acid.

Attribute Scoring

For each contaminant in the training data set and for each of the validation test cases, values between 1 and 10 were assigned to each of five health effects and occurrence attributes. The committee used the contaminant attributes and associated scoring metrics and guidance outlined in Chapter 4. It is important to note that the contaminant attribute scores for chemicals and microorganisms in the training data set are considered rough estimates because they were generated in a very rapid fashion using limited sources of health effects and occurrence information. Thus, they are not provided in this report. However, the committee gained a number of important insights by going through this exercise; these insights form the basis for the "lessons learned" section at the end of Chapter 4. For the five regulated contaminants that were used as validation test cases, which are described later in this chapter, details of the attribute scoring scheme used by the committee are explained in the Box 5-1.

Despite the considerable uncertainty in attribute values in its training data set, the committee made every effort to be as precise and consistent as possible within the time frame allowed and feels that this analysis provides some very valuable insights into the usefulness of the approach. The first component of the analysis is an examination of the extent to which the attribute values are correlated (Figure 5-1). For the training data set constructed by the committee, there is no significant correlation between any of the attributes. This is interesting because the committee had expected at the outset that there would be some redundancy between the prevalence scores and the persistence-mobility scores, reasoning that if something persists in the environment and is mobile in water bodies, it is more likely to be prevalent in drinking water sources. Further, the absence of correlation between the attributes is encouraging because it implies that each contributes unique information that may be useful in the classification of PCCL contaminants. Figure 5-1 also shows that the values of each of the attributes are fairly well distributed over the assigned range of 1 to 10.

EPA will have to collect and organize available data and research for each PCCL contaminant and document the attribute scoring scheme used to help ensure a transparent and defensible process. One way in which EPA is encouraged to expand the training data set and classification algorithm is to allow for the expected case of missing data—that is, to purposefully include in the training data set contaminants for which values

---

BOX 5-1
Attribute Scoring for Validation Test Cases[1]

Arsenic

Arsenic is an element that occurs naturally in rocks, soil, water, air, plants, and animals. It is a metalloid that exhibits both metallic and non-metallic chemical and physical properties and has several valence states. Although arsenic is found in nature to a small extent in its elemental form (0 valence), it most often occurs as inorganic and organic compounds in either the As(III) (+3) or As(V) (+5) valence states (see more below). There are numerous natural sources (e.g., geologic formations and volcanic activity) as well as anthropogenic sources (e.g., manufacture of semiconductors and animal feed additives (EPA, 2000i) of arsenic.

The severity score was assigned based on the health end point associated with the potency score. For arsenic, the potency score associated with the lowest observed adverse effect level (LOAEL) for noncancer effects was higher than the potency score based on its cancer end point (EPA, 2000c). The adverse health effects at the LOAEL were hyperpigmentation, keratosis, and possible vascular complications in humans. Since these effects were considered irreversible changes, leading to a treatable disease, arsenic was assigned a severity score of 6.

The reference dose (RfD) given in EPA's Integrated Risk Information System (IRIS) database for arsenic is 3×10^{-4} mg/kg (EPA, 2000c). This is based on a no observed adverse effect level (NOAEL) of 8×10^{-4} mg/kg in humans. As noted above, the effect at the LOAEL is hyperpigmentation, keratosis, and possible vascular complications in humans. The range of LOAELs for the chemicals that were scored varied from a low of 2×10^{-8} mg/kg (dioxin) to a high of 1×10^{3} mg/kg (di(2-ethylhexyl) adipate). Based on the range of LOAEL values and the LOAEL for arsenic, it was assigned a potency score of 6.

---

[1]This box provides several examples of how the attributes of various drinking water contaminants used in the training data set for this demonstration were individually and expeditiously scored using publicly and readily available environmental databases as described in Chapter 4. As such, these scores do not in any way represent an independent or systematic evaluation of their health effects and occurrence data and should not be interpreted or cited as such.

continues

BOX 5-1 Continued

The data used for obtaining arsenic's prevalence score were taken from the Endocrine Disruptor Priority-Setting Database (EDPSD) currently being developed for use by EPA (ERG-EPA, 2000). The database contains information from the National Drinking Water Contaminant Occurrence Database (NCOD). Information from the EDPSD-NCOD about the estimated population exposed (127,350) to arsenic and the number of analyses with detectable levels (57) of arsenic was used to assign a prevalence score of 4. The range of population exposed in this particular database for the chemicals scored was 250 to 327,600, and the range in analyses with detectable levels was 0 to 2,970.

The EDPSD-NCOD drinking water database also contains information about contaminant concentration. The EDPSD-NCOD reported a weighted average concentration in drinking water for arsenic of 410 µg/L. The weighted average concentration in drinking water for the chemicals scored in this database ranged from a low of 1 µg/L to a high of 8,343 µg/L. A magnitude score of 10 was assigned to arsenic using information on the weighted average concentration and the potency score.

Scoring the persistence and mobility of arsenic exemplifies some of the difficulty of this exercise for contaminants exhibiting complex speciation under environmental conditions. Under oxidizing conditions, the stable form of arsenic is pentavalent (arsenate), whereas the trivalent form (arsenite) and various organoarsenic compounds are more prevalent in reducing environments. While arsenite is more mobile than arsenate, chemical or biological oxidation-reduction reactions can convert one form to the other (Nriagu, 1994). Since arsenate adsorbs rather strongly to soils, the overall mobility of arsenic was scored rather low. However, the overall persistence of arsenic was scored as high because most mechanism for detoxifying arsenic appears to be reversible. Thus, the resulting score for the persistence-mobility attribute was 6.

Nitrate

Inorganic nitrates often enter drinking water supplies through runoff from fertilizer use, leaching from septic tanks, sewage, and erosion of natural deposits (EPA, 2000a). The severity score for nitrate was based on the health effect associated with the potency score, (i.e., methemoglobinemia; see Chapter 4 for further information). Since this health effect is associated with significant, but reversible functional changes, a severity score of 5 was assigned to nitrate.

continues

BOX 5-1 Continued

The RfD for nitrate given in EPA's IRIS database is 1.6 mg/kg (EPA, 2000d). This is based on a NOAEL of 1.6 mg/kg for early clinical signs of methemoglobinemia in excess of 10 percent in 0- to 3-month-old infants. A potency score of 4 was assigned for nitrate and was based on its LOAEL of 1.6 mg/kg and the range of LOAEL values. The scoring for nitrates was based on an effect in a vulnerable population that contains many individuals, and the committee considered this reasonable; this is also consistent with EPA's current approach for evaluating nitrates.

The data used to estimate nitrate's prevalence score were taken from EDPSD-NCOD (ERG-EPA, 2000). The estimated population exposed to nitrate was given as 118,800 with the number of analyses with detectable concentrations given as 55. The range of information about population exposed and number of detects for all of the chemicals considered, along with this same information for nitrate, resulted in a prevalence score of 3.

The EDPSD-NCOD reported a weighted average concentration for nitrate in drinking water of 821 µg/L. This average concentration along with potency information was used to assign a magnitude score for nitrate of 8.

Many otherwise useful databases (e.g., the Hazardous Substances Database in TOXNET; NLM, 2000) are inconveniently organized for the purposes of this exercise since they contain no entry for the free aqueous nitrate anion—only entries for the various salts of nitrate (KNO_3, etc.). Most of these salts are very soluble, and since sorption of nitrate to most mineral surfaces is not especially strong, it was considered highly mobile. The persistence of nitrate varies greatly with the microbiology of the local environment because nitrate reduction can be quite rapid under anaerobic conditions but is usually negligible under aerobic conditions. This led the committee to score nitrate's persistence as intermediate. Combined with the highest possible score for mobility, this resulted in a combined persistence-mobility score of 8 for nitrate.

Atrazine

Atrazine is a herbicide that often enters drinking water supplies through runoff from its use in agriculture. The severity score was based on the health effects associated with the potency score for atrazine (degradation products were not considered) (i.e., a decrease in body weight gain compared to controls, cardiac toxicity, moderate to severe dilation of

continues

BOX 5-1 Continued

the right atrium). Since the cardiac toxicity and moderate to severe dilation of the right atrium are a single organ system pathology and function loss, atrazine was assigned a severity score of 7 (EPA, 2000e). The RfD for atrazine is 3.5×10^{-2} mg/kg and is based on a NOAEL of 3.5 mg/kg in rats from a two-year feeding study (EPA, 2000e). The LOAEL from this study was 25 mg/kg for a decrease in body weight gain. A one-year feeding study in dogs was used as support for this RfD. The second study had a NOAEL of 34 mg/kg and a LOAEL of 4.97 mg/kg, with the adverse effect being cardiac toxicity and moderate to severe dilation of the right atrium. Atrazine's potency score was based on its LOAEL of 25 mg/kg. The range of LOAELs for the chemicals that were scored varied from a low of 2×10^{-8} mg/kg (dioxin) to a high of 1×10^{3} mg/kg (di(2-ethylhexyl) adipate). Based on these LOAEL values, atrazine was assigned a potency score of 3.

The data used for obtaining atrazine's prevalence score were taken from EDPSD-NCOD (ERG/EPA, 2000). Information from EDSPD-NCOD about the estimated population exposed (223,550) to atrazine and the number of analyses with detectable levels (24) of atrazine was used to assign a prevalence score for atrazine of 3. The range for population exposed in this particular database for the chemicals scored was 250 to 327,600, and the range in analyses with detectable levels was 0 to 2,970.

The EDPSD-NCOD reported a weighted average concentration value for atrazine of 1 µg/L. This information along with potency data was used to assign a magnitude score for atrazine of 2.

The persistence and mobility of atrazine and other triazine herbicides have been studied and reviewed extensively (Ballantine and McFarland, 1998; NLM, 2000). Atrazine is a nonionogenic but moderately polar organic molecule, so it has a moderate solubility, relatively low volatility, and moderately high tendency to adsorb to soils. Atrazine is subject to photodegradation and biodegradation where conditions are favorable. Reported half-lives for biodegradation of atrazine in soils are typically on the order of months, whereas half-lives in groundwater are estimated to be in years. The moderate mobility and substantial persistence of atrazine resulted in an overall persistence-mobility score of 7.

Tetrachloroethylene (PCE)

Tetrachloroethylene is a solvent that can reach drinking water supplies through industrial discharges from factories and dry cleaners (EPA,

continues

BOX 5-1 Continued

2000a). PCE causes liver tumors in mice when administered by gavage (ATSDR, 1997). The oral cancer potency factor (CPF) given by EPA's Region III for PCE is 5.2×10^{-2} mg/kg/day (EPA, 1999i). Because PCE causes cancer, its severity score was 9.

The potency score for PCE was based on its CPF (EPA, 1999i). The range in oral CPFs for the chemicals that were scored varied from $1.56 \times 10^{+5}$ mg/kg/day (dioxin) to 1.2×10^{-3} mg/kg/day (di(2-ethylhexyl) adipate). Based on the CPFs, the potency score for PCE was assigned a value of 3.

The data used for obtaining PCE's prevalence score were from EDPSD-NCOD (ERG-EPA, 2000). The estimated population exposed to PCE was given as 227,600, and the number of analyses with detectable levels was given as 124. Using this information along with information from the other chemicals scored resulted in a prevalence score for PCE of 10.

The EDPSD-NCOD gave a weighted average concentration for PCE of 4 μg/L. This information along with potency information was used to assign a magnitude score for PCE of 4.

The environmental fate of chlorinated ethenes has been reviewed from many perspectives (NLM, 2000; Pankow and Cherry, 1996). PCE is regarded as moderately mobile in natural waters, even though its solubility in water is fairly low, because retardation due to adsorption is also relatively low. In general, PCE is regarded as persistent, especially under aerobic conditions, although both aerobic and anaerobic pathways of PCE biodegradation are well documented. Combining a moderately high persistence with moderately mobility resulted in a combined persistence-mobility score of 7.

Giardia Lamblia

Giardia lamblia is a protozoan parasite that may reach drinking water supplies through human and animal fecal waste. It induces mild to severe diarrhea over a moderately prolonged (one-to-two week) period, with most cases either self-limiting or amenable to therapy (Steiner et al., 1997). There do not appear to have been significant reports of chronic sequelae.[2] Thus, this organism was assigned a severity score of 6.

---

[2]The term "chronic sequelae" is poorly understood and often misapplied as related to the study of waterborne pathogens. For the purposes of this report, it can be defined as a secondary adverse health outcome that (1) occurs as a result of a previous infection by a microbial pathogen *and* (2) is clearly distinguishable from the health events, if any, that initially result from the causative infection *and* (3) lasts three months or more after recognition (Parkin et al., 2000).

continues

BOX 5-1 Continued

There are only two pathogens other than *G. lamblia* for which regulations are set (or proposed): *Cryptosporidium parvum* and enteric viruses. The median infectious dose (N_{50}) of rotavirus is 6.2 plaque-forming units (Regli et al., 1991), while that for *C. parvum* is 165 oocysts (Haas et al., 1996). The median infectious dose of *G. lamblia* is 34 cysts (Rose et al., 1991). Thus, the potency of *Giardia* is intermediate between *C. parvum* and rotavirus. To obtain a percentile, examination of a broader spectrum of human pathogens for which dose-response assessments have been made must be undertaken. The table below, adapted from Haas et al. (1999), shows that *G. lamblia* is the 3rd most potent of 11 organisms or classes of organisms. Assigning the most infectious (adenovirus 4) a score of 10 and the least infectious (nonenterohemorrhagic *Escherichia coli*) a score of 1, the potency score based on rank order would be 8.18, rounded to 8, for *G. lamblia*.

Based on measurements of *G. lamblia* in source waters (LeChevallier et al., 1991, 1997; Rose et al., 1991) a spatial prevalence of 50-75 percent (accounting for both groundwater and surface water) and a temporal prevalence of 75-90 percent appear to be reasonable estimates. Thus, a prevalence value of 9 was assigned.

To determine the score for magnitude first involved ranking the occurrence of *Giardia* versus other waterborne pathogens. In comparison with the two other regulated microorganisms (enteric viruses and *Cryptosporidium*), the median levels of *Giardia* in source waters are higher.[3] Thus, it is considered to be in the ninth decile for concentration. The score, noted above for potency, is 8. The overall score for magnitude would be $\sqrt{8 \cdot 9} = 8.5$, rounded to 9.

The two applicable subattributes for the evaluation of persistence-mobility of *G. lamblia* are amplification and stability. Since *G. lamblia* is an obligate parasite, there is no reproduction under environmental conditions and the score for this property is 0 (out of 3). Studies on persistence of the cyst in natural waters (DeRegnier et al., 1989) indicate a survival time in excess of weeks; thus, the score on the property of stability is 3 (out of 3). The average of these two scores, expressed on a scale of 10, is 5, which is taken as the score for the overall persistence-mobility attribute.

---

[3]Based on data collected in response to the Information Collection Rule (i.e., source waters from communities serving in excess of 100,000 persons).

continues

BOX 5-1 Continued

Median Infection Doses of Waterborne Pathogens

Organism	N_{50}
Adenovirus 4	1.66
Rotavirus	6.3
Giardia lamblia	34.8
Cryptosporidium parvum	165
Vibrio cholerae	243
Campylobacter jejuni	896
Salmonella (5 nontyphoid strains)[a]	23,600
Salmonella typhosa	3.60×10^6
Escherichia coli (6 nonenterohemorhagic strains)[b]	8.60×10^7

[a] *Salmonella newport, derby, bareilly, anatum,* and *meleagridis.*
[b] *E. coli* O124, O143, O6:H16, O148:H28, O78:H11, and O55.
SOURCE: Adapted from Haas et al., 1999.

---

of some of the attributes are unknown and develop a scheme that allows prediction for contaminants for which some of the attributes are unknown. Statistical schemes have been developed to deal with missing and incomplete data (e.g., Little and Rubin, 1987; Weiss and Kulikowski, 1990). Some of the general techniques include filling in the missing values with the means of values for other cases in the same class, incorporating Boolean logic structures that allow for redundancy in expression of an attribute (i.e., A or B), and using smoothing methods to interpolate values based on assumed underlying data structures. There are, of course, risks in including incompletely characterized contaminants in the training data set because biases may be introduced in the mathematical treatment of missing values. However, these risks can be outweighed by the benefits of having a very large, information-rich training data set.

Prototype Classification Functions

The simplest function to represent the mapping between contaminant attributes and the binary classification variable is a linear model:

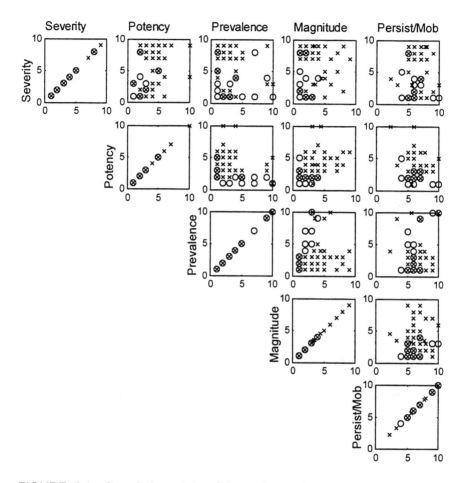

FIGURE 5-1 Correlation plots of the values of the five attributes for contaminants in the training data set. Crosses represent T = 1 contaminants and circles represent T = 0 contaminants.

$$Y = w_0 + w_1 X_1 + w_2 X_2 + w_3 X_3 + w_4 X_4 + w_5 X_5, \qquad (5\text{-}3)$$

where w_i is the weight for attribute i. The optimal parameters (i.e., weights) are estimated, for example, by minimizing the *mse* (Equation 5-2). The linear model is an attractive alternative because the mapping function is readily understandable and the values of the weights are easy to interpret. Furthermore, calibrating a linear classification model can be done with very simple statistical procedures that are widely available. The disadvantage of the linear model is that its performance is poor if the training data are not "linearly separable," as explained later in this chapter. To achieve good performance with linearly nonseparable data, one must use a model that is capable of nonlinear dependencies.

Neural networks provide the flexibility to capture linear as well as nonlinear dependencies (Hornik et al., 1989). Neural networks were originally conceived in the 1960s and were more formally developed in the 1980s. Their use has become widespread in the last decade, and a number of excellent textbooks have been written on the applications of neural networks in a variety of fields (Garson, 1998; Weiss and Kulikowski, 1990; Zupan and Gasteiger, 1993). Widely cited introductory articles include Bailey and Thompson (1990) and Hinton (1992).

A neural network is a mathematical representation of a network of biological neurons. Input data are fed into the network, and output from the network is computed based on the architecture of the network and the operative mathematical functions. The simplest neural network is a single neuron with a vector input and single output (Figure 5-2). In this network, the sum of the weighted inputs is passed through a transfer function $f( )$. If the transfer function is linear, then this neural network is mathematically equivalent to the linear classifier in Equation 5-3. This neuron has a bias that is equivalent to w_0, the intercept in Equation 5-3. More complex neural networks can be constructed by having multiple layers of neurons, multiple neurons within a layer, complex connectivity between the layers, and nonlinear transfer functions mapping the neuron input to the output. For example, a multilayer neural network has "hidden" layers, which are additional layers of neurons between the input and output layers.

One of the attractive advantages of using a neural network is that it is not necessary to specify a priori the mathematical relationship between input and output data. One chooses the architecture, which specifies the number of neurons and their organization, and the transfer functions op-

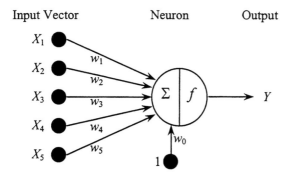

Input Vector   Neuron   Output

FIGURE 5-2 Single-neuron model with a vector input and single output.

perative at each information node. The more elaborate the architecture, the more flexible is the model in capturing the functionalities between input and output and the possibly numerous interactions in variables. It is precisely this advantage that leads to the primary disadvantage of using neural networks—the resulting classification algorithm is not readily extracted, and there is a necessary loss in transparency in exactly how the input variables determine the classification output.

A cautionary statement is appropriate at this point. In all prototype classification schemes, the user should be aware of the danger in overfitting the training data. Overfitting occurs when a modeler has undue confidence in the precision of the training data set and is overzealous in finding an algorithm that produces no classification error in representing these data. This can impose "false structure" on the mapping, which does not truly capture the functional dependencies. The danger of overfitting is especially present in neural network modeling because of the tremendous flexibility in the underlying mathematical relationships. The result is a sacrifice of generalization (predictive) ability. This issue has been discussed extensively in the literature of statistical learning theory and information theory (Vapnik, 1995).

The following sections present classification results for the committee's illustrative example training data set. The committee presents results for both a linear classification model and a neural network. The classification algorithms were developed using Matlab and the Matlab Neural Network Toolbox (Mathworks Inc., Natick, Massachusetts). The Matlab computer codes used for classification, error analysis, and prediction are included in Appendix B.

Classification Results Using a Linear Classifier

Using the model in Equation 5-3 and the training data set, a linear regression produced a mean squared error of 0.094. The resulting weights are listed in Table 5-2. The most important and statistically significant indicators are severity, potency, and magnitude. This implies that these are the metrics that have, in the past, determined whether a contaminant is appropriate for regulatory action. Although in principle prevalence and persistence-mobility are important indicators of human health hazard, the analysis did not show this. Either these factors have not been given significant weight in past regulatory decision making for drinking water safety or one's ability to estimate these attribute scores accurately given available data, is poor. This finding may change when EPA constructs a formal training data set, but it illustrates the type of conclusion that can be derived.

The resulting distributions of Y_i values for each of the two types of contaminants in the training data set are shown in Figure 5-3. Clearly, there is not a perfect separation between the two categories, which indicates that these data are not linearly separable. However, there is a clear

TABLE 5-2 Linear Regression Results for Illustrative Example

Attribute	Weight	Regression Estimate	Significantly Different from Zero at the 95% Confidence Level?
—	w_0	0.018	No
Severity	w_1	0.043	Yes
Potency	w_2	0.062	Yes
Prevalence	w_3	−0.029	No
Magnitude	w_4	0.044	Yes
Persistence-Mobility	w_5	0.040	No

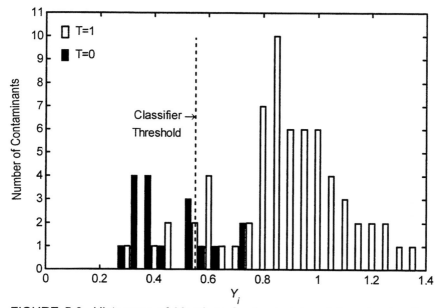

FIGURE 5-3 Histogram of Y_i values for the training data set using the linear classifier.

trend that contaminants in the $T = 0$ category tend to have smaller predicted values of Y_i. This result alone is interesting because it serves to verify that past regulatory decisions do indeed separate contaminants in a manner consistent with the factors that the committee believes to be important indicators of human health risk.

The next step is the determination of an appropriate threshold value that separates the objects into the two categories. The committee decided to optimize the value of the threshold by minimizing the total number of misclassified contaminants. Figure 5-4 is a plot of the number of misclassified contaminants as a function of the threshold value. Because two values of the threshold (0.4 and 0.55), produce a minimum in the total number of misclassified contaminants, the committee employed a secondary criterion that minimized the sum of the percent errors for each of the categories (see Figure 5-5). A threshold value of 0.55 produces a smaller percent error in both categories, so this was chosen as the optimal threshold.

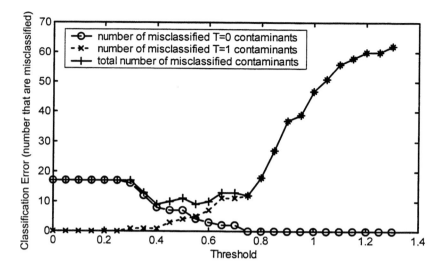

FIGURE 5-4   Classification error as a function of threshold value, in which classification error is defined as the number of misclassified contaminants linear classifier).

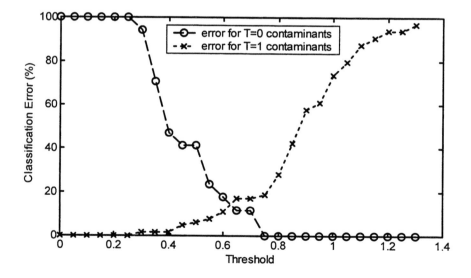

FIGURE 5-5   Classification error as a function of threshold value, in which classification error is defined as the percentage of the number of contaminants within a category that are misclassified (linear classifier).

The ability of the classification scheme to separate the training data set is one way to estimate the classification error that is expected when used for prediction. With a threshold value of 0.55, the error in misclassifying $T = 1$ contaminants is 8 percent (5 out of 63) and the error in misclassifying $T = 0$ contaminants is 24 percent (4 out of 17). The larger error in misclassifying $T = 0$ contaminants reflects the fact that this portion of the training data set was smaller, so there is less confidence that the contaminants used are representative of the population of contaminants in this category. These errors can be interpreted as follows: If this classification algorithm is used for prediction, 92 percent of the time a contaminant that should be on the CCL will be classified correctly. This represents the "sensitivity" of the classification. The other characteristic is the "specificity," which is that 76 percent of the time a contaminant that should not be on the CCL will be classified correctly. That is, the probability of a false negative is 8 percent and the probability of a false positive is 24 percent. This estimation of errors is essentially a demonstration of what the committee discussed in Appendix A of its first report (NRC, 1999a).

Classification Results Using a Neural Network Classifier

The neural network used for this classification problem has two layers connected in a feed-forward configuration (Figure 5-6). The first is a hidden layer containing two nodes (neurons). A hyperbolic tangent sigmoidal function was chosen as the transfer function for each node in this layer. This transfer function is one of several commonly used nonlinear functions. The second is the output layer with a single node and a linear transfer function. All nodes have biases. Other possible network architectures could have been used for this problem (e.g., additional nodes in the hidden layer or different transfer functions). The committee chose this architecture because it is one of the simplest but has sufficient flexibility to capture nonlinear dependencies.

The training algorithm used to calibrate the neural network was a conjugate gradient method that constitutes a family of efficient search algorithms. This search method converges much faster than the simpler gradient descent methods, but as is true with all nonlinear optimization problems, care must be taken to ensure robustness in the solution by running several training sessions with different initial conditions. Network performance is measured according to the minimum of *mse* (Equation 5-2).

Using the committee's training data set, the resulting mean squared error was 0.018, which is considerably smaller than that achieved using the linear classifier. This clearly demonstrates the improvement in fitting capabilities of a neural network model over a linear model. The classification results using the neural network model are shown in Figure 5-7. The enhanced ability of the neural network classifier to separate the training data is clearly seen by comparing the histograms in Figures 5-3 and 5-7. The improved performance of the neural network is rather remarkable considering that the neural network architecture (Figure 5-6) is one of the simplest possible for this problem. Classification error analysis indicated that the optimum threshold value of Y for the neural network classifier is 0.55, which coincidentally is the same as the resulting optimal threshold for the linear classifier. The predicted classification error for the neural network classifier is 3 percent for false negatives (2 out of 63). Because there were no misclassifications of the $T = 0$ contaminants, the false-positive rate is estimated to be near zero.

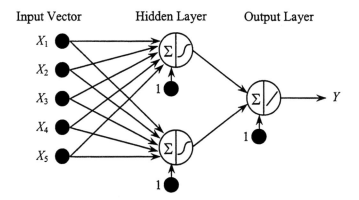

FIGURE 5-6 Multilayer neural network used for contaminant classification. Weights are not shown, for simplicity.

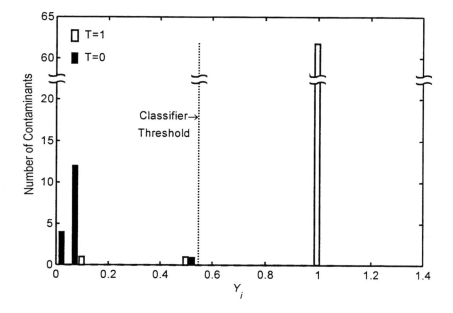

FIGURE 5-7   Histogram of Y_i values for the training data set using the neural network classifier.

For the linear classifier it was possible to examine the values of the weights and their statistical significance to determine the relative importance of the different attributes in determining the classification outcome. Because of the greater complexity of the neural network model, there is less transparency in the functional mapping. In most computer programs, the weights can be examined, but it is very difficult to extrapolate these weights mentally to readily understandable rules. For example, in this neural network, there are 10 weights in the first layer, 2 weights in the second layer, and a total of 3 bias weights. Because these parameters relate to cross-products and nonlinear functions of the attributes, it is not immediately obvious what the values mean. One way to probe the importance of various attributes in a neural network is to leave out certain attributes in the training data set and examine the effect on the classification of the training data. Indeed, this practice is discussed in Chapter 2 as a means to enhance the transparency of the approach, and the committee recommends that EPA conduct such a sensitivity analysis on any classification model it develops and intends to use to assist in the creation of future CCLs.

DEMONSTRATED USE OF THE TRAINED CLASSIFIER

Examination of Misclassified Contaminants

Misclassification of contaminants in the training data set can be interpreted in three ways: Either (1) the training data (i.e., the attribute scores) do not capture the information that determines regulatory action for drinking water contaminants; (2) the model relating the input to the output does not adequately capture the process by which this information is used in regulatory decision-making; or (3) the target values are wrong, implying that some of the regulatory decisions made in the past are inconsistent with regulatory decisions for the bulk of drinking water contaminants. If one operates on the presumption that the training data are accurate, precise, and complete, then classification errors can be reduced by exploring modeling alternatives. That is precisely what was done in the analysis in this chapter. A large number of classification errors resulted from the linear model, so a neural network model was used that greatly reduced classification error. One can continue to try to eliminate all classification errors by using more and more elaborate neural networks (or other classification models such as support vector machines, cluster algorithms, radial basis functions). However, as mentioned previously, this endeavor may lead the analyst down the potentially dangerous path of overfitting the data. Thus, an analyst must question whether persistent errors are indicative of true classification errors.

If one operates on the assumption that the attribute scores should combine in a linear fashion to determine classification output, then some insights can be gained by examining which of the contaminants in the training data set were misclassified using the linear classifier. These are listed in Table 5-3. Total coliforms and heterotrophic plate count (HPC) are misclassified because these contaminants are not inherently hazardous, but rather are indicators of the potential presence of hazardous microorganisms. For this reason, the committee believes it is appropriate for these two contaminants to fall below the threshold. The linear classifier also misclassified toluene, *o*-dichlorobenzene, and *trans*-1,2-dichloroethylene, which are currently regulated chemicals. These chemicals score relatively low on severity and potency because their health effects are smaller than those of other regulated drinking water contaminants that are of greater concern possibly because of their carcinogenic potential or their potential to cause health effects at low

TABLE 5-3   Contaminants in the Training Data Set That Were Misclassified Using the Linear Classifier

Misclassified $T = 1$ Contaminants	Y_i	Misclassified $T = 0$ Contaminants	Y_i
o-Dichlorobenzene	0.47	Ethanol	0.57
trans-1,2-Dichloroethylene	0.54	Folic acid	0.72
Toluene	0.43	Olestra	0.63
HPC	0.28	Saccharin	0.70
Total coliforms	0.42		

concentrations. Toluene is a chemical that is generally known to be rather prevalent, but the occurrence data available were insufficient to represent this fact. In general, the data used to score prevalence for all contaminants in the training data set were found to be lacking in several respects (see Chapter 4). These misclassifications may be indicative of a paucity of good information on which to base occurrence metrics. Of the $T = 0$ contaminants that were misclassified in the linear classifier, the committee notes that ethanol, folic acid, and saccharin have potentially severe health impacts, and Olestra has significant potential for persistence and mobility in the environment. Like other substances in the $T = 0$ category, however, these are substances that many people purposefully and regularly ingest.

Rather than placing emphasis on the misclassifications obtained using the linear classifier, one can operate on the assumption that the underlying process by which the attribute scores determine classification output is complex and requires nonlinear functionalities to represent it mathematically. This makes the case for the use of neural networks rather than linear classifiers. The misclassified contaminants for the neural network classifier are listed in Table 5-4. The neural network classifier had a much smaller number of misclassified contaminants, indicating that it was able to capture the data mapping process mathematically. It is interesting to note that the misclassified contaminants in this case are not a subset of those misclassified in the linear classification. Here, ethylbenzene has been misclassified, whereas it had not been misclassified in the linear classification. This indicates the strong underlying nonlinearity that is being modeled by the neural network.

TABLE 5-4   Contaminants in the Training Data Set That Were Misclassified Using the Neural Network Classifier

Misclassified $T = 1$ Contaminants	Y_i	Misclassified $T = 0$ Contaminants
Ethylbenzene	0.50	—
HPC	0.08	—

Validation Test Cases

The contaminants in the training data set in the $T = 1$ category did not include all those that have MCLs. Five such chemical and microbial contaminants were withheld as validation test cases to examine the predictive accuracy of the classification algorithm as required in the second phase of study (see Preface to this report). Details of how health effect and occurrence attributes were scored for these regulated contaminants are discussed earlier in this chapter. The predicted values of Y_i for the five validation test cases are listed in Table 5-5. All contaminants are correctly classified as being in the $T = 1$ category because their Y_i values are well above the thresholds. These correct predictions, albeit few in number, provide additional supporting evidence of the validity of the classification algorithm. EPA should make every effort to increase the number of both types of validation test cases (especially for $T = 0$ contaminants) to assess more thoroughly the predictive accuracy of any classification algorithm developed for use in the creation of future CCLs.

Prediction for Interesting Test Cases

The committee selected five potential drinking water contaminants for which data were available that may be of interest in the future (Table 5-6). Two of these, aluminum and methyl-t-butyl ether (MTBE), are currently included on the 1998 CCL (EPA, 1998b). The linear classifier predicts that all five should be considered for regulatory action. However, the neural network classifier predicts that silver, chloroform, aspirin, and MTBE should be placed on the CCL, but aluminum should not (based on data available at this time). The committee emphasizes that these results do not indicate a recommendation that any of these con-

TABLE 5-5 Classification Prediction Accuracy for Validation Test Cases

Validation Test Cases	Predicted Y_i Using Linear Classifier (Threshold = 0.55)	Predicted Y_i Using Neural Network (Threshold = 0.55)
Arsenic	1.2	1.00
Nitrate	1.1	1.00
Atrazine	0.79	1.00
Tetrachloroethylene	0.76	0.99
Giardia lamblia	1.1	1.00

TABLE 5-6 Classification Prediction for Interesting Test Cases

Interesting Test Cases	Predicted Y_i Using Linear Classifier (Threshold = 0.55)	Predicted Y_i Using Neural Network (Threshold = 0.55)
Aluminum	0.61	0.08
Silver	1.2	1.00
Chloroform	0.8	1.00
Aspirin	1.0	1.00
MTBE	0.98	1.00

taminants be placed on a future CCL or removed from the 1998 CCL. Rather, the results are intended to demonstrate how the EPA can develop and use a classification scheme to help select PCCL contaminants for inclusion on the CCL. The committee also believes that this demonstrates the sensitivity of the results to choices made in constructing the classification algorithm.

SUMMARY: CONCLUSIONS AND RECOMMENDATIONS

The purpose of this analysis was to demonstrate how existing contaminant data and past regulatory decisions could be used to develop a prototype classification algorithm to determine, in conjunction with expert judgment, whether a particular drinking water contaminant is of regulatory concern or not. More specifically, the committee has demonstrated a prototype classification approach that must first be trained (calibrated) using a training data set containing prototype contaminants and can then be used in conjunction with expert judgment to predict whether a new (PCCL) contaminant should be placed on the CCL or not. The use of the majority of currently regulated drinking water contaminants in the training data set can be described simply as "making decisions that are consistent with and build upon what has been done in the past." If this is deemed defensible, the prototype classification approach can be regarded as valid. It is important to realize that this approach is then constrained by the data (i.e., past regulatory decisions).

What has been presented in this chapter is a framework and demonstration of how EPA might develop its own prototype classification scheme for use in the creation of future CCLs. In this regard, the committee makes the following recommendations:

- A linear model and a neural network are discussed and demonstrated for potential use in a prototype classification scheme. Although the neural network performed better than the linear model (with respect to minimizing the number of misclassified contaminants), at this time the committee cannot make a firm recommendation as to which model EPA should use because of the aforementioned uncertainties in the training data set. Thus, the committee recommends that EPA explore alternative model formulations and be cognizant of the dangers of overfitting and loss of generalization.

- To adopt and implement the recommended approach for the creation of future CCLs, EPA will have to employ or work with persons knowledgeable of prototype classification methods and devote appreciable time and resources to develop and maintain a comprehensive training data set. In this regard, the committee recommends strongly that EPA greatly increase the size of the training data set that is used illustratively in this chapter to improve predictive capacity. One way in which EPA can expand the training data set and classification algorithm is to allow for the expected case of missing data—that is, to purposefully include in the training data set contaminants for which values of some of the attributes are unknown and develop a scheme that allows prediction of contaminants for which some of the attributes are unknown.

- EPA will also have to accurately and consistently assign attribute scores for all contaminants under consideration. To do this, it will have to collect and organize available data and research for each PCCL contaminant and document the attribute scoring scheme used to help ensure a transparent and defensible process, the importance of which is discussed in Chapter 2. As recommended in Chapter 3, the creation of a consolidated database that would provide a consistent mechanism for recording and retrieving information on the contaminants under consideration would be of benefit.

• EPA will also have to withhold contaminants from inclusion in the training data set to serve as validation test cases that can assess the predictive accuracy of any classification algorithm developed. While the committee was able to withhold five contaminants presumed worthy of regulatory consideration (T = 1) for this purpose (see Table 5-5), it had insufficient numbers of contaminants presumed not worthy of regulatory consideration (T = 0) to similarly withhold. All withheld validation contaminants were classified correctly as belonging in the T = 1 category and such results provide (albeit limited) additional support for the validity of the classification algorithm approach. EPA should make every effort to increase the number of both types of validation test cases (especially for T = 0 contaminants) to assess more thoroughly the predictive accuracy of any classification algorithm developed for use in the creation of future CCLs.

• If neural networks are used for prototype classification, the transparency in understanding which contaminant attributes determine the category of a contaminant will be less than that of a linear model or a more traditional rule-based scheme. However, if one acknowledges that the underlying process that maps attributes into categorical outcomes is very complex, then there is little hope that an accurate rule-based classification scheme can be constructed. The fact that the nonlinear neural network performed better than the linear classifier is a strong indicator that the underlying mapping process is complex, and it would be a difficult task for a panel of experts to accurately specify the rules and conditions of this mapping. Furthermore, the loss in transparency in using a neural network is not inherent, but rather derives from the difficulty in elucidating the mapping.

• The underlying mapping in a neural network classifier can be examined just as one would conduct experiments to probe a physical system in a laboratory. Through numerical experimentation, one can probe a neural network to determine the sensitivity of the output to various changes in input data. Although a sensitivity analysis was not conducted because of time constraints, the committee recommends that EPA should use several training data sets to gauge the sensitivity of the method as part of its analysis and documentation if a classification approach is ultimately adopted and used to help create future CCLs.

• Finally, EPA should realize that the committee is recommending a prototype classification scheme to be used in conjunction with expert judgment for the future selection of PCCL contaminants for inclusion on a CCL. Thus, transparency is less crucial (though no less desired) at this juncture than when selecting contaminants from the CCL for regulatory activities as discussed in the committee's first report (NRC, 1999a).

6
Virulence-Factor Activity Relationships

INTRODUCTION

The term "virulence-factor activity relationship," or VFAR (formerly referred to as virulence-activity relationship or VAR; NRC, 1999a), is rooted in a recognition of the utility of using structure-activity relationships (SARs) to compare the structure of newly identified or produced chemicals to known chemical structures to enable prediction of their toxicity and other physical properties. In essence, the committee believes the same principle can be applied to waterborne pathogens. It is important to state that many sections of this chapter necessarily include more extensive use of scientific terms and language than might typically be found in the body of a National Research Council (NRC) report. That is, rather than deleting, simplifying, or relegating such relevant technical language to an appendix, the committee decided to keep all information related to VFARs in one comprehensive chapter. This chapter should be read with that qualification in mind.

For microorganisms, there are many levels of structure, such as the cell or organism itself and the larger internal components that comprise the microorganism (e.g., nucleus, micronemes, flagellae). These morphological components can sometimes be used to identify pathogenic microorganisms. Beyond these relatively large structures, there are smaller, biochemical components of the organism, including proteins, carbohydrates, and lipids. Many of these biochemical building blocks are directly related to how a particular microorganism causes disease. Some examples of these include the outer coat of some bacteria (the lipid polysaccharide coat), attachment and invasion factors, and bacterial toxins. Thus, the central premise of VFARs is to relate the architectural and biochemical components of microorganisms to potential human disease.

Virulence can be defined as the quality of being poisonous or injurious to life (i.e., virulent). For an organism to be virulent, it must be able to infect its human host, reproduce, and/or cause a disease. This broad definition of virulence is more inclusive than the narrow definition commonly used by microbiologists (i.e., virulence is solely the severity of the disease produced after exposure and infection). Each of the microbiological attributes that contribute to virulence can in general be linked to specific architectural elements or biochemical compounds within the organism. Together, these elements and compounds can generally be termed "virulence factors," and the blueprints for them are included in the genetic code of an organism. For this reason, a principal topic of this chapter is the genetic structure of various microorganisms because of its direct relationship to virulence factors.

Owing to recent advances in molecular biology, the genetic structures of many thousands of organisms (especially bacteria and viruses) have been identified, reported, and stored in what are called gene banks. Sophisticated computer programs allow for the sorting and matching of genetic structures and specific genes. The discipline that organizes and studies these genes is known as *bioinformatics*, while the study of genes and their function is known as *genomics*. In addition, a growing area of related interest is *functional genomics*, that is, understanding the specific role of genes in terms of the function of the organism. The ability to use these and related tools to address the microbial contamination of drinking water is illustrated by some of the following observations:

- The genetic structures of most known waterborne pathogens have been characterized at least partially, with the information stored in gene databanks. The complete genome of several important waterborne pathogens, such as *Vibrio cholerae* (the agent of cholera), is now known, and many more will be characterized in the near future (Heidelberg et al., 2000).

- Other related information is accumulating that allows the use of these databanks to determine or predict the ability of a microorganism to produce virulence factors, such as toxins, attachment factors, and other surface proteins, and genes that encode bacterial resistance to antibiotics.

- On a more basic level, these data can be used to characterize similarities and differences between a microorganism of interest and known pathogens.

• Data of this kind can also be used to identify sources of, and thus exposures to, microorganisms through molecular "fingerprinting."
• The *functional genomics* or *bioinformatics* expertise needed to establish a nationwide VFAR program already exists in the private and public sectors.

Thus, the committee concludes that a VFAR concept, with many parallels to the SAR concept used for chemicals, would be a powerful approach to examining emerging waterborne pathogens, opportunistic microorganisms, and other newly identified microorganisms.

STATEMENT OF THE PROBLEM

As noted in the committee's first report (NRC, 1999a), the current approach to identifying and controlling waterborne disease is limited. It has followed a similar path since cholera was first linked to transmission via water ("from the Broad Street pump") in London, England, nearly a century and an half ago, and since Koch first proposed his famous postulates regarding causation (see Okun, 1999). Typically, a disease outbreak is reported only when a significant portion of a community is recognized to have been affected, the responsible microorganism has been identified, and an epidemiological study is undertaken to determine possible sources of exposure to the agent in the community. If any of these three elements is lacking, the outbreak is generally missed and goes unreported. If the consumption of drinking water is identified as a potential source of exposure, a public health advisory to boil water may be issued. Alternatively, the culpable part of the system may be identified and isolated until the cause of contamination is eliminated. However, for most of the waterborne outbreaks in the United States, the etiology is never determined, the responsible microorganism is never identified, and public water systems are not easily fixed or shut off. The identification of pathogens is thus unnecessarily related to the recognition of an outbreak. Under the amended Safe Drinking Water Act, microbial contamination, regardless of whether it is associated with an outbreak or not, must be addressed.

Hundreds if not thousands of microorganisms have the potential to be spread through drinking water supplies and distribution systems. While data on health effects for many of these are described in the medical literature, there are no occurrence databases or even routine methodologies for developing these databases (NRC, 1999a). One of the principal dilemmas to be addressed is that current regulatory practice requires that methods to culture organisms of interest be developed before occurrence data can be gathered. Thus, a microorganism ordinarily must first be identified as a pathogen, and be capable of in vitro culture, before occurrence data are acquired. This long-standing paradigm makes it very difficult or impossible to develop a database of potential or emerging pathogens.

There is also no widely accepted approach for prioritization of waterborne pathogens, other than through expert judgment. For example, and as noted earlier, the U.S. Environmental Protection Agency (EPA) and the American Water Works Association Research Foundation have jointly sponsored a series of expert workshops since 1996 for the development of a decision process for prioritizing emerging waterborne pathogens that is nearing completion. These expert judgments must be made, of necessity, by a very small number of researchers in the discipline of health-related environmental microbiology. This approach to the process makes transparency very difficult to achieve, the importance of which is discussed in Chapters 2 and 5 of this report.

The committee believes strongly that if EPA continues to rely on exposure and health effects as two primary data categories for screening potential microbial drinking water contaminants, progress will continue to be unacceptably slow. Current efforts are able to address only one or two microorganisms every 5 to 10 years with the current CCL development and implementation approach. To illustrate the dilemma, consider that of the ten microorganisms and groups of related microorganisms on the 1998 CCL, nine are in the "research priorities" category (see Table 1-3) and will go unregulated in the first CCL cycle. Of these nine microbial contaminants, only one, *Aeromonas hydrophila*, is slated for delayed screening level monitoring during the first cycle of the Unregulated Contaminant Monitoring Regulation (UCMR) (EPA, 1999c) (see Table 1-4).

It is clear that a severe bottleneck exists in identifying and addressing important microbial contaminants in drinking water. Thus, a new approach to assessing pathogens could help overcome this ongoing problem.

VFAR ANALOGY TO SARS AND QUANTITATIVE SARS

A variety of terminology has developed in the literature to identify various classes of correlations useful for predicting the properties of agents in environmental and health sciences.

For example, chemical properties are amenable to prediction through use of structure-activity relationships, which can be distinguished from property-activity relationships (PARs) and structure-property relationships (SPRs). Although careful classification along these lines certainly has heuristic value (e.g., Brezonik, 1990), few researchers adhere to these distinctions rigorously. Instead, only a few terms are commonly used and these are often applied to a wider range of correlation types than strict use of each expression would allow (Tratnyek, 1998). One example of this is the term linear free energy relationship (LFER), which originally referred to a specific type of correlation used by physical organic chemists but eventually came to represent the entire field of correlation analysis in organic chemistry (Shorter, 1973). Similarly, the term quantitative structure-activity relationship (QSAR) was originally coined for use in drug design but is now commonly used to refer to many types of correlations employed in the pharmaceutical, toxicological, and environmental sciences. By analogy to the above discussion, the committee has coined the term "virulence-factor activity relationship" and defined it as the known or presumed linkage between the biological characteristics of a microorganism and its real or potential ability to cause harm (pathogenicity).

FRAMEWORK

The central concept is to use microbial characteristics to predict virulence via what the committee terms a virulence-factor activity relationship. Microbial VFARs would function in much the same way as QSARs do, namely to assist in the early identification of at least several potential elements of virulence. Research increasingly has shown certain common characteristics among virulent pathogens, such as the production of specific toxins, specific surface proteins, and specific repair mechanisms that enhance their ability to infect and inflict damage in a host. Recently some of these "descriptors" (the terminology often used in QSARs) have been tied to specific genes, and it has become evident that the same can be done for others. Identification of these descriptors, either directly or through analysis of genetic databases, could become a powerful tool for estimating the potential virulence of a microorganism. This is particularly true for two important aspects of virulence: potency and persistence in the environment. The committee conceives of VFAR as being the relationship that ties specific descriptors to outcomes of concern (see Figure 6-1).

FORMULATING VFARS

Conceptually, pathogens of interest must be related in that they exhibit pathogenicity through a common mechanism but are also likely to be distinguished through secondary characteristics that cause virulence to be variable. Since virulence is the target property to be predicted by the VFAR, it is by definition the dependent or "response" variable in a VFAR. Variability in the virulence of pathogens may be characterized by one or more independent variables (i.e., variability in the genetic makeup)—referred to as "descriptor variables"—that can be conven-

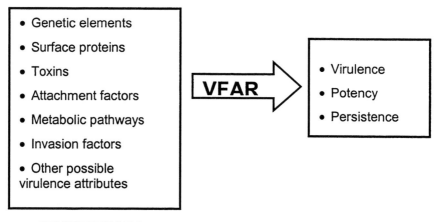

DESCRIPTORS   OUTCOMES

FIGURE 6-1 Schematic drawing of VFAR predicting outcomes of concern (virulence, potency, persistence) using the presence or quality of "descriptor" variables.

iently measured or otherwise determined. When correlation of the response and descriptor variables yields a consistent relationship, the result can be used as a (quantitative) model for comparing and predicting properties of related pathogens.

Note that there are many potential ways in which response and descriptor variables may be defined, and this gives flexibility to the VFAR approach, such that it should in principle be able to accommodate many complicating factors. For example, when variability in a pathogen's virulence is related substantially to host factors (e.g., when the host is in an immuno-compromised state) then an "interaction effect" could generate cases that do not obey a VFAR. However, if the response variable (virulence) is defined in such a way that it is unaffected by the behavior of opportunistic pathogens, or if descriptor variables are used that incorporate opportunistic behavior, then a VFAR can incorporate this effect and outliers can be avoided. Such subtleties suggest that developing and validating robust and reliable VFARs will require considerable research, but the committee believes that the promise of VFARs should make them a high priority for such research.

Response (Outcome) Variables

As noted previously, the response variable of concern in VFARs is virulence. Narrowly defined, pathogenicity can be characterized as the ability to cause disease and clinical virulence as a measure of the severity of disease. A broader definition is used in this report, where virulence (with respect to VFARs) incorporates both the concept of pathogenicity and the narrower concept of clinical virulence. Viewed in this manner, it may be useful to include attributes of persistence in the environment as contributing to virulence. It is also conceivable that pathogenicity, clinical virulence, and environmental persistence could be considered separate response variables that work together to contribute to the broadly defined "virulence" of a pathogenic organism.

There are a number of potential metrics of virulence (broadly defined) that may be used as a quantitative outcome measure. These include the duration of symptomatic illness and the intensity of symptoms (perhaps using a disability-weighted scale).

Descriptor Variables

Descriptor variables, in this context, are those attributes of a micro-organism that may prove useful in predicting their virulence. For example, the presence of toxins, adherence factors, adhesins, invasins, capsular components, fimbria, hemolysins, metabolic pathways, and antibiotic resistance could prove to be effective descriptors of microbial virulence. Alternatively, association with certain families of pathogenic microorganisms may be sufficient as a descriptor (e.g., for viruses), and species and genotype may be all that is necessary for protozoa. As our knowledge of pathogens improves, the definition and calibration of specific descriptors will evolve as well.

For many pathogens, the specific mechanisms or virulence descriptors that underlie the range of virulence from one genotype to the next are not well understood. Because of this circumstance, it has already been demonstrated in waterborne pathogens that a genetically based VFAR approach could be particularly powerful. For example, recent studies suggest that various isolates or species of *Cryptosporidium* are virulent to varying degrees in humans (e.g., Okhuysen et al., 1999; Widmer et al., 1998). The ability to recognize and differentiate the genomic content of these different isolates or species, and thus recognize differences in virulence, is based upon the same intellectual concepts that underlie the recognition of toxin-encoding bacterial genes. The power of a VFAR approach is that it has the ability to genuinely reflect the true biological diversity found in human pathogens, even when the exact mechanisms that shape this diversity are not yet understood (Morgan et al., 1999a; Sulaiman et al., 2000).

The committee anticipates that the VFAR paradigm is robust enough to accommodate the reality that sometimes the mere presence of a protozoan in drinking water is not of public health concern. For example, there is now abundant evidence that the species *Cryptosporidium parvum* is, in fact, made up of a number of genotypes, each with different virulence where the human population is concerned (Xiao et al., 2000). Furthermore, one study (Morgan et al., 1999a) used genetic methods to identify eight different species of *Crytposporidium*: *parvum* (many mammals), *muris* (rodents, cattle), *felis* (cats), *wrairi* (guinea pigs), *meleagridis* and *baileyi* (birds), *serpentis* (reptiles), and *nasorum* (fish). The same study demonstrated seven genotypes of *parvum*: genotype 1 infects humans only; genotype 2 infects cattle, sheep, goats, and humans; genotype 3 infects mice and bats; genotype 4 infects pigs; genotype 5 infects koalas and kangaroos; genotype 6 infects dogs; and genotype 7 infects ferrets. Subsequent studies indicate the existence of an eighth genotype (Sulaiman et al., 2000). Of these, only genotypes 1 and 2 are believed to infect immuno-competent humans, but several genotypes have been found to infect immuno-compromised individuals (Morgan et al., 1999b). In addition, several non-*parvum* species (*C. felis*, *C. meleagridis*) have been found to infect people with AIDS (Morgan et al., 2000).

Genomics and Proteomics

Proteomics, a discipline within functional genomics, is the study of protein sets made (expressed) when the genomic blueprint of an organism is actually translated into functional molecules. When faced with changing environmental conditions, organisms will respond by making different sets of proteins to help them survive. For example, it has been estimated that *Vibrio cholerae* is capable of making approximately 3,900 different proteins depending on environmental conditions (Heidelberg et al., 2000). These proteins are the actual molecules that build other important structural molecules, such as lipids, deoxyribonucleic acid (DNA), and ribonucleic acid (RNA), and are capable of having both structural and catalytic or enzymatic functions. It is known that some important bacterial toxins (such as Shiga toxin, discussed later in this chapter) are maximally produced under very specific conditions (Acheson et al., 1991). Faced with a hostile environment, many bacteria will shift production of a protein set that is associated with growth to another set associated with a viable but nonculturable state or to the formation of spores as discussed later in this chapter. Thus, knowledge of the set of proteins being made by an organism can impart information far more revealing that that gained from studying the expression of a single protein.

The committee anticipates that because the state of the art of genomics is currently more advanced than that of proteomics, the initial emphasis in VFAR formulation will be genetic. While much is already known about the growing field proteomics, the committee believes it would be premature to discuss or make recommendations about how much research and data will be needed to examine this aspect of developing VFARs, particularly under changing environmental conditions. Nonetheless, the logical extension of identifying and understanding the entire genome of an organism is ascertaining how this is translated into the expression of proteins and other structural building blocks. In this regard, the committee anticipates that the same rationale that exists for using genomics also exists for proteomics. For example, in a subsequent section of this chapter the committee discusses the use of DNA chips that act as sensors for finding the characteristic DNA elements that encode a particular virulence factor. These chips function via a binding interaction between a section of DNA spotted onto the chip and the complementary strand of a target DNA molecule, such as one from a pathogenic organism. Protein chips that bind the actual virulence protein factors could work in an analogous fashion. Under such a scenario, binding molecules known to attach to specific bacterial toxins (e.g., monoclonal antibodies) could be spotted onto a chip and used to sift through the proteins expressed by a novel bacterium to see if a protein of concern is made by the targeted organism.

CURRENT LEVEL OF GENETIC CHARACTERIZATION

In this section, three existing, major bodies of endeavor that have relevance to the development and implementation of VFARs are discussed.

Microbial Genome Projects and Comparative Databases

The first major endeavor to be discussed in this section is the set of single-organism genome projects and the large genomic databases that are used for comparing the genes of one organism with those of others. The genome projects are comprehensive attempts to sequence the entire genomes of organisms, such as yeast, pathogenic microorganisms, and humans. Computerized analysis and the growing use of automated polymerase chain reaction (PCR) techniques have allowed for tremendous gains in the study of microbial genomics as well as of whole organisms. The databases that exist to store such information are large and expanding daily. For example, the Institute for Genomic Research (TIGR) maintains a collection of databases containing DNA, protein and gene expression, and taxonomic data for microbes, plants, and even humans (see http://www.tigr.org for further information). TIGR also provides links to worldwide genome sequencing projects.

A number of microorganisms are listed in Table 6-1 whose genomes have already been studied; the results of much of this work are available in the published literature. A number of these organisms are associated

TABLE 6-1   Examples of Microbial Genome Databases for Waterborne Pathogens

Microorganism	Size (Million Base Pairs)
Campylobacter jejuni	1.7
Encephalitozoon cuniculi	2.9
Enterococcus faecalis	3.0
Escherichia coli	4.6
Giardia lamblia	12
Helicobacter pylori	1.66
Klebsiella pneumoniae	
Legionella pneumophila	4.0
Leptospira interrogans serovar *icterohaemorrhagiae*	4.8
Mycobacterium avium	4.7
Pseudomonas aeruginosa	5.9
Salmonella paratyphi A	4.5-4.8
Salmonella typhi	
Salmonella typhimurium	
Shigella flexneri	4.7
Vibrio cholerae	4.0

SOURCE: TIGR (see http://www.tigr.org).

with waterborne disease. For example, studies on the *Giardia* genome have recently been published (Adam, 2000), and the complete sequence of *Vibrio cholerae* was recently announced with great acclaim (Heidelberg et al., 2000). The *Cryptosporidium* genome is being sequenced by investigators at the University of Minnesota (http://www.cbc. umn.edu/ResearchProjects/AGAC/Cp/index.htm), with other important work being conducted in the United Kingdom (http://www.mrc-lmb.cam.ac.uk/happy/CRYPTO/Ref.html), California (http://medsfgh. ucsf.edu/id/cpTags/), and elsewhere. Notably, funding for the *Vibrio cholerae* and *Cryptosporidium* genome projects was provided by the National Institute of Allergy and Infectious Diseases (NIAID) at the National Institutes of Health (see http://www.niaid.nih. gov/dmid/ genomes/genome.htm for a listing of genome projects currently supported by NIAID).

On May 30, 2000, an important report entitled *Interagency Report on the Federal Investment in Microbial Genomics* was published by the Biotechnology Research Working Group—a subcommittee of the National Science and Technology Council (BRWG, 2000). The charge for the Subcommittee on Biotechnology was to summarize the activities in microbial genetics of a number of federal agencies; identify each federal agency's areas of interests; and identify opportunities for, and limitations to, research in microbial genetics.[1] One of the main findings of this report is that the current effort in microbial genomics in each federal agency is based on the mission of the specific agency, and, thus, there are clear research gaps—or opportunities for cooperation—in the area of microbial genomics.

Notably, despite EPA's clear mandate for the surveillance of water supplies and developing a rational and transparent scheme for regulating pathogenic water contaminants to date, it has not yet participated in these interagency genome project efforts. Indeed, the research gaps and opportunities identified in this important report (BRWG, 2000) did not even mention the field of waterborne pathogens, possibly because the participating federal agencies do not address this particular area of public health and EPA has not yet participated in this forum. However, the report did identify the problem of pathogens that are difficult to culture—the importance of which is discussed elsewhere in this chapter—highlighting the potential for synergism between federal agencies. In this regard, the committee strongly recommends the future participation of EPA in such cooperative interagency programs.

The U.S. Department of Energy (DOE) has been involved extensively in building genetic databases on microorganisms. Although much of DOE's focus has been on bioremediation and not on waterborne pathogens per se, the methodologies for building, using, and interpreting genetic databases are applicable (DOE, 2000). More specifically, much of DOE's research in this field has recently turned to address functional genomics. As noted previously, breakthroughs in genome sequencing, along with characterization of proteins through use of supercomputers, make this possible.

The uses of large genetic databases are many, but most important to this report is their role in identifying similar genes—and thus virulence

---

[1] Agencies that contributed to this report include the Departments of Defense, Agriculture, and Energy; the National Aeronautics and Space Administration; the National Institutes of Health; the National Institute of Standards and Technology; and the National Science Foundation. Within the National Institutes of Health, the National Centers for Research Resources, Human Genome Research Institute, National Institute of Allergy and Infectious Diseases, Dental and Cranial Research, and General Medical Sciences, as well as the National Library of Medicine's National Center for Biotechnology Information, participated.

factors—in different organisms. As discussed later in this chapter, many well-recognized waterborne pathogens share the same or very similar genes that encode virulence factors. However, it is not possible to predict all of the insights that may result from the use of these databases. To illustrate this point, when the genome of *Vibrio cholerae* was compared to other organisms in the database (Heidelberg et al., 2000), the largest number of similarities was found to *Escherichia coli* (the common enteric pathogen), but the second largest number was unexpectedly to *Haemophilus influenzae* (a respiratory pathogen). Although the latter is not known to be transmitted via water, this finding aptly demonstrates the surprising ability of pathogens to share common components that may or may not relate to overall virulence.

Molecular Methods for Characterization of Waterborne Microorganisms

The second major arena of endeavor to be discussed is the use of molecular methods, particularly PCR, for the detection and characterization of waterborne pathogens (NRC, 1999a; Wiedenmann et al., 1998). Perhaps because the recognized and known bacterial pathogens are culturable, the major recent focus has been on microorganisms that are not yet culturable (e.g., protozoan agents, certain viruses). In this regard, PCR is an attractive diagnostic procedure because it is rapid, sensitive, and pathogen specific (DiGiovanni et al., 1999; Johnson et al., 1995; Kostrzynska et al., 1999; Rochelle et al., 1997b). Independent of this report, Rochelle et al. (1997b) have recommended that PCR should become a more widely accepted method of pathogen detection and monitoring within the water industry and should be used in parallel with conventional techniques (e.g., cultivation) to improve detection capabilities for existing and newly emerging pathogens.

Although it is beyond the scope of this report to discuss genetics in a substantive way, a very concise overview of molecular genetics as related to virulence factors is appropriate. All living organisms carry with them a complete genetic code, the genome, which serves as a master blueprint for all cellular structures and activities for the lifetime of the cell or organism. An organism's genome consists of DNA and associated protein molecules, except for RNA viruses, which use RNA rather than DNA. Each DNA molecule contains many genes—the basic functional units of heredity and what makes each organism individually distinct. Genes in turn are comprised of specific sequences of four nucleotide bases (adenine, thymidine, cytosine, and guanine represented as A, T, C, and G, respectively). Each strand of DNA is bound to a complementary strand of DNA. Every individual base in one DNA strand is matched in the complementary strand by the base that binds to it to form a base pair (bp). These pairs of DNA bases are formed from As and Ts or from Gs and Cs (see Figure 6-2). Copies of individual genes are made by an organism by separating the two strands, and then making a new complementary strand of DNA using one strand as a template. By convention, an organism's genome size is expressed as the total number of base pairs (see Table 6-1). Some organisms use slightly different nucleotides, but the principle is the same. Genes specify the exact genetic instructions required to create individual organisms with unique traits (e.g., eye color in humans, the toxins of *Escherichia coli* O157:H7). They also provide the information needed to produce an incredible variety of proteins through an indirect process that utilizes a transient intermediary molecule called messenger RNA (mRNA). When the DNA code is to be translated, the two intertwined strands of DNA are separated, and an RNA copy is made of one of the strands. This RNA copy is then sent to the cell "machinery" that translates the code into proteins. Proteins provide the structural components of cells and tissues, and enzymes for essential biochemical reactions, but they can also act as toxins as illustrated below.

	Transcription		*Translation*		*Infection*	
Genes	⟶	Messenger RNA	⟶	Proteins (toxins)	⟶	Disease

PCR techniques are based on the principle that genetic elements such as DNA or RNA, which are present at very low concentrations in water or other materials, can be copied many times by specific enzymes (polymerases) and subsequently detected via fairly standard biochemical methods. This amplification process is fundamentally the same process used by living creatures to duplicate their genes. A primer, or small stretch of DNA known to match a portion of the target organism's genome, is added to the concentrated water (or other sample) to be tested. If it finds a match (i.e., if the organism's DNA is present), the polymerase chain reaction can take place, and the products can be detected after amplification. It is typical for PCR to amplify the targeted DNA by a factor of 10,000 to a millionfold. The products of the copy (amplification) process are called amplicons.

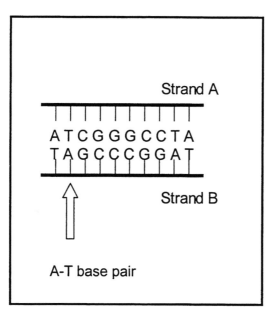

Strand A

ATCGGGCCTA
TAGCCCGGAT

Strand B

A-T base pair

FIGURE 6-2   Illustration of two complementary strands of DNA forming
A-T and G-C base pairs.

Protozoa

Several recent papers have described a variety of PCR-based protocols for the detection of waterborne pathogens, including *Cryptosporidium* (Champliaud et al., 1998; DiGiovanni et al., 1999; Kimbell et al.,
1999; Kostrzynnska et al., 1999; Sulaiman et al., 1999; Xiao et al.,
1999a,b), microsporidia (Dowd et al., 1998a,b), *Cyclospora* (Jinneman et
al., 1996), and *Giardia* (Rochelle et al., 1997a,b) in environmental samples. A comprehensive review of the use of PCR techniques for the detection of protozoa has recently been published (Morgan and Thompson,
1998).

The primers of PCR protocols for *Cryptosporidium* parasites are
based on undefined genomic sequences (Laxer et al., 1991; Morgan and
Thompson, 1998) or specific genes (Johnson et al., 1995; Leng et al.,
1996; Rochelle et al., 1997a,b). Recent molecular studies have shown

that there are extensive genetic differences among different *Cryptosporidium* species, as well as within *C. parvum* (Sulaiman et al., 2000). These inter- and intraspecies differences have been used in the development of molecular diagnostics tools for *Cryptosporidium* spp. and for genotype differentiation. For example, Xiao et al. (1999a,b) evaluated several PCR techniques to determine whether they could accurately detect *C. parvum* in environmental samples. The authors concluded that two nested-PCR-restriction fragment length polymorphisms (RFLPs) based on the small-subunit ribosomal RNA (rRNA) (Xiao et al., 1999a,b) and dihydrofolate reductase genes (Gibbons et al., 1998) were more sensitive than single-round PCR or PCR-RFLP protocols for detection and *Cryptosporidium* species differentiation.

Using a slightly different approach, Kozwich et al. (2000) have capitalized on the observation that a double-stranded RNA molecule, which is apparently found only in *C. parvum* but not in other *Cryptosporidium* species (Khramtsov et al., 2000); can be used as a "signature" sequence that is specific for this organism. Using a novel solid-phase capture material and PCR, they were able to detect levels of oocysts as low as one per liter in environmental samples. This technology provides a simple reading that looks very much like the commercially available pregnancy test.

For the water industry to make accurate human health risk assessments for *C. parvum*, it is essential to have methods to detect viable, infectious oocysts in water samples. DiGiovanni et al. (1999) described a new strategy for the detection of infectious *C. parvum* oocysts in water samples, which combines immunomagnetic separation (IMS) techniques for recovery of oocysts with in vitro cell culturing and PCR. This method, by its very nature, requires that the oocysts be viable if cell culture and subsequent PCR are to detect anything. Assays that use dyes appear to overestimate the viability of oocysts after disinfection with ozone, as judged by mouse infectivity studies (Bukhari et al., 2000).

Not all of the molecular methods of interest are based on PCR techniques. A fluorescent in situ hybridization (FISH) technique has been developed recently that shows considerable promise as an indicator of *C. parvum* oocyst viability (Vesey et al., 1998). The basic premise is that a viable oocyst, but not a dead one, has genetic elements that can be found with a colored tag that is visible when examined under a microscope. Technically, a fluorescent DNA probe is targeted to the 18S rRNA of *C. parvum* on the premise that 18S rRNA is usually present in viable organisms and is degraded by cellular ribonucleases (RNases) in dead or dying cells. Another proposed target for this kind of simple visual confirmation of viability is β-tubulin mRNA (Widmer et al., 1999). While existing FISH techniques are limited to measuring the viability of *C. parvum* oocysts and not their infectivity (Neuman et al., 2000), as our understanding of the *Cryptosporidium* genome becomes more sophisticated, the latter may become possible.

Organisms other than *Cryptosporidium* have also been investigated with PCR methods. *Giardia*-specific primers used in published reports amplify a 183-bp product from the small subunit rRNA gene (Weiss et al., 1992); 218- and 171-bp amplicons from a giardin gene (Mahbubani et al., 1992); and a 163-bp product from a heat shock protein gene (Abbaszadegan et al., 1993). Rochelle et al. (1997a) reported a PCR assay based on primers that are specific for *G. lamblia* in water samples and that amplify a 218-bp product. A PCR-based test to detect *Cyclospora* has been developed by Jinneman et al. (1996). This method amplifies a region of the *Cyclospora* 18S ribosomal RNA gene. Specific nucleotide differences in the amplified segment can be used to differentiate amplicons of two closely related genus of coccidian parasites (*Cyclospora* sp. and *Eimeria* sp.) by digestion with the restriction endonuclease *Mnl* I. Dowd et al. (1999b) assessed two methods for isolating microsporidia DNA from water for use in PCR amplification of microsporidia target sequences. Both of the DNA isolation methods when combined with PCR showed the ability to detect less than 10 spores of human pathogenic microsporidia in water.

Capitalizing on these advances, Orlandi and Lampel (2000) of the U.S. Food and Drug Administration have published an extraction-free, filter-based PCR template preparation technique for the detection of *Cryptosporidium, Cyclospora*, and pathogenic microsporidia. This methodology does not require DNA extraction; is rapid, efficient, and reproducible; and can be used in multiplex PCR applications designed to detect multiple parasitic protozoa.

Viruses

The most frequently identified viruses in drinking water and/or associated with waterborne outbreaks are hepatitis A, Norwalk virus and other caliciviruses, coxsackievirus, rotavirus, and echovirus (Jaykus, 1997). The cultivatable enteroviruses, which include poliovirus, echovirus, and coxsackievirus, make up only a small percentage of the viruses present in wastewater. The standard culture method is to inoculate mammalian cells with these viruses or potentially contaminated water and watch for damage to the cells (a "cytopathic effect"). Unfortunately, this method has been shown to be insensitive for many viruses, which replicate but do not destroy cells. Thus, PCR is now being utilized in cell culture to detect noncytopathic viruses, and it has been used to screen for viruses in groundwater (Abbaszadegan et al., 1999). In addition, new viruses (e.g., caliciviruses) are constantly being identified that are nonculturable causes of gastroenteritis. These human enteric viruses will have to be investigated in water using PCR methods or their equivalent.

Hepatitis E virus (HEV) is the most common cause of acute hepatitis in humans in many parts of the world, especially Asia, and is also found in wild and domestic animals. Although mortality rates for this infection in humans are generally low (<1 percent) as many as 25 percent of pregnant women who acquire this infection will die (Aggarwal and Krawczynski, 2000). Waterborne epidemics as well as person-to-person spread of this virus have been reported. Recent genetic sequencing studies have found that human and pig HEV are very similar genetically in the United States as well as in Nepal (Meng et al., 1997, 1998; Tsarev et al., 1999). Thus, zoonotic transmission seems very possible (Smith, 2001). Although the cultivation of HEV has recently been reported (Smith, 2001), reverse transcriptase PCR is the method of choice in water and has been used successfully to detect HEV RNA in sewage (Jothikumar et al., 1993; Pina et al., 1998).

The Norwalk-like caliciviruses (NLVs) are noncultivatable enteric viruses (also known as small round structured viruses) that have been reported to cause numerous waterborne outbreaks (Jaykus, 1997; Kaplan et al., 1982; Schaub and Oshiro, 2000). A diverse group of RNA viruses, they are a common cause of gastroenteritis, with diarrhea and or vomiting lasting approximately two days. These viruses may be quite prevalent in the environment and have been reported in sewage at 10^7 RNA-containing particles per liter using PCR techniques (Lodder et al., 1999).

Bacteria

Because of their relative ease in manipulation in the laboratory, rapid growth, and sophistication of our understanding of bacterial genomes, most of the published literature dealing with the molecular characterization of pathogens is focused on culturable bacteria. Indeed, the insights developed in this particular field have led to the whole-organism genomic sequencing projects discussed earlier in this chapter.

However, it is now apparent that even bacteria of very major public health concern are not always culturable. This important issue is also discussed at length later in this chapter under virulence factor "persistence." One of the best paradigms in this regard is the agent of cholera, *Vibrio cholerae.* This organism's favored natural environment is estuarine areas. It can enter a viable but not culturable dormant state wherein it has greatly reduced needs for nutrients and oxygen (see reviews by Colwell and Huq, 1994; Sanchez and Taylor, 1997). The ingestion of these nonculturable forms by humans is believed to allow for reversion to the highly pathogenic form, leading to cholera disease and potential outbreaks. These forms can be detected via PCR methods, as well as epifluorescent microscopy and acridine orange staining. Of note, it has been shown directly that PCR methods can detect the presence of cholera toxin genes even when the organisms are in a viable but nonculturable state (Colwell and Huq, 1994). It is not generally appreciated that a number of other highly pathogenic microorganisms such as *Campylobacter jejuni, Salmonella enteritidis, Escherichia coli, Helicobacter,* and *Legionella* have the same ability to enter into nonculturable form. These examples help support the conclusion of the Biotechnology Research Working Group—a subcommittee of the National Science and Technology Council (BRWG, 2000)—and this committee, that methods *other* than culture must be used to fully evaluate microbial contamination of drinking water.

A recent example of the successful application of PCR methods and the use of genetics for waterborne pathogens was reported by Kingombe et al. (1999) for the bacteria *Aeromonas. Aeromonas hydrophila* is included on the 1998 CCL (EPA, 1998a) and as previously noted is the only CCL microorganism on the UCMR (EPA, 1999f,g) that will be monitored in the first cycle of the UCMR. Yet the methodology proposed to evaluate and identify this pathogen in water is based on a cultivation technique (Havelaar et al., 1987) and will yield little information on the virulence or the pathogenic nature of the isolates (EPA, 1999f). *Aeromonas* spp. are ubiquitous in nature and only recently have the bacteria been associated with human illness. A large number of virulence factors for this microorganism have been described in the literature. The similarity between the cytolytic enterotoxin gene of *A. hydrophila* and the aerolysin genes of *Aeromonas* spp. was recently used to characterize the distribution of virulence in water (Kingombe et al., 1999), with 58 percent of the isolates associated with potential health threats. The particularly clever aspect of this work by Kingombe et al. (1999) is their use of molecular techniques to detect virulence factors in a variety of *Aeromonas* species that are of concern to humans.

There are more than 100 serotypes of *Escherichia coli* that are capable of producing Shiga toxins (STXs) (Nataro and Kaper, 1998). The genes encoding for STXs are located on bacteriophages and thus, may be spread from one serotype to another. Law (2000) reports that the pathogenicity of any given *E. coli* is likely related to a number of virulence factors in addition to the STX gene. This finding supports the premise that it may be possible to identify the potential for emerging types of pathogenic bacteria by understanding the array of virulence genes that are present in environmental waters.

Gene Microarrays and Genomics

Gene chip technology (microarrays), has been used in research laboratories since the late 1990s to study gene expression and is the subject of recent and intense scientific interest. DNA microarrays are immobilized pieces of single-stranded manufactured DNA, typically spotted onto glass or nylon substrates, that are used to capture key genetic targets.

The premise is that the DNA is spotted using an arrayer device that places it on the slide in a known position. The arrayer device can be an expensive robotic device or a simple ink-jet spotter (e.g., see "How to Build Your Own Microarrayer" at http://cmgm.stanford.edu/pbrown/ mguide). The DNA spotted onto the chip is designed to bind a sequence of DNA that may or may not be in the sample to be tested. Currently, most studies using this technology are examining the entire spectrum of genes of an organism (its genome) to see how the entire set of genes varies under different metabolic conditions or when stressed by a malignancy or other circumstance (e.g., Aach et al., 2000; DeRisi and Iyer, 1999). However, that need not be the only way in which this technology is used.

For example, a chip could catch several thousand bits of DNA from pathogenic microorganisms that are, or may be, waterborne. The chip would be incubated in a water sample that had been treated to liberate the DNA from any microorganisms. If the pathogenic microorganism of concern was present in the sample, its DNA would bind to the bit of DNA that matched its own on the chip (i.e., a complementary strand). This bound DNA could then be amplified using PCR and subsequently labeled (e.g., with fluorescent molecules) and detected using a variety of means such as spectroscopy. Alternatively, DNA spotted onto the slide could act as a "molecular beacon," or a piece of DNA that becomes intensely fluorescent once the target DNA binds to it (Tan et al., 2000). This once conceptual method has already been used clinically to identify specific bacteria found in the bloodstream of hospital patients (Anthony et al., 2000).

By 1998, microarrays were manufactured to assay 500 to 5,000 genes (Marshall and Hodgson, 1998; Ramsay, 1998), and chips that can assay up to 100,000 genes are predicted to be available in the near future (Lander, 1999). Although the experimental power of such arrays is considerable, current costs for complete systems range from $25,000 to $135,000. Commercially available systems are currently being produced for what is known as "gene discovery" (i.e., rapid identification of targets in infectious disease).

The committee anticipates that in a very short period of time, microarrays could be developed that are labeled with all of the genes for a variety of virulence factors identified within enteric bacteria, pathogenic viruses, opportunistic protozoa, and other (waterborne) microorganisms. Examples of some of these are provided in the next section of this chapter. These gene chips could be used to assay environmental and drinking water samples for the presence of genetic virulence factors of concern. If such virulence factors were present, the sample could be assayed further if needed to better identify the microorganism. Thus, the commercial and public health implications are enormous.

VIRULENCE AND POTENCY RESPONSE—HEALTH ASPECTS

Introduction

Historically, it has been well recognized that the virulence of a microbial pathogen can be correlated with some observable feature. In this section, several examples of the current state of knowledge concerning the molecular basis for variation in virulence, and what is known about some of the underlying mechanisms of virulence itself, are discussed. This section is intended to give the reader an overview of some of the microbial virulence factors that have already been identified and could act as virulence factors in the future development of a VFAR.

Viral Examples

Influenza—Mutation is Associated with Virulence

Influenza can be considered as a prototypic emerging disease. Although it is not known to be waterborne, it is discussed here to support the contention that specific virulence attributes can be mapped to an important and well-understood pathogen that is widely recognized by the public. Influenza virus is zoonotic (i.e., it infects and is maintained in other animals, chiefly birds and swine) and is capable of mutating so frequently that immunity to one strain will not be protective against another strain. It can also result in an innocuous infection or a lethal one. In 1918, influenza was responsible for a worldwide pandemic that killed more than 20 million people (Webster et al., 1992). More recently, a well-publicized outbreak in Hong Kong in 1997 resulted in the deaths of 6 of 18 people who were confirmed to have been infected with a new serotype of influenza (H5N1) (Snacken et al., 1999). For influenza, it became clear that the outer surface proteins of the virus are closely linked to the degree of disease that humans suffer.

Serotypes of influenza are classified by the neuraminidase (N) and hemagglutinin (H) protein molecules on the surface of the virus. These are encoded by the RNA-based genome of the virus. Several isolates of influenza can infect the same animal at the same time, leading to gene reassortment events in which the progeny virus are a mixture of the two parental strains. Each of the major families of the neuraminidase and the hemagglutinin molecules on the surface of the virus has a specific subtype name, such as N1, N2, H1, H2, and so forth. Every year, a decision is made by U.S. public health authorities regarding which subtypes to concentrate on for vaccine production based upon infection information from elsewhere in the world. Once a decision is made to manufacture a specific vaccine using specific serotypes, the vaccine must be grown, inactivated, and packaged for delivery. In the case of the Hong Kong outbreak, the new isolate was so virulent that it killed the chickens and chicken eggs that are typically used to grow influenza virus for vaccine production (Snacken et al., 1999). Thus, the Hong Kong isolate was so virulent that to protect the human population adequately would have been extremely difficult. Fortunately, its high virulence was apparently not matched by high transmissibility, and it did not spread beyond Hong Kong.

Influenza thus represents a virus whose surface molecules correlate with virulence, but researchers do not yet know why this is the case. Nonetheless, genetic recognition of the molecules associated with virulence can serve as an important public health tool.

Hepatitis E—An Emerging Waterborne Infection in the United States

Hepatitis E virus is the third leading cause of hepatitis, after hepatitis A and B. It occurs worldwide, but rarely in developed countries such as the United States (Labrique et al., 1999). As discussed earlier in this chapter, HEV is predominantly a waterborne disease since direct transmission from person-to-person is uncommon (~2 percent of cases; Labrique et al., 1999). Disturbingly, it now appears that transmission is occurring in the United States. Tsang and colleagues (2000) reported a case of HEV in California. A man, who had not traveled outside the United States for more than 10 years, drank water from a well and a lake one month before becoming ill. In El Paso, Texas, 0.4 percent of pregnant women (the group most at risk of death during acute infection) were reported to have had serological evidence of prior exposure to this agent (Redlinger et al., 1998). In Iowa, 4.9 percent of patients with non-A, non-B hepatitis were seropositive for HEV (Karetnyi et al., 1999). In other developed countries such as the United Kingdom, it has also become apparent that HEV is a cause of acute hepatitis and is underdiagnosed (McCrudden et al., 2000). Since HEV is principally a waterborne disease elsewhere in the world, it is appropriate to be concerned about waterborne transmission in the United States.

Two people in the United States have been diagnosed as having HEV with strains that are genetically different from the other HEVs that occur in less developed countries (Kwo et al., 1997; Meng et al., 1997, 1998b). However, these strains were nearly identical genetically to the recently discovered swine HEV, which is found throughout the United States in swine populations. Other mammals can also be infected with HEV in the United States. In a recent nationwide survey by the Centers for Diseases Control and Prevention, 806 rodents (26 species in 15 genera) were tested and 60 percent of rats were seropositive for HEV (Favorov et al., 2000). Tying these data to information about transmission of HEV in the United States is the fact that actual clinical differences have been reported between HEV strains within a genotype (Labrique et al., 1999; Ticehurst, 1999; Tsarev et al., 1999).

Thus, it is probable that modern molecular surveillance of U.S. drinking water could detect HEV of animal and potentially human origin. Furthermore, analysis of strains and genotypes in the detected HEV would probably lead to further information regarding the potential for this pathogen to infect humans who ingest such water. Moreover, tracking different genotypes could assist in establishing dispersion patterns of HEV into the aquatic environment.

Poliovirus and Other Enteroviruses

Enteroviruses account for 10 million to 15 million infections per year in the United States (Sawyer, 1999) and are easily detected in surface waters (Melnick and Gerba, 1980). They are spread by waterborne transmission, direct person-to-person contact, and common-source exposures such as swimming pools. Paralytic poliomyelitis is often the dreaded consequence of infection by a common enterovirus, poliovirus. This enteric virus has historically been transmitted both in waterborne epidemics and through person-to-person contact. The majority of children infected with polio have a simple undifferentiated febrile illness or no symptoms, while others will develop aseptic meningitis or paralysis. Despite virtual eradication of this endemic disease in the western hemisphere through universal vaccination, it unfortunately remains common in Africa and parts of Asia. Since 1980, all cases of poliomyelitis in the United States have actually been caused by vaccine strains of polio, which is exceedingly rare (Strebel et al., 1992). Any region with wild-type poliovirus can act as a reservoir for reintroducing virulent poliovirus to areas that no longer have endemic transmission problems, and this has happened frequently over the past three decades (Kubli et al., 1987). Thus, continued surveillance as well as vaccination for this virus is clearly warranted throughout the United States.

Three serotypes of poliovirus exist (Bodian et al., 1949). They share some antigens but are characterized by marked intertypic differences (Melnick, 1996). Protection against this virus in conferred when a person has antibodies to the three main structural proteins VP1, VP2, and VP3 that make up the viral surface of all three serotypes. A fourth protein, VP4, is internal. Vaccination with one serotype does not, however, confer adequate protection against the other serotypes of polio (Melnick, 1955). Most of the epitopes, or sites that are recognized by antibodies, lie on VP1. These VP proteins vary markedly between serotypes and even within a given serotype. The tendency for poliovirus to infect the nervous system (and not just the intestine) is called neurotropism. Although all three serotypes of poliovirus can infect the nervous system, some isolates are more or less neurotropic. Indeed, the original Sabin (live, oral) vaccine was developed and used because it lacked neurotropism (Sabin, 1985). Specific mutations that are associated with the lack of neurotropism have been identified (Mento et al., 1993; Ren et al., 1991).

The discovery of enteroviruses was closely linked to the poliovirus control effort. Animal and tissue culture virus isolation studies, looking for poliovirus isolates, often revealed other viruses of the poliovirus family, or enteroviruses (Pallansch and Anderson, 1998). These include other groupings, such as the coxsackievirus A, coxsackievirus B, and echovirus groups. Since it became clear that all of these viral agents actually belonged to one family, all new isolates have simply been classified as enteroviruses and numbered sequentially. These agents cause diseases marked by rash (hand-foot-and-mouth disease, herpangina); cardiac disease (myocarditis and pericarditis, which can be fatal); respiratory tract infections; central nervous system disease including paralysis identical to that of poliovirus; and a variety of other diseases. Epidemiologic and observational studies have suggested that the development of insulin-requiring diabetes mellitus is related to infection with enteroviruses (e.g., Roivainen et al., 1998). The entire genome of any given enterovirus, including polioviruses, is encoded by a single strand of RNA that is about 7,500 nucleotides long, and the entire genome of many enteroviruses is already known. Moreover, the structure and physical properties of enteroviruses are nearly identical to those of polioviruses (Pallansch and Anderson, 1998). Thus, the very major variances in virulence and tissue tropism of all of the enteroviruses are encoded in this one relatively short molecule.

At this time, the mere detection in the United States of a wild-type poliovirus in a drinking water supply would be of very major public health importance because endemic transmission is believed to have ended in this hemisphere. Similarly, the monitoring of public drinking waters for the presence of enteroviruses is likely to lead to important information regarding the causal role of these viruses in a number of chronic diseases such as diabetes mellitus. While traditional cell culture techniques required the (prohibitively expensive) use of at least four cell types to screen for all enteroviruses (Dagan and Menegus, 1986), the committee notes that powerful PCR methods have recently been developed to detect enteroviruses in surface waters collected under the Information Collection Rule (Chapron et al., 2000). This methodology has been developed at the same time that similar PCR techniques have been evaluated and found to be cost-effective for the rapid diagnosis of enterovirus infections in humans (Nigrovic and Chiang, 2000). Thus, the use of VFAR molecular methods for monitoring enterovirus infections would (1) take advantage of the immense knowledge base about virulence characteristics that exists at the viral level and (2) tie into new clinical technologies that could be used to confirm actual human disease characteristics with specific virulence attributes.

Bacterial Examples

Although the previous discussion may have suggested that the knowledge base for viral pathogens is extensive, the most robust knowledge about pathogens actually lies in the realm of bacterial pathogens. This set of examples, like the viral ones, begins with a pathogen that is generally recognized by all members of the public—streptococcal infection.

Streptococcal Infections

Group A streptococci (*Streptococcus pyogenes*) are the bacteria that cause "strep throat," scarlet fever, and rheumatic fever, as well as the emerging "flesh-eating" syndromes with rapidly spreading infection and loss of limb and life (necrotizing fasciitis). They have very well characterized exterior proteins that are recognized as distinct serotypes (Lancefield, 1928).[2] These serotypes are determined by exterior cell wall M, T, and R antigens, which are glycoproteins (proteins with sugars attached) encoded by the bacterial genome (Stollerman, 1998). The M protein, a major surface antigen, is the predominant virulence attribute that predicts pathogenicity. It acts to prevent ingestion of the bacteria by human phagocytic cells.

Acute glomerulonephritis, or renal failure, frequently follows a group A streptococcal infection, and a very limited number of M and T serotypes are associated with this form of kidney disease. Similarly, only specific serotypes commonly cause rheumatic fever. Thus, there is an excellent correlation between the presence of specific markers of

---

[2] "Serotype" here refers to the common laboratory method of distinguishing between strains of streptococci by using serological testing with antibodies.

virulence—the M and T antigens—and actual adverse human outcomes. Rheumatic heart disease was once one of the leading causes of death in the United States, and it remains a major cause of morbidity and death in many developing countries (Stollerman, 1998).

Streptococci also produce a very large number of toxins. Some of these cause the bright red rash of scarlet fever, whereas others destroy and literally dissolve human tissues. One set of these toxins causes toxic shock syndrome and belongs to a family of toxins that is shared with an otherwise unrelated bacterium *Staphylococcus aureus*. These pyrogenic toxins are relatively small (molecular weight 20,000 to 30,000) and are similar on a genetic basis (Bohach et al., 1989). They also provide an excellent example of how a virulence attribute in one organism predicts virulence in an organism of a different genus and species. Thus, there are well-known virulence attributes that predict pathogenicity within species (M proteins) and across species (toxic shock toxins).

Enteric Bacteria

Most of the bacteria that cause diarrhea or dysentery (bloody diarrhea) do so after a set of interactions with the human host. These interactions include (1) ingestion by the host; (2) survival after passage through the acidic environment of the stomach; (3) attachment to the lining of the host's intestine (epithelium); and (4) production of compounds that induce the host to secrete fluid that leads to diarrhea and/or to envelop the invading bacteria so it can enter the host cell. Bacteria are far more complex than typical viruses and have the capacity to devote energy and part of their genome to accomplish each of the above tasks successfully. Moreover, bacteria have the ability to share the genes for these tasks with each other.

This sharing of toxin genes and other virulence factors means that bacteria detected within the United States may have their native representatives that are just as harmful. For example, *Shigella* bacteria (a cause of dysentery) are now rarely of major concern in the United States because hygienic standards are generally high. *Shigella dysenteriae* produces a highly lethal toxin called Shiga toxin (Acheson, 1998; Acheson et al., 1991; Conradi, 1903; Keusch, 1998; Keusch et al., 1972). Other *Shigella* species (e.g., *S. sonnei, flexneri, boydii*) are unlikely to make this toxin in similar quantities (Keusch, 1998). STX is composed of one A unit and five B subunits. The five B subunits first attach to a host cell, the toxin penetrates; and then the A subunit kills the cell. Although originally described from the bacterium *Shigella dysenteriae* type 1, an essentially identical set of toxins is made by *Escherichia coli* O157:H7, which is why this and other *E. coli* strains that make the toxin are of such public health concern.

Escherichia coli O157:H7 is frequently carried in cattle, has been implicated in many raw beef or hamburger-related epidemics, and has been implicated as the causative lethal bacterium involved in a number of waterborne disease outbreaks (Anonymous, 1999; Swerdlow et al., 1992). Haas et al. (2000) estimated that the median infectious dose is 5.96×10^5 organisms in drinking water and that ingestion of only 4,000 organisms would result in a 1 percent attack rate. Nevertheless, average ingested doses below this level can still pose a significant public health threat, particularly if exposure of large population occurs. For example, Tuttle et al. (1999) found that the median "most probable" number of organisms in contaminated hamburger patties involved in a recent widespread outbreak in Canada was only 67.5.

A very closely related toxin called Shiga toxin 2 (STX2) is also produced by *E. coli* and has three major known biological variants (WHO, 1998). The majority of STX-type genes are actually present on a bacteriophage that infects the *E. coli* bacteria, fostering transfer between bacteria. It is these toxins that are thought to cause the bloody diarrhea and frequent death of people who have shigellosis or who are infected with *E. coli* strains that produce these toxins. The mere presence of these genes and the ability to make this toxin may not, however, always be sufficient to cause disease. The bacteria often attach to the human host intestine after having entered the digestive tract, and this requires a set of genes that facilitate this type of interactions.

The attachment of these bacteria to the intestinal wall is through a characteristic attaching and effacing (A/E) cytopathic lesion. The ability to attach and efface is encoded by 41 genes in a "pathogenicity island" or "locus for enterocyte effacement" (LEE). This island or locus encodes the adhesin called intimin on the eaeA gene, as well as other factors that are needed for secretion of these molecules into the space between the bacterium and the host cell. This group of genes can be shared among all of the bacteria that adhere to the intestine via this mechanism (Acheson, 1998; Goosney et al.,1998; WHO, 1998).

Some enteric bacteria invade the host cell and evade the immune response, essentially "hiding" within the host. This is a very dangerous property of such bacteria, which is very strongly correlated with virulence. These bacteria include *Shigella, Salmonella, Yersinia, Listeria,* and others. Some of these enteric bacteria literally blow a hole in the host cell as they move into an adjacent cell and accomplish this by causing host proteins to jell behind them and force them forward like a jet-propelled object. These genes are shared between bacteria that are as unrelated as *Shigella* (Goosney et al., 1998) and *Listeria* (Chakraborty et al., 1995). The genes that encode for such destructive characteristics are known and are highly associated with virulence. They also represent an example of how a VFAR relationship, which ties specific genes that encode for virulence factors, can correspond to pathogenic effects in humans.

Summary

It is beyond the scope of this chapter to comprehensively review the very extensive knowledge base that already exists regarding microbial genes that are associated with virulence. However, several examples have been discussed and serve to help make the following points:

- Because of their public health risks, for more than a century scientific interest has existed in pathogens and their associated virulence factors, and the scientific foundation for these measures of virulence is appreciable.
- Virulence is often clearly and easily linked to known genetic elements.
- The genetic elements associated with virulence vary somewhat among isolates of specific pathogens, and this variation has been linked directly to the genetic variation within many species of bacteria or viruses (e.g., polioviruses, influenza, *Shigella* toxins).
- These genetic elements are frequently shared among waterborne pathogens having a similar ecological niche that warrants public health concern (e.g., *Salmonella*, *Shigella*, *Vibrio*, *Escherichia* bacteria).
- The ease of identification of these genetic elements, their sequencing, and comparison has increased dramatically in the past decade due to advances in molecular biology and bioinformatics.

PERSISTENCE RESPONSES

When pathogens are released into the aquatic environment they may die, multiply, or enter a dormant state. Each of these has implications for subsequent human exposure and health. The factors responsible for pathogen decay are reviewed below. It is important to note at the outset that the assessment of pathogen survival is dependent on the assay used for analysis. This relationship has been particularly well documented for bacteria (Roszak and Colwell, 1987). Further discussion of this issue is provided later in the chapter. It is one of the committee's central assertions that the assessment of persistence (survival) in the environment using molecular techniques may be superior to some of the older methods.

Mechanisms Responsible for Decay

The factors that can cause removal of pathogens from the aquatic environment can be grouped broadly into abiotic and biotic factors, based on the mediation of other organisms in the process. In any environment, overall pathogen loss rates reflect the combination of these factors (Auer and Niehaus, 1993; Canale et al., 1993; Chamberlin and Mitchell, 1978).

Abiotic Factors

A number of abiotic factors may be responsible for microbial loss in the aquatic environment. Perhaps the most straightforward is sedimentation. Although environmental pathogens have quite low settling velocities by virtue of their size and density, many organisms can become attached to particles in the water column and increase their effective settling velocity to that of the aggregate. This process has been demonstrated clearly for *Cryptosporidium* (Medema et al., 1998), and similar phenomena are likely to occur with other microorganisms.[3]

Although, the physical removal of microorganisms via sedimentation represents a loss process from the water column, it does not result in total elimination of the pathogens from the aquatic environment. In fact, there is strong circumstantial evidence that the transport of pathogens into sediments may create a reservoir for recontamination of the water column. Furthermore, microorganisms in sediments may have lower net inactivation rates than microorganisms in the water column (Burton et

---

[3] For example, there is information that bacteria stick to solid surfaces in the milieu of filtration in aquifer-like conditions (Bolster et al., 1998).

al., 1987; Davies et al., 1995; Laliberte and Grimes, 1982; Matson et al., 1978; Palmer, 1988; Smith et al., 1978). The effect of visible light on increasing decay rates of pathogens (and indicator organisms) in water is well documented (Chamberlin and Mitchell, 1978; Davies-Colley et al., 1994; Mancini, 1978; Muela et al., 2000). It is known that the penetration of sunlight into natural waters can produce a variety of photochemical oxidants, including hydroxyl radicals and hydrogen peroxide. Thus, the promotion of pathogen decay by light may involve direct, as well as indirect (oxidant-mediated), mechanisms (Arana et al., 1992).

Biotic Factors

Interactions between pathogens and other organisms in water may result in loss of viability of the pathogens. Among the more commonly documented processes is the predation of bacteria by indigenous protozoan organisms (Davies et al., 1995; Enzinger and Cooper, 1976; Sibille et al., 1998). The obligate parasitic bacteria *Bdellovibrio* may also serve to diminish pathogenic (and indicator) bacterial levels (Fry and Staples, 1974). Predation of bacteria by bacterioviruses (phage) may also occur in natural waters (Bergh et al., 1989). Although the evidence for this is not well documented, it is known that phage exist for many pathogenic bacteria.

However, a recent review by Wommack and Colwell (2000) focusing primarily on viral interactions with indigenous bacterioplankton (most of which are nonpathogenic), stated that "less than 20% of bacterioplankton and phytoplankton [in natural waters] is attributable to viral infection." They concluded that mortality loss from infection tends to increase as the density of the host bacteria increases. Thus, it would be anticipated that the persistence of pathogenic bacteria (or other potential hosts, such as algae or protozoa) would be impacted minimally by the potential for viral infection.

Mechanisms Affording Protection to Microorganisms

There are several potential mechanisms that protect microorganisms against adverse environmental conditions. Foremost among these is association with solids that confer protection from die-off (Gerba et al., 1978). The mechanism whereby this protection occurs has not been

well-characterized but may result from protection against biotic antago-
nists or from transport of inhibitory substances to the solid-associated
microbe. Some microorganisms are able to enter dormant stages (e.g.,
bacterial spores), which affords a measure of protection against adverse
environmental conditions. For example, the relatively strong persistence
of nonpathogenic *Clostridium perfringens* in water has been well documented (Cabelli, 1977; Fujioka and Shizumura, 1985).

The formation of cysts in protozoa such as *Giardia* (Adam, 1991) or
oocysts by *Cryptosporidium* (O'Donoghue, 1995) results in a life stage
that is able to survive for extended periods in the environment. Helmin-
thic ova also represent a similar dormant or protective stage, and *Ascaris
lumbricoides* ova have been documented to survive for years and even
decades in the soil (Bergstrom and Langeland, 1981; Buts, 1969;
Kizeval'ter and Derevitskaia, 1968; Kransnonos, 1978).

In some cases, microorganisms may occupy habitats that offer
unique protection against environmental agents. For example, it is has
been established that intracellular association with aquatic protozoa may
be important in protecting *Legionella pneumophila* from adverse environmental conditions (Barker et al., 1992; Fields et al., 1984). This association may also assist in the resuscitation of "viable nonculturable" *Legionella* (see more below) (Steinert et al., 1997). Other bacteria (and
perhaps other nonbacterial pathogens) may be harbored protectively in
this manner. For example, King et al. (1988) reported that the protozoan
Tetrahymena could harbor and protect cells of *Escherichia coli, Citro-
bacter freundii, Enterobacter agglomerans, E. cloacae, Klebsiella pneu-
moniae, K. oxytoca, Salmonella typhimurium, Yersinia entercolitica,
Shigella sonnei, Legionella gormanii,* and *Campylobacter jejuni* for at
least several hours. The relative importance of pathogen harboring by
indigenous protozoa versus diminution of pathogen levels through predation in aquatic environments deserves further study. The committee
contends that the molecular methods discussed in this chapter are likely
to prove useful in assessing the viability of "harbored" pathogens.

Although the concept is controversial (Bogosian et al., 1996; Bogosian et al., 1998; Kell et al., 1998), a number of researchers have indicated that bacteria can enter a dormant stage, generally termed "viable
nonculturable." This was first shown in studies on *Vibrio cholerae*, in
which the viable nonculturable state apparently plays an important role in
the maintenance of the pathogen in the water column (Brayton et al.,
1987; Colwell, 1996; Ravel et al., 1995). (This topic is discussed earlier
in this chapter; however, the focus there is on the value of PCR tech-

niques in detecting nonculturable bacteria rather than on persistence responses.)

In some cases, however, the pathogenicity of the putative viable nonculturable organisms may be low, as reported by Caro et al. (1999) for *Salmonella typhimurium*. In this dormant state, assessment of microbial levels by plate counts may indicate little occurrence (unless resuscitation has been triggered), while other assays such as total microscopic count or nucleic acid assay may indicate higher levels. Table 6-2 summarizes some published reports of the occurrence of viable nonculturable states in bacteria.

Range of Decay Rates

Regardless of the mechanism(s) promoting loss of viability of microorganisms in aquatic systems, several researchers have reported the observed rate of disappearance under different conditions as summarized below.

TABLE 6-2 Viable Nonculturable States in Bacteria

Microorganism	References
Campylobacter jejuni	Buswell et al., 1998
	Rollins and Colwell, 1986
Coliforms	McFeters et al., 1986
Escherichia coli O157:H7	Rigsbee et al., 1997
Klebsiella pneumoniae	Byrd et al., 1991
Enterobacter aerogenes	
Agrobacterium tumefaciens	
Streptococcus faecalis	
Micrococcus flavus	
Salmonella enteriditis	Chmielewski and Frank, 1995
Salmonella dysenteriae	Islam et al., 1993
Enterococcus faecalis	Lleo et al., 1998
Legionella pneumophila	Steinert et al., 1997
Vibrio vulnificus	Weichart and Kjelleberg, 1996

Determination of Viability

For studies that measure decay rates in microorganisms, the particular assays used for assessment of viability become important. In most cases, but particularly for data obtained before the mid-1990s, the assessment of viability was based on culturing methods such as agar plate growth of bacteria and most-probable-number assays for bacteria or viruses (in the form of the $TCID_{50}$ determination [i.e., tissue culture infectious dose, or dose required to infect 50 percent of the tissue culture in which a sample is inoculated]).

As noted previously, however, bacteria may form viable nonculturable stages that by definition are not readily enumerated using culture techniques. Therefore, reliance on culture techniques may incorrectly estimate the true decay rates. In more recent years, some investigators have used molecular genetic techniques such as PCR (Abbaszadegan et al., 1999; DiGiovanni et al., 1999; Shieh et al.,1997; Sturbaum et al., 1998) to assess occurrence or decay of pathogens in environmental systems. Although PCR and other molecular methods may allow more efficient data collection, they may also overestimate the occurrence or persistence of viable microorganisms (Deere et al., 1996; Dupray et al., 1997). Thus, any reports of survival times (or occurrences) of pathogens in water should be accompanied by a description of the methods used to assess viability.

Data for Established Pathogens

As part of a mid-1980s reevaluation of the coliform standards for drinking water, a comprehensive review of the decay of indicators and pathogens in water was performed under the sponsorship of EPA. A summary of these decay values is provided in Table 6-3. The original tabulated values of times required for 50, 90, 99, or 99.9 percent reduction are indicated—this is preferable to conversion to a single metric (e.g., half-life), since in many cases the underlying data differed from ideal first-order decay. The information in this table reflects microorganism survival under diverse conditions ranging from raw water (of various sources) to finished drinking water (although in no circumstances was there any disinfectant residual present).

Data for More Recent Pathogens

There have been studies of additional microorganisms since the efforts summarized below in Table 6-3. Although a comprehensive review of such studies is beyond the objective of this report, a brief synopsis of findings for some emerging pathogens is appropriate. DeRegnier et al. (1989) suspended *Giardia muris* in river water and lakewater at ambient temperature to monitor viability using propidium iodide and animal infectivity. As measured by infectivity, cysts remained viable at least 40 days. It should be noted, however, that the small number of test animals did not likely permit measurement of inactivation beyond one log. The authors concluded

> . . . *G. muris* cysts suspended in environmental water remained viable for 2 to 3 months, and their survival was enhanced by exposure to low water temperature, despite the fact that the cysts were suspended in the fecal biomass within the sample vial.

TABLE 6-3 Survival Times for Pathogens in Raw or Finished Waters[a]

Microorganism	Temperature (°C)	Time for Indicated Die-off (Days) T_{50}	T_{99}	$T_{99.9}$	Reference
Campylobacter jejuni	25			2-3	Blaser et al., 1980
Campylobacter jejuni	4			3-18	Blaser et al., 1980
Coxsackievirus A9	19-25		>21		Herrmann et al., 1974
Coxsackievirus B1	4-8		2.4		O'Brien and Newman, 1977
Coxsackievirus B3	20			6-8	Hurst and Gerba, 1980
Echovirus 7	20			3	Hurst and Gerba, 1980
Entamoeba histolytica	4			55-60	Chang, 1943
Entamoeba histolytica	6-8			38-42	Chang, 1943
Entamoeba histolytica	21-22			7-8	Chang, 1943
Poliovirus 1	19-25		>21		Herrmann et al., 1974
Poliovirus 1	4-8		2		O'Brien and Newman, 1977
Poliovirus 1 and 3	23-27		1, 1.8		O'Brien and Newman, 1977
Rotavirus SA-11	20			10-14	Hurst and Gerba, 1980
Salmonella enteritidis	9.5-2.5	0.66-0.79			McFeters et al., 1974
Shigella flexneri	23-25			4-21	Mohadjer and Mehrabian, 1975
Vibrio cholerae	9.5-12.5	0.29			McFeters et al., 1974

[a] Underlying data obtained using culture techniques.
SOURCE: Adapted from Sobsey and Olson, 1983.

Robertson et al. (1992) used a differential dye inclusion assay to monitor viability decay of two strains of *Cryptosporidium parvum* oocysts. One was originally isolated from deer and cultured in sheep, and the other was a bovine isolate. The organisms were held in membrane diffusion chambers in river water under ambient conditions. Their results indicate that 1-log inactivation is estimated to occur at 100 and 180 days for the two strains examined. More recently, Jenkins et al. (1997) determined that the survival of oocysts in fecal material (as measured by vital dyes) correlates well with the ability of the oocysts to excyst. However there is continuing controversy about the suitability of dye incorporation assays versus other techniques with respect to assessing oocyst viability (Belosevic et al., 1997; Bukhari et al., 2000). As noted earlier in this chapter, FISH techniques that use mRNA or other targets may be superior to estimate microbial viability. Enriquez et al. (1995) reported that adenovirus held for 60 days in dechlorinated tap water produced only a 2-log reduction at 23°C as measured through tissue culture assays.

Intrinsic Factors Influencing Decay

A key question is to what degree the persistence or decay of pathogens in water can be predicted quantitatively and how this information could be used in the construction of VFARs. Based on the preceding information, it is clear that a wide range of variation exists in the removal rates of pathogens in aquatic systems. However, beyond some broad generalizations, a fully quantitative model that incorporates effects of adverse conditions on a range of pathogens has eluded investigators. It is encouraging, however, that in some cases for specific microorganisms, an overall predicted model can be developed (Auer and Niehaus, 1993; Auer et al., 1998; Canale et al., 1993; Chamberlin and Mitchell, 1978; Mancini, 1978).

Nonetheless, there are identifiable differences between microorganisms that should allow for a semiquantitative assessment of environmental persistence; these are

- ability to sorb suspended solids;[4]
- ability to form dormant stages, including viable nonculturable;

---

[4] Assuming that sorption to suspended solids does not result in increased decay rates.

- ability to survive and/or multiply within aquatic protozoa or other microbial hosts;
- ability to survive freezing;
- ability to survive desiccation;
- ability to survive wastewater treatment and to reenter drinking water; and
- ability to survive in anaerobic sediment.

INTERPRETATION OF ISSUES

Data Information and Management Issues

Although the technology, methodology, and even the genetic data-banks exist, the application of a VFAR approach to assess waterborne pathogens would require considerable effort and expenditure of resources by EPA in conjunction with the Centers for Disease Control and Prevention, National Institutes of Health, and other federal and state health organizations (NRC, 1999b). Such an interagency "Waterborne Microbial Genomics" (WMG) project would also require extensive expertise in bioinformatics, molecular microbiology, environmental microbiology, and infectious disease. Initially, existing gene banks would have to be screened and evaluated for key targets. For example, the National Center for Biotechnology Information jointly established by the National Library of Medicine and the National Institutes of Health maintains Gen-Bank (www.ncbi.nlm.nih.gov). However, the available sequence data are not error free, and greater quality control and quality assurance would have to go into screening the genetic information. Of course, new data on genetic sequences would have to be added to the WMG as they are reported in the clinical literature. As a start, this would require the evaluation of literature for references to microorganisms having the potential to be waterborne, found in feces or urine, and naturally occurring in the water environment.

Furthermore, protocols would have to be established and tested regarding data entry, validation, and use in the development of microbial VFARs. Background levels and determination of prevalence, persistence, and quantity of key target genes would have to be gathered for analysis and interpretation of health risk and/or exposure potential. Outbreaks and contamination events would provide useful information to enhance the database. Once key parameters had been established, the possibility of screening hundreds of water samples for thousands of key microbial hazards could be achieved through development of custom chip arrays.

The use of appropriate data and sophisticated data management would be crucial to the development and validation of VFARs. Because VFARs have the potential to be very powerful, they will require thorough validation and careful use, with attention to the limits of their validity. Validation can proceed in a variety of ways, such as the statistical measure of how well a VFAR fits into the descriptor or response data, the use of sensitivity analysis to validate VFAR data that are already available, using a VFAR with new data after it has been established with older data, and comparing the predictions of one VFAR to those of another. All of these will require the development of appropriate data sets and data management tools. The committee also notes that the use of prototype classification methods to help select PCCL contaminants for inclusion on a CCL can obviously be applied to VFARs. That is, training sets of descriptor and response variables could be developed and used in conjunction with prototype classification methods to help derive VFARs. This again implies that such training sets would have to be appropriate and robust.

The committee fully recognizes that just the initial establishment of such a program (excluding maintenance and expansion) is likely to require at least a five-year commitment and significant cooperation and expenditure of resources by EPA and other participating organizations. However, the opportunities for rapid identification of microbial hazards in water afforded by such a program would greatly improve the ability of EPA to quickly and successfully protect public health and improve water quality.

FEASIBILITY

For the VFAR concept to be ultimately adopted and used by EPA in its drinking water program, it must be feasible. Several aspects of feasibility are discussed below, including scientific validity and applicability; actual technological feasibility; application of these technologies to studying disease in humans (validation); the degree to which these methodologies are being universally adopted within the scientific community; and the need for their development and use to adhere to the principles of transparency, public participation, and other sociopolitical considerations reviewed in Chapter 2. To one extent or another, each of these elements affects the ability of the VFAR concept to be developed, used, or validated. Since these elements either are present or can reasonably be expected to be available in the near future, the committee strongly concludes that the development and use of VFARs is indeed feasible. Having carefully noted some caveats and limitations in the preceding text, the committee remains enthusiastic about the utility of developing and using VFARs in the protection of the nation's drinking water.

First, the underlying concept must be scientifically valid and robustly applicable. As previously noted, the relationship between specific microbial attributes and human disease has been known for more than a century. This linkage has become increasingly documented and precise as our knowledge of microorganisms and human disease has dramatically improved in the past few decades. While the illustrative examples provided in this chapter are by no means exhaustive, they certainly speak to the power of specific microbial attributes to predict virulence in humans. It is not only possible, but in fact now routine, to associate very specific human disease outcomes with the presence, absence, or variability of specific microbial characteristics (or "descriptors" in the language of SARs). To state that the concept is robustly applicable, the committee means that it is neither limited nor narrow, but is in fact valid across a very large number of microorganisms and remains valid when small variations in a single organism are explored in great depth. The fact that this is indeed the case, and is considered a paradigm of biomedical science, provides a convincing demonstration of the validity and robustness of the concept. Thus, the committee deems that the first necessary condition for feasibility exists.

For the VFAR concept to be useful, it must be able to extend a known relationship between a virulence attribute and human disease to a situation in which the attribute is found in a new or unexpected circumstance or in microorganisms that have not heretofore been recognized as potentially pathogenic. The profound scientific revolution associated with the unraveling of DNA's double helix speaks to this second aspect of feasibility—the disciplines of bioinformatics, proteomics, and genomics. The ability to rapidly, and completely, sequence the genome of entire organisms, and to use bioinformatic techniques to compare gene sequences of different organisms, provides this mechanism for comparison. The committee adds that the time and cost required for sequencing a microorganism have both declined markedly in just the past few years. Independent of any judgment made by this committee, a number of biotechnology and pharmaceutical companies have chosen to aggressively pursue opportunities that rely on comparative genomics, which the committee regards as confirming its judgment of the adequacy, power, and affordability of the methodology. The committee thus warrants that the necessary condition of technological feasibility also exists.

Although the committee is unclear as to whether compelling logic currently exists for the development of VFARs based on genomic techniques that can be extended to proteomics, it fully acknowledges the potential for this in the near future. The possibility for proteomics to also play a role in the development of VFARs adds both depth and an additional dimension to ways in which VFARs might operate in the future within EPA's drinking water program.

A third element by which to judge feasibility is the likelihood that adverse human outcomes (e.g., diseases) will continue to be discovered in association with the action or presence of a microbial contaminant, microbial gene, or gene product in the clinical setting. This clinical linkage between diseases and specific microorganisms or their products has been a hallmark of medical sciences for the past two centuries. There is no indication that the accelerating pace of these medical discoveries is abating; one need only consider prions and mad cow disease, Ebola virus, *Escherichia coli* O157:H7, *Helicobacter pylori*, and nanobacteria to be reminded of important pathogens that were unknown to science until a few decades ago. As discussed previously, the intent of the VFAR is to characterize, categorize, and make scientific the potential linkage, as outlined in Figure 6-3 below.

This external element represents both a validation of the linkage for those organisms already known to cause disease and an element that will be helpful in validating the discovery of emerging waterborne pathogens through the use of VFARs. For "established" waterborne microoorganisms such as *Vibrio cholerae*, *Salmonella*, and the pathogenic protozoa, this linkage was, and is, made easily. That is, these microorganisms are already easily cultured or visible in human specimens—no new technological or scientific advances are required for them to be linked to human disease. In the case of emerging microorganisms that are often unsuspected agents of disease, or are difficult to detect using traditional methods of culture or microscopy, it is likely that the novel molecular detection techniques discussed in this chapter (e.g., PCR, gene chips) will continue to lead to new medical associations. Identification of some viruses (e.g., herpes simplex virus) or specific microbial antigens through PCR techniques has now become commercially viable and widespread in the medical setting, replacing earlier methods. Many diagnostic kits are now available to detect antigens shed by pathogenic bacteria and viruses in urine, blood, and spinal fluid. Viruses that were once "too expensive"

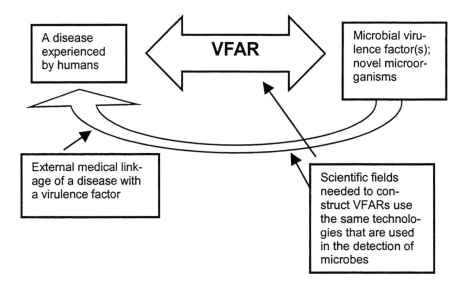

FIGURE 6-3   Linkage between microbial virulence factors and human disease.

to look for on a routine basis (e.g., rotavirus) are now tested routinely for in the clinical microbiology laboratory using simple ELISA (enzyme-linked immunosorbent assay) methods. Indeed, ELISA kits that recognize *Giardia* and *Cryptosporidium* antigens are already available (e.g., Alexon-Trend's ProSpecT® assays). Thus, the committee can foresee the likelihood that the same technologies needed for constructing VFARs will already be used in the clinical setting to detect microorganisms or their products, further strengthening the utility of the VFAR relationship.

A fourth element regarding feasibility is the likelihood that EPA's movement to adopt VFARs for use in its drinking water program will be congruent with the direction that other government, private, and public agencies are taking. In simplest terms, is such an effort likely to be adopted solely by EPA, or is it likely to be a direction that other agencies will follow? Resoundingly, all evidence points to a massive public and private investment in genomics, bioinformatics, and proteomics, which are the key disciplines behind developing and using VFARs. Furthermore, the specific needs of EPA are likely to be recognized by others as being of crucial importance to shared problems. For example, the "identification" problem that exists for EPA—identifying potentially pathogenic microbial water contaminants that are difficult or impossible to culture—has already been recognized by other government agencies as a high-priority area for research (BRWG, 2000). There is every reason to believe that the path EPA must follow to develop VFARs will be similar to one already blazed by many other agencies. Indeed, it can be argued persuasively that EPA will benefit very substantially from the synergistic efforts of other agencies and independent outside researchers as recommended in the committee's second report (NRC, 1999a). In all likelihood, the resources of EPA will have to be directed primarily to (1) focusing its own internal efforts and the attention of other government agencies on waterborne pathogens and (2) integrating a tremendous knowledge base (in large part developed outside the agency) with the purpose of VFAR construction, validation, and use in EPA's drinking water program. Thus, adoption of the technologies behind VFARs by the wider scientific community considerably improves the feasibility of any related EPA efforts to develop and use VFARs. The high-priority issues identified in this report are well recognized by other agencies that have similar needs but different applications in mind.

Lastly, the committee's (Chapter 2) recommendations that the process for selecting drinking water contaminants for future CCLs be systematic, scientifically sound, transparent, and involve broad public participation should also be met in the development and use of VFARs.

CONCLUSIONS AND RECOMMENDATIONS

Despite the identification and discussion of some necessary caveats and limitations, the committee concludes that the construction and eventual use of VFARs in EPA's drinking water program are feasible and merit careful consideration. More specifically, the committee makes the following recommendations:

• Establish a scientific VFAR Working Group on bioinformatics, genomics, and proteomics, with a charge to study these disciplines on an ongoing basis and periodically inform the agency as to how these disciplines can affect the identification and selection of drinking water contaminants for future regulatory, monitoring, and research activities. The committee acknowledges the importance of several practical considerations related to the formation of such a working group within EPA, including how it should be administered and supported (e.g., logistically and financially) or where it could be located. However, the committee did not have sufficient time in its meetings to address these issues or make any related recommendations.

• The findings of this report, and especially those of the Biotechnology Research Working Group (BRWG, 2000) should be made available to the VFAR Working Group at its inception. The committee views the activities of such a working group as a continuing process in which developments in the fields of bioinformatics, genomics, and proteomics can be assessed rapidly and adopted for use in EPA's drinking water program.

• The working group should be charged with the task of delineating specific steps and related issues and time lines needed to take VFARs beyond the conceptual framework of this report to actual development and implementation by EPA. All such efforts should be made in open cooperation with the public, stakeholders, and the scientific community

• With the assistance of the VFAR Working Group, EPA should identify and fund pilot bioinformatic projects that use genomics and proteomics to gain practical experience that can be applied to the development of VFARs while it simultaneously dispatches the charges outlined in the two previous recommendations.

• EPA should employ and work with scientific personnel trained in the fields of bioinformatics, genomics, and proteomics to assist the agency in focusing efforts on identifying and addressing emerging waterborne microorganisms.

• EPA should participate fully in all ongoing and planned U.S. government efforts in bioinformatics, genomics, and proteomics as potentially related to the identification and selection of waterborne pathogens for regulatory consideration.

References

Aach, J., W. Rindone, and G. M. Church. 2000. Systematic management and analysis of yeast gene expression data. Genome Research 10:431–445.

Abbaszadegan, M., M. S. Huber, C. P. Gerba, and I. L. Pepper. 1993. Detection of enteroviruses in groundwater with the polymerase chain reaction. Applied and Environmental Microbiology 59:1318–1324.

Abbaszadegan, M., P. Stewart, and M. LeChevallier. 1999. A strategy for detection of viruses in groundwater by PCR. Applied and Environmental Microbiology 65(2):444–449.

Acheson, D. W. 1998. Nomenclature of enterotoxins [comment]. Lancet 351(9108):1003.

Acheson, D. W. K, A. Donohue-Rolfe, and G. T. Keusch. 1991. The family of Shiga and Shiga-like toxins. Pp. 415–433 in Alouf, J. E, and J. H. Freer (eds.) Sourcebook of Bacterial Protein Toxins. London: Academic Press.

Adam, R. 1991. The biology of *Giardia* spp. Microbiological Reviews 55(4):706–732.

Adam, R. D. 2000. The *Giardia lamblia* genome. International Journal for Parasitology 30:475–484.

Aggarwal, R., and K. Krawczynski. 2000. Hepatitis E: An overview and recent advances in clinical and laboratory research. Journal of Gastroenterology and Hepatology 15(1):9–20.

Anderson, C. W. 1993. Recommending a scheme of reason: Political theory, policy science, and democracy. Policy Sciences 26:215–227.

Anonymous. 1999. Outbreak of *Escherichia coli* O157:H7 and *Campylobacter* among attendees of the Washington County Fair-New York, 1999. MMWR 48(36):803–805.

Anthony, R. M., T. J. Brown, and G. L. French. 2000. Rapid diagnosis of bacteremia by universal amplification of 23S ribosomal DNA followed by hybridization to an ologonucleotide array. Journal of Clinical Microbiology 39:781–788.

Arana, I., A. Muela, J. Iriberri, L. Egea, and I. Barcina. 1992. Role of hydrogen peroxide in loss of culturability mediated by visible light in *Escherichia coli* in a freshwater ecosystem. Applied and Environmental Microbiology 58(12): 3903–3907.

Arneson, T., and E. Nord. 1999. The value of DALY life: Problems with ethics and validity of disability adjusted life years. British Medical Journal 319:1423–1425.

ATSDR (Agency for Toxic Substances and Disease Registry). 1997. Toxicological Profile for Tetrachloroethylene (Update). Atlanta, Ga.: U.S. Department of Health and Human Services, U.S. Public Health Service.

Auer, M. T., and S. L. Niehaus. 1993. Modeling fecal coliform bacteria—I. Field and laboratory determination of loss kinetics. Water Research 27(4): 693–701.

Auer, M. T., S. T. Bagley, D. A. Stern, and M. J. Babiera. 1998. A framework for modeling the fate and transport of *Giardia* and *Cryptosporidium* in surface waters. Journal of Lake and Reservoir Management 14(2–3):393–400.

AWWA (American Water Works Association). 1997. Workshop Report: Mission Definition for the National Contaminant Occurrence Database (NCOD). Preliminary Draft Report. Prepared by M. M. Frey, and J. S. Rosen. Denver, Colo.: AWWA.

AWWARF (American Water Works Association Research Foundation). 2000. Chapter 1 and 5 In Research Needs Report: Report from Expert Workshop on Drinking Water Research. Denver, Colo.: AWWARF.

Bailey, D., and D. Thompson. 1990. How to develop neural-network application. AI Expert 5(6):38–47.

Balbus, J, R. Parkin, and M. Embrey. 2000. Susceptibility in microbial risk assessment: Definitions and research needs. Environmental Health Perspectives 108(9):901–905.

Ballantine, L. G., and J. E. McFarland (eds.). 1998. Triazine Herbicides: Risk Assessment. Washington, D.C.: American Chemical Society.

Barke, R. P., and H. C. Jenkins-Smith. 1993. Politics and scientific expertise: Scientists, risk perception, and nuclear waste policy. Risk Analysis 13:425–439.

Barker, J., M. R. Brown, P. J. Collier, I. Farrell, and P. Gilbert. 1992. Relationship between *Legionella pneumophila* and *Acanthamoeba polyphaga*—Physiological status and susceptibility to chemical inactivation. Applied and Environmental Microbiology 58(8):2420–2425.

Barnes, D. G., and M. Dourson. 1988. Reference dose (RfD): Description and use in health risk assessments. Regulatory Toxicology and Pharmacology 8:471–486.

Baxt, W. G. 1995. Application of artificial neural networks to clinical medicine. Lancet 346:1135–1138.

Beierle, T. C. 1998. Public participation in environmental decisions: An evaluation framework using social goals. Resources for the Future, November 1998, Discussion Paper 99–06. Available at http://www.rff.org (November 1998).

Belosevic, M., R. A. Guy, R. Taghi-Kilani, N. F. Neumann, L. L. Gyurek, L. R. J. Liyanage, P. J. Millard, and G. R. Finch. 1997. Nucleic acid stains as indicators of *Cryptosporidium parvum* oocyst viability. International Journal for Parisitology 27(7):787–798.

Bennett, D. H., T. E. McKone, and W. E. Kastenberg. 2000. Evaluating multimedia chemical persistence: Classification and regression tree analysis. Environmental Toxicology and Chemistry 19:810–819.

Bennett, P. 1999. Understanding responses to risk: Some basic findings. Pp. 3–19 in Bennett, P., and S. K. Calman (eds.) Risk Communication and Public Health. New York, NY: Oxford University Press.

Bergh, O., K. Y. Borsheim, G. Bratbak, and M. Heldal. 1989. High abundance of viruses found in aquatic environments. Nature 340: 467–469.

Bergstrom, K., and G. Langeland. 1981. Overleving av spolormegg, salmonellabakterier og termostabile koliforme bakterier i jord og pa gronnsaker dyrket i infisert jord [Survival of ascaris eggs, salmonella and fecal coli in soil and on vegetables grown in infected soil]. Nordisk Veterinaermedicin 33:23–32.

Blaser, M. J., H. L. Hardesty, B. Powers, and W. L. Wang. 1980. Survival of *Campylobacter fetus* subsp. jejuni in biological milieus. Journal of Clinical Microbiology 11(4): 309–313.

Bodian, D., I. M. Morgan, and H. A. Howe. 1949. Differentiation of three types of poliomyelitis viruses. III. The grouping of fourteen strains into three immunological types. American Journal of Hygeine 49:234.

Bogosian, G., L. E. Sammons, P. J. Morris, J. P. O'Neil, M. A. Heitkamp, and D. B. Weber. 1996. Death of the *Escherichia coli* K-12 strain W3110 in soil and water. Applied and Environmental Microbiology 62(11): 4114–4120.

Bogosian, G., P. J. Morris, and J. P. O'Neil. 1998. A mixed culture recovery method indicates that enteric bacteria do not enter the viable but nonculturable state. Applied and Environmental Microbiology 64(5):1736–1742.

Bohach, G. A., D. J. Fast, R. D. Nelson, and P. M. Schlievert. 1989. Staphylococcal and streptococcal pyrogenic toxins involved in toxic shock syndrome and related illnesses. Critical Reviews in Microbiology 17:251.

Bolster, C. H., G. M. Hornberger, A. L. Mills, and J. L. Wilson. 1998. A method for calculating bacterial deposition coefficients using the fraction of bacteria recovered from laboratory columns. Environmental Science and Technology 32(10):1329–1332.

Bowie, C., S. Beck, G. Bevan, J. Raftery, F. Silverton, and A. Stevens. 1997. Estimating the burden of disease in an English region. Journal of Public Health Medicine 19(1):87–92.

Bowker, G. C., and S. L. Star. 1999. Sorting Things Out: Classification and Its Consequences. Cambridge, Mass.: Massachusetts Institute of Technology Press.

Brayton, P. R., M. L. Tamplin, A. Huq, and R. R. Colwell. 1987. Enumeration of *Vibrio cholerae* O1 in Bangladesh waters by fluorescent-antibody direct viable count. Applied and Environmental Microbiology 53(12):2862–2865.

Brezonik, P. L. 1990. Principles of linear free-energy and structure-activity relationships and their applications to the fate of chemicals in aquatic systems. Pp. 113–143 in Stumm, W. (ed.) Aquatic Chemical Kinetics: Reaction Rates of Processes in Natural Waters. New York: Wiley-Interscience.

Brown, E. R., V. D. Ojeda, R. Wyn, and R. Levan. 2000. Racial and Ethnic Disparities in Access to Health Insurance and Health Care. Los Angeles, Calif.: UCLA Center for Health Policy Research and the Henry J. Kaiser Family Foundation.

Brown, P. 1992. Popular epidemiology and toxic waste contamination: Lay and professional ways of knowing. Journal of Health and Social Behavior 33:267–281.

Brown, P. 1997. Popular epidemiology revisited. Current Sociology 45:137–156.

BRWG (Biotechnology Research Working Group). 2000. Interagency Report on the Federal Investment in Microbial Genomics. Washington, D.C.: National Science and Technology Council.

Buchanan, K. L., and J. W. Murphy. 1998. What makes *Cryptococcus neoformans* a pathogen? (synopsis). Emerging Infectious Diseases 4:71–83.

Bukhari, Z, M. M. Marshall, D. G. Korich, C. R. Fricker, H. V. Smith, J. Rosen, and J. L. Clancy. 2000. Comparison of *Cryptosporidium parvum* viability and infectivity assays following ozone treatment of oocysts. Applied and Environmental Microbiology 66:2972–2980.

Bullard, R. D. 1994. Dumping in Dixie: Race, Class, and Environmental Quality. Boulder, Colo.: Westview Press.

Burton, G. A., Jr., D. Gunnison, and G. R. Lanza. 1987. Survival of pathogenic bacteria in various freshwater sediments. Applied and Environmental Microbiology 53(4):633–638.

Buswell, C. M., Y. M. Herlihy, L. M. Lawrence, J. T. McGuiggan, P. D. Marsh, C. W. Keevil, and S. A. Leach. 1998. Extended survival and persistence of *Campylobacter* spp. in water and aquatic biofilms and their detection by immunofluorescent antibody and -rRNA staining. Applied and Environmental Microbiology 64(2):733–741.

Buts, F. I. 1969. O dlitel'nosti vyzhivaniia iaits ascaris lumbricoides v pochve trekh zon Adygeiskoi avtonomnoi Krasnodarskogo kraia [On the duration of survival of eggs of *Ascaris lumbricoides* in the soil of three zones of the Adygei Autonomous District of the Krasnodar Territory]. Meditsinskaia Parazitologiia i Parazitarnye Bolezni 38:241–242.

Byrd, J. J., H. S. Xu, and R. R. Colwell. 1991. Viable but nonculturable bacteria in drinking water. Applied and Environmental Microbiology 57(3):875–878.

Cabelli, V. J. 1977. *Clostridium perfringens* as a water quality indicator. In Hoadley, A., and B. Dutka (eds.) Bacterial Indicators/Health Hazards Associated with Water. Philadelphia, Pa.: American Society for Testing and Materials.

Canale, R. P., M. T. Auer, E. M. Owens, T. M. Heidtke, and S. W. Effler. 1993. Modeling fecal coliform bacteria—II. Model development and application. Water Research 27(4):703–714.

Caro, A. P. Got, J. Lesne, S. Binard, and B. Baleux. 1999. Viability and virulence of experimentally stressed nonculturable *Salmonella typhimurium*. Applied and Environmental Microbiology 65(7):3229–3232.

Chakraborty, T., F. Ebel, E. Domann, K. Niebuhr, B. Gerstel, B. Gerstel, S. Pistor, C. J. Temm-Grove, B. M. Jockusch, M. Reinhard, U. Walter, and J. Wehland. 1995. A focal adhesion factor directly linking intracellularly motile *Listeria monocytogenes* and *Listeria ivanovii* to the actin-based cytoskeleton of mammalian cells. European Molecular Biology Organization Journal 14:1314–1321.

Chamberlin, C., and R. Mitchell. 1978. A decay model for enteric bacteria in natural waters. Chapter 12 in Mitchell, R. (ed.) Water Pollution Microbiology. New York: Wiley-Interscience..

Champliaud, D., P. Gobet, M. Naciri, O. Vagner, J. Lopez, J. Christophe-Buison, I. Varga, G. Harly, R. Mancassola, and A. Bonnin. 1998. Failure to differentiate *C. parvum* from *C. meleagridis* based on PCR amplification of eight DNA sequences. Applied and Environmental Microbiology 64(4):1454–1458.

Chang, S. L. 1943. Studies on *Entamoeba histolytica*, II. Observations concerning encystation, maturation and excystation of *E. histolytica* and on the longevity of culture induced cysts in various fluids and at different temperatures. Journal of Infectious Diseases 72:232–241.

Chapron, C. D., N. A. Ballester, J. H. Fontaine, C. N. Frades, and A. B. Margolin. 2000. Detection of astroviruses, enteroviruses, and adenovirus types 40 and 41 in surface waters collected and evaluated by the information collection rule and an integrated cell culture-nested PCR procedure. Applied and Environmental Microbiology 66:2520–2525.

Chess, C. 2000. Improving public participation in solving environmental health problems. Journal of Environmental Health 63:24–27.

Chmielewski, R. A., and J. F. Frank. 1995. Formation of viable but nonculturable *Salmonella* during starvation in chemically defined solutions. Letters in Applied Microbiology 20(6):380–384.

Colwell, R. R. 1996. Global climate and infectious disease: The cholera paradigm. Science 274(5295):2025–2031.

Colwell, R. R., and A. Huq. 1994. Vibrios in the environment: Viable but nonculturable *Vibrio cholerae*. Pp. 117–133 in Wachsmuth, I. K., P. A. Blake, and O. Olsvik (eds.) *Vibrio cholerae* and Cholera: Molecular to Global Perspectives. Washington, D.C.: American Society for Microbiology.

Conradi, H. 1903. Ueber lösliche durch aseptische Autolyse erhalten Giftstoffe von Ruhr und Typhusbazillen. Deutsch Med Wochenschr 29:26–28.

Crump, K. S. 1995. Calculation of benchmark doses for continuous data. Risk Analysis 15(1):79–89.

Dagan, R., and M. A. Menegus. 1986. A combination of four cell types for rapid detection of enteroviruses in clinical specimens. Journal of Medical Virology 19:219.

Dahinden, U., C. Querol, J. Jager, and M. Nilsson. 1999. Using Computer Models in Participatory Integrated Assessment—Experiences Gathered in the ULYSSES Project and Recommendations for Futher Steps. ULYSSES WP-99-2. Available online at: http://zitl.zit.tu-darmstadt.de/ulysses/index. htm.

Dalkey, N. C. 1969. Analyses from a group opinion study. Futures 1:541–551.

Davies, C. M., J. A. Long, M. Donald, and N. J. Ashbolt. 1995. Survival of fecal microorganisms in marine and freshwater sediments. Applied and Environmental Microbiology 61(5):1888–1896.

Davies-Colley, R. J., R. G. Bell, and A. M. Donnison. 1994. Sunlight inactivation of *Enterococci* and fecal coliforms in sewage effluent diluted in seawater. Applied and Environmental Microbiology 60(6):2049–2058.

Deere, D., J. Porter, R. W. Pickup, and C. Edwards. 1996. Survival of cells and DNA of *Aeromonas salmonicida* released into aquatic microcosms. Journal of Applied Bacteriology 81(3):309–318.

DeRegnier, D. P., L. Cole, D. G. Schupp, and S. L. Erlandsen. 1989. Viability of *Giardia* cysts suspended in lake, river and tap water. Applied and Environmental Microbiology 55(5):1223–1229.

DeRisi, J. L., and V. R. Iyer. 1999. Genomics and array technology. Current Opinion in Oncology 11:76–79.

DiGiovanni, G. D., F. H. Hashemi, N. J. Shaw, F. A. Abrams, M. W. LeChevallier, and M. Abbaszadegan. 1999. Detection of infectious *Cryptosporidium parvum* oocysts in surface and filter backwash water samples by immunomagnetic separation and integrated cell culture PCR. Applied and Environmental Microbiology 65(8):3427–3432.

DOE (U.S. Department of Energy). 2000. Microbial Genome Project. Available online at: http://www.sc.doe.gov/production/ober/microbial.

Dowd, S., C. P. Gerba, F. Enriquez, and I. Pepper. 1998a. PCR amplification and species determination of microsporidia in formalin-fixed feces after immunomagnetic separation. Applied and Environmental Microbiology 64(1):333–336.

Dowd, S., C. P. Gerba, and I. Pepper. 1998b. Confirmation of the human-pathogenic microsporidia *Enterocytozoon bieneusi, Encephalitozoon intestinalis*, and *Vittaforma corneae* in water. Applied and Environmental Microbiology 64(9):3332–3335.

Dupray, E., M. P. Caprais, A. Derrien, and P. Fach. 1997. Salmonella DNA persistence in natural seawaters using PCR analysis. Journal of Applied Microbiology 82(4):507–510.

EDSTAC (Endocrine Disruptor Screening and Testing Advisory Committee). 1999. Final Report: Volume I. Washington, D.C.: U.S. Environmental Protection Agency.

Einsiedel, E. F., and D. L. Eastlick. 2000. Consensus conferences as deliberative democracy. Science Communication 21:323–343.

Enriquez, C. E., et al. 1995. Survival of enteric adenoviruses 40 and 41 in tap, sea and waste water. Water Research 29(11):2548–2553.

Enzinger, R. M., and R. C. Cooper. 1976. Role of bacteria and protozoa in the removal of *Escherichia coli* from estuarine waters. Applied and Environmental Microbiology 31(5):758–763.

EPA (U.S. Environmental Protection Agency). 1995. Guidance for Risk Characterization. Washington, D.C.: Science Policy Council.

EPA. 1996a. Safe Drinking Water Act Amendments of 1996: General Guide to Provisions. EPA/810/S/96/001 Washington, D.C.: Office of Water.

EPA. 1996b. The Conceptual Approach for Contaminant Identification (working draft). EPA/812/D/96/001. Washington, D.C.: Office of Ground Water and Drinking Water.

EPA. 1996c. The Model Plan for Public Participation. Developed by the Public Participation and Accountability Subcommittee of the National Environmental Justice Advisory Council, a Federal Advisory Committee to the US EPA. EPA 300-K-96-003. Washington, D.C.: Office of Environmental Justice.

EPA. 1997a. Announcement of the Draft Drinking Water Contaminant Candidate List; Notice. Federal Register 62(193):52194–52219.

EPA. 1997b. EPA Drinking Water Microbiology and Public Health Workshop. Washington, D.C.: Office of Ground Water and Drinking Water.

EPA. 1997c. Meeting Summary: EPA National Drinking Water Contaminant Occurrence Data Base. Contract No. 68-W4-0001 prepared for Office of Ground Water and Drinking Water. Washington, D.C.: RESOLVE, Inc.

EPA. 1997d. Options for Developing the Unregulated Contaminant Monitoring Regulation: Background Document (working draft). EPA/815/D/97/003. Washington, D.C.: Office of Ground Water and Drinking Water.

EPA. 1998a. Announcement of the Drinking Water Contaminant Candidate List; Notice. Federal Register 63(40):10274–10287.

EPA. 1998b. Definition of a Public Water System in SDWA Section 1401(4) as Amended by the 1996 SDWA Amendments. Federal Register 63(150):41939.

EPA. 1998c. U.S. EPA Response to Comment Document: Draft Drinking Water Contaminant Candidate List. Washington, D.C.: Office of Ground Water and Drinking Water.

EPA. 1999a. A Review of Contaminant Occurrence in Public Water Systems. Washington, D.C.

EPA. 1999b. America's Drinking Water in 1997. EPA 816-F-99-001. Washington, D.C.: Office of Water.

EPA. 1999c. Final Revisions to the Unregulated Contaminant Monitoring Regulation; Fact Sheet. Washington, D.C.: EPA, Office of Ground Water and Drinking Water.

EPA. 1999d. Issue Papers for Stakeholder Meeting of November 16, 1999. Washington, D.C.: Office of Ground Water and Drinking Water.

EPA. 1999e. National Drinking Water Advisory Council Factsheet. EPA 816-F-99-009. Washington, D.C.: Office of Ground Water and Drinking Water.

EPA. 1999f. Revisions to the Unregulated Contaminant Monitoring Regulation for Public Water Systems; Final Rule. Federal Register 64(180):50556–50620.

EPA. 1999g. Revisions to the Unregulated Contaminant Monitoring Regulation for Public Water Systems: Proposed Rule. Federal Register 64(83):23397–23458.

EPA. 1999h. Risk Assessment Guidance for Superfund: Volume 3 (Part A, Process for Conducting Probabilistic Risk Assessment). Draft Revision No. 5. Washington, D.C.

EPA. 1999i. Risk-Based Concentration Table. Region III. Superfund Technical Support.

EPA. 2000a. Current Drinking Water Standards. Available online at http://www.epa. gov/safewater/mcl.html.

EPA. 2000b. Draft Research Plan for the Drinking Water Contaminant Candidate List. Washington, D.C.: EPA, Science Advisory Board Review Draft.

EPA. 2000c. Integrated Risk Information System (IRIS); Arsenic, inorganic. Available online at http://www.epa.gov/iris/subst/0278.htm.

EPA. 2000d. Integrated Risk Information System (IRIS); Nitrate. Available online at http://www.epa.gov/iris/subst/0076.htm.

EPA. 2000e. Integrated Risk Information System (IRIS); Atrazine. Available online at http://www.epa.gov/iris/subst/0209.htm.

EPA. 2000f. Integrated Risk Information System (IRIS). Available online at http://www.epa.gov/iris.

EPA. 2000g. National Drinking Water Contaminant Occurrence Database: Introduction. Online. EPA. Available online at http://www.epa.gov/ncod.

EPA. 2000h. National Drinking Water Contaminant User's Guide Release Two. EPA. Available online at: http://www.epa.gov/ncod/html/ncod_userguide.html.

EPA. 2000i. National Primary Drinking Water Regulations; Arsenic and Clarifications to Compliance and New Source Contaminants Monitoring; Proposed Rules. Federal Register 65(121):38887–38983.

EPA. 2000j. Unregulated Contaminant Monitoring Regulation for Public Water Systems; Analytical Method for List 2 Contaminants and Clarification; Proposed Rule, Federal Register 65(178):55361–55398.

EPA. 2000k. Unregulated Contaminant Monitoring for Public Water Systems: Analytical Methods for Perchlorate and Acetochlor; Announcement of Laboratory Approval and Performance Testing (PT) Program for the Analysis of Perchlorate; Final Rule and Proposed Rule. Federal Register 65(42):11372–11385.

ERG (Eastern Research Group, Inc.)-EPA. 2000. Endocrine Disruptor Priority-Setting Database. Version 2 Beta. Available online at http://www.ergweb.

com/endocrine/.

Favorov, M. O., M. Y. Kosoy, S. A. Tsarev, J. E. Childs, and H. S. Margolis. 2000. Prevalence of antibody to hepatitis E among rodents in the United States. Journal of Infectious Diseases 181:449–455.

Fields, B. S., E. B. Shotts, J. C. Feeley, G. W. Gorman, and W. T. Martin. 1984. Proliferation of *Legionella pneumophila* as an intracellular parasite of the ciliated protozoan *Tetrahymena pyriformis*. Applied and Environmental Microbiology 47:467–471.

FIFARS (Federal Interagency Forum on Aging-Related Statistics). 2000. Older Americans 2000. Hyattsville, Md.

Finkelstein, N. D. 2000. Introduction: Transparency in public policy. Pp. 1–9 in Finkelstein, N. D. (ed.) Transparency in Public Policy. New York: St Martin's Press.

Fiorino, D. J. 1990. Citizen participation and environmental risk: A survey of institutional mechanisms. Science, Technology, and Human Values 15:226–243.

Franz, C. R., and K. G. Jin. 1995. The structure of group conflict in a collaborative work group during information systems development. Journal of Applied Communication Research 23:108–127.

Fry, J. C., and D. G. Staples. 1974. The occurrence and role of *Bdellovibrio* bacteriovirus in a polluted river. Water Research 8:1029–1035.

Fujioka, R. S., and L. K. Shizumura. 1985. *Clostridium perfringens*, a reliable indicator of stream water quality. Journal of the Water Pollution Control Federation 57(10):986–992.

Garson, G. D. 1998. Neural Networks: An Introductory Guide for Social Scientists. Thousand Oaks, Calif.: Sage Publications.

Gaylor, D., L., Ryan, D. Krewski, and Y. Zhu. 1998. Procedures for calculating benchmark doses for health risk assessment. Regulatory Toxicology and Pharmacology 28(2):150–164.

Gerba, C. P., et al. 1978. Characterization of sewage solid-associated viruses and behavior in natural waters. Water Research 12:805–812.

Gibbons, C. L., B. G. Gazzard, M. Ibrahim, Morris-Jones, C. S. L. Ong, and F. M. Awad-El—Kariem. 1998. Correlation between markers of strain variation in *Cryptosporidium parvum*: Evidence of clonality. Parasitology Int 47:139–147.

Gibbs, L. M., and CCHW (Citizens Clearinghouse for Hazardous Waste). 1995. Dying from Dioxin. Boston, Mass.: South End Press.

Gibson, M. C., S. M. deMonsabert, and J. Orme-Zavaleta. 1997. Comparison of noncancer risk assessment approaches for use in deriving drinking water criteria. Regulatory Toxicology and Pharmacology 26:243–256.

Gilliom, R.J., and D. R. Helsel. 1986. Estimation of distributional parameters for censored trace level water quality data. 1. Estimation techniques. Water Resources Research 22(2):135–146.

Golub, M. S. 2000. Adolescent health and the environment. Environmental Health Perspectives 108:355–362.

Goosney, D. L., D. G. Knoechel, and B. B. Finlay. 1998. Enteropathogenic *E. coli, Salmonella* and *Shigella*: Masters of host cell cytoskeletal exploitation. Emerging Infectious Diseases 5:216–223.

Gouin, T., D. Mackay, and F. Wania. 2000. Screening chemicals for persistence in the environment. Environmental Science and Technology 34:881.

Haas, C. N., and P. A. Scheff. 1990. Estimation of averages in truncated samples. Environmental Science and Technology 24:912–919.

Haas, C. N., C. Crockett, J. B. Rose, C. Gerba, and A. Fazil. 1996. Infectivity of *Cryptosporidium parvum* oocysts. Journal of the American Water Works Association 88(9):131–136.

Haas, C. N., J. B. Rose, and C. P. Gerba. 1999. Quantitative Microbial Risk Assessment. New York: John Wiley.

Haas, C. N., A. Thayyar-Madabusi, J. B. Rose, and C. P. Gerba. 2000. Development of a dose-response relationship for *Escherichia coli* O157:H7. International Journal of Food Microbiology 56(2–3):153–159.

Hampton, G. 1999. Environmental equity and public participation. Policy Sciences 32:163–174.

Hattis, D., and E. L. Anderson. 1999. What should be the implications of uncertainty, variability, and inherent "biases"/"conservatism" for risk management decision-making? Risk Analysis 19:95–107.

Havelaar, A. H., M. During, and J. F. Versteegh. 1987. Ampicillin-dextrin agar medium for the enumeration of *Aeromonas* species in water by membrane filtration. Journal of Applied Bacteriology 62(3):279–287.

Havelaar, A. H., A. E. De Hollander, P. F. Teunis, E. G. Evers, H. J. Van Kranen, J. F. Versteegh, J. E. Van Koten, and W. Slob. 2000. Balancing the risks and benefits of drinking water disinfection: Disability adjusted life-years on the scale. Environmental Health Perspectives 108(4):315–321.

Heidelberg, J. F, J. A. Elsen, W. C. Nelson, R. A. Clayton, M. L. Gwinn, R. J. Dodson, H. H. Haft, E. K. Hickey, J. D. Peterson, L. Umayam, S. R. Gill, K. E. Nelson, T. D. Read, H. Tettelin, D. Richardson, M. D. Ermolaeva, J. Vamathevan, S. Bass, H. Qin, I. Dragoi, P. Sellers, L. McDonald, T. Utterback, R. D. Fleishmann, W. C. Nierman, O. White, S. L. Salzberg, H. O. Smith, R. R. Colwell, J. J. Mekalanos, J. C. Venter, and C. M. Fraser. 2000. DNA sequence of both chromosomes of the cholera pathogen *Vibrio cholerae*. Nature 406:477–484.

Helsel, D. R., and T. A. Cohn. 1988. Estimation of descriptive statistics for multiply censored water quality data. Water Resources Research 24(12):1997–2004.

Herrmann, J. E., K. D. Kostenbader, and D. O. Cliver. 1974. Persistence of enteroviruses in water. Applied Microbiology 28:895–896.

Hinton, G. E. 1992. How neural networks learn from experience. Scientific American 267:144–151.

Hornik, K., M. Stinchombe, and H. White. 1989. Multilayer feedforward networks are universal approximators. Neural Networks 2:359–366.

Hurst, C. J., and C. P. Gerba. 1980. Stability of simian rotavirus in fresh and estuarine water. Applied and Environmental Microbiology 39(1):1–5.

Hyder, A. A., G. Rotllant, and R. H. Morrow. 1998. Measuring the burden of disease: Healthy life-years. American Journal of Public Health 88(2):196–202.

IOM (Institute of Medicine). 1988. Medical Technology Assessment Directory. A Pilot Reference to Organizations, Assessments, and Information Resources. Washington, D.C.: National Academy Press.

IOM. 1992. Setting Priorities for Health Technologies Assessment: A Model Process. Washington, D.C.: National Academy Press.

IOM. 1995. Setting Priorities for Clinical Practice Guidelines. Washington, D.C.: National Academy Press.

IOM. 1999. Toward Environmental Justice: Research, Education, and Health Policy Needs. Washington, D.C.: National Academy Press.

Islam, M. S., M. K. Hasan, M. A. Miah, G. C. Sur, A. Felsenstein, M. Venkatesan, R. B. Sack, and M. J. Albert. 1993. Use of the polymerase chain reaction and fluorescent-antibody methods for detecting viable but nonculturable *Shigella dysenteriae* type 1 in laboratory microcosms. Applied and Environmental Microbiology 59(2):536–540.

Jaykus, L.-A. 1997. Epidemiology and detection as options for control of viral and parasitic foodborne disease. Emerging Infectious Diseases 3:529–539.

Jenkins, M. B., L. J. Anguish, D. D. Bowman, M. J. Walker, and W. C. Ghiorse. 1997. Assessment of a dye permeability assay for determination of inactivation rates of *Cryptosporidium parvum* oocysts. Applied and Environmental Microbiology 63(10):3844–3850.

Jinneman, K. C., J. H. Wetherington, A. M. Adams, J. M. Johnson, B. J. Tenge, N. L. Dang, and W. E. Hill. 1996. Differentiation of *Cyclospora* sp. and *Eimeria* spp. by using the polymerase chain reaction products and restriction fragment length polymorphisms. FDA Lab Information Bulletin 4044:4.

Johnson, D. W., N. J. Pieniazek, D. W. Griffin, L. Misener, and J. B. Rose. 1995. Development of a PCR protocol for sensitive detection of *Cryptosporidium* oocysts in water samples. Applied and Environmental Microbiology 61(11):3849–3855.

Jothikumar, N., K. Aparna, S. Kamatcdhiammal, R. Paulmurugan, S. Saravandadevi, and P. Khanna. 1993 Detection of hepatitis E virus in raw and treated wastewater with the polymerase chain reaction. Applied and Environmental Microbiology 59:2558–2562.

Kaplan, J. E., R. A. Goodman, L. B. Schonberger, E. C. Lippy, and G. W. Gary. 1982. Gastroenteritis due to Norwalk virus: An outbreak associated with a municipal water system. Journal of Infectious Diseases 146(2):190–197.

Karetnyi, Y. V., M. J. Gilchrist, and S. J. Naides. 1999. Hepatitis E virus infection prevalence among selected populations in Iowa. Journal of Clinical Virology 14:51–55.

Kell, D. B., A. S. Kaprelyants, D. H. Weichart, C. R. Harwood, and M. R. Barer. 1998. Viability and activity in readily culturable bacteria: A review and discussion of the practical issues. Antonie Van Leeuwenhoek 73(2):169–187.

Keller, P. E., S. Hashem, L. J. Kangas, and R. T. Kouzes. 1995. Applications of Neural Networks in Environment, Energy, and Health. Proceedings of the 1995 Workshop on Environmental and Energy Applications of Neural Networks. River Edge, N.J.: World Scientific Publishing.

Keusch, G. T. 1998. Shigella. Pp. 1804–1810 In Gorbach, S. L., J. G. Bartlett, and N. R. Blacklow (eds.) Infectious Diseases. Philadelphia, Pa.: W.B. Saunders.

Keusch, G. T., G. F. Grady, L. J. Mata, and J. M. McIver. 1972. The pathogenesis of *Shigella* diarrhea. 1. Enterotoxin production by *Shigella dysenteriae 1*. Journal of Clinical Investigation 51:1212–1218.

Khramtsov, N. V., P. A. Chung, C. C. Dykstra, J. K. Griffiths, U. M. Morgan, M. J. Arrowood, and S. J. Upton. 2000. Presence of double-stranded RNAs in human and calf isolates of *Cryptosporidium parvum*. Journal of Parasitology 86(2):275–282.

Kimbell, L. M., D. L. Miller, W. Chavez, and N. Altman. 1999. Molecular analysis of the 18S rRNA gene of C. serpentis in a wild-caught corn snake (*Elaphe guttata guttata*) and a five-species restriction fragment length polymorphism-based assay that can additionally discern C. parvum from C. wrairi. Applied and Environmental Microbiology 65(12):5345–5349.

King, C. H., E. B. Shotts, R. E. Wooley, and K. G. Porter. 1988. Survival of coliforms and bacterial pathogens within protozoa during chlorination. Applied and Environmental Microbiology 53(12):3023–3033.

Kingombe, C. I., G. Huys, M. Tonolla, M. J. Albert, J. Swings, R. Peduzzi, and T. Jemmi. 1999. PCR detection, characterization, and distribution of virulence genes in *Aeromonas* spp. Applied and Environmental Microbiology 65(12):5293–5302.

Kizeval'ter, I. S., and V. V. Derevitskaia. 1968. Vyzhivaemost' iaits askarid v pochve v usloviiakh Moskovskoi oblasti [Survival of ascarid eggs in soil under conditions of the Moscow region]. Meditsinskaia Parazitologiia i Parazitarnye Bolezni 37:527–529.

Kostrzynska, M., M. Sankey, E. Haack, C. Power, J. E. Aldom, A. H. Chagla, S. Unger, G. Palmateer, H. Lee, J. T. Trevors, and S. A. De Grandis. 1999. Three sample preparation protocols for polymerase chain reaction based detection of *Cryptosporidium parvum* in environmental samples. Journal of Microbiological Methods 35:65–71.

Kozwich, D., K. A. Johansen, K. Landau, C. A. Roehl, S, Woronoff, and P. A. Roehl . 2000. Development of a novel, rapid integrated *Cryptosporidium parvum* detection kit. Applied and Environmental Microbiology 66(7):2711–2717.

Kransnonos, L. N. 1978. Mnogoletniaia vyzhivaemost' iaits askarid (*Ascaris lumbricoides* L., 1758) V pochve Samarkanda [Long-term survival of ascarid eggs (*Ascaris lumbricoides* L., 1758) in the soil of Samarkand]. Meditsinskaia Parazitologiia i Parazitarnye Bolezni 47:103–105.

Kraus, N, T. Malmfors, and P. Slovic. 1992. Intuitive toxicology: Expert and lay judgments of chemical risks. Risk Analysis 12:215–232.

Kubli, D., R. Steffen, and M. Schär. 1987. Importation of poliomyelitis to industrialized nations between 1975 and 1984: Evaluation and conclusions for vaccination recommendations. British Medical Journal 295:169.

Kwo, P. Y., G. G. Schlauder, H. A. Carpenter, P. J. Murphy, J. E. Rosenblatt, G. J. Dawson, E. E. Mast, K. Krawczynski, and V. Balan. Acute hepatitis E by a new isolate acquired in the United States. Mayo Clinic Proceedings 72:1133–1136.

Labrique, A.B., D. L. Thomas, S. K. Stoszek, and K. E. Nelson. 1999. Hepatitis E: An emerging infectious disease. Epidemiologic Reviews 21:162–179.

Laird, F. N. 1993. Participatory analysis, democracy, and technological decision making. Science, Technology, and Human Values 18:341–361.

Laliberte, P., and D. J. Grimes. 1982. Survival of *Escherichia coli* in lake bottom sediment. Applied and Environmental Microbiology 43(3):623–628.

Lancefield, R. C. 1928. The antigenic complex of *Streptococcus haemolyticus*. I. Demonstration of a type-specific substance in extracts of *Streptococcus haemolyticus*. Journal of Experimental Medicine 47:91–103.

Lander, E. S. 1999. Array of hope. Nature Genetics 21(Suppl. 1):3–4.

Law, D. 2000. Virulence factors of *Escherichia coli* O157 and other Shiga toxin-producing *E. coli*. Journal of Applied Microbiology 88:729–745.

Laxer, M. A., B. K. Timblin, and R. J. Patel. 1991. DNA sequences for the specific detection of *C. parvum* in raw milk by PCR and oligonucleotide probe hybridization. Applied and Environmental Microbiology 62:3259–3264.

LeChevallier, M. W., W. D. Norton, and R. G. Lee. 1991. Occurrence of *Giardia* and *Cryptosporidium* spp. in surface water supplies. Applied and Environmental Microbiology 57(9):2610–2616.

LeChevallier, M. W., W. Norton, M. Abbaszadegan, T. Atherholt, and J. Rosen. 1997. Variations in *Giardia* and *Cryptosporidium* in Source Water: Statistical Approaches to Analyzing ICR Data. Denver, Colo.: American Water Works Association.

Lenaghan, J., B. New, and E. Mitchell. 1996. Setting priorities: Is there a role for citizens' juries? British Medical Journal 312:1591–1593.

Leng, X., D. A. Mosier, and R. D. Oberst. 1996. Differentiation of *C. parvum*, *C. muris* and *C. baileyi* by PCR-RFLP analysis of the 18S rRNA gene. Veterinary Parasitology 62:1–7.

Linstone, H., and M. Turoff (eds.). 1975. The Delphi Method: Techniques and Applications. Reading, Mass.: Addison-Wesley.

Little, R. J. A., and D. B. Rubin. 1987. Statistical Analysis with Missing Data. New York: John Wiley & Sons.

Lleo, Md., M. C. Tafi, and P. Canepari. 1998. Nonculturable *Enterococcus faecalis* cells are metabolically active and capable of resuming active growth. Systematic and Applied Microbiology 21(3):333–339.

Lodder, W. J., J. Vinje, R. van de Heide, A. M. de Roda Husman, E. J. T. M. Leenen, and M. P. G. Koopmans. 1999. Molecular detection of Norwalk-like caliciviruses in sewage. Applied and Environmental Microbiology 65:5624–5627.

Lopez, C. J., and G. M. Gonzalez. 1996. Lay knowledge and public participation in technological and environmental policy. Philosophy and Technology 2:53–72.

Mahbubani, M., A. K. Bej, M. H. Perlin, F. W. Schaeffer, W. Jakubowski, and R. M. Atlas. 1992. Differentiation of *G. duodenalis* from other *Giardia* spp. by using polymerase chain reaction and gene probes. Journal of Clinical Microbiology 30:74–78.

Malone, M. J. 1994. Small disagreements: Character contests and working consensus in informal talk. Symbolic Interaction 17(2):107–127.

Mancini, J. L. 1978. Numerical estimates of coliform mortality under various conditions. Journal of the Water Pollution Control Federation 50:2477–2484.

Marshall, A., and J. Hodgson. 1998. DNA chips: An array of possibilities. Nature Biotechnology 16 :27–31.

Matson, E. A., S. G. Horner, and J. D. Buck. 1978. Pollution indicators and other microorganisms in river sediment. Journal of the Water Pollution Control Federation (1):13–19.

Mauskopf, J. A., and M. T. French. 1991. Estimating the value of avoiding morbidity and mortality from foodborne illnesses. Risk Analysis 11(4):619–631.

McCrudden, R., S. O'Connell, T. Farrant, S. Beaton, J. P. Iredale, and D. Fine. 2000. Sporadic acute hepatitis E in the United Kingdom: An underdiagnosed phenomenon? Gut 46:732–733.

McFeters, G. A., G. K. Bissonnette, J. J. Jezeski, C. A. Thomson, and D. G. Stuart. 1974. Comparative survival of indicator bacteria and enteric pathogens in well water. Applied Microbiology 27:823–829.

McFeters, G. A., J. S. Kippin, and M. W. LeChevallier. 1986. Injured coliforms in drinking water. Applied and Environmental Microbiology 51(1):1–5.

Medema, G. J., F. M. Schets, P. F. Teunis, and A. H. Havelaar. 1998. Sedimentation of free and attached *Cryptosporidium* oocysts and *Giardia* cysts in water. Applied and Environmental Microbiology 64(11): 4460–4666.

Melnick, J. L. 1955. Antigenic crossings within poliovirus types. Proceedings of the Society for Experimental Biology and Medicine 89:131–133.

Melnick, J. L. 1996. Enteroviruses: Polioviruses, coxsackieviruses, echoviruses, and newer enteroviruses. Chapter 22 in Fields, B. N., D. M. Knipe, and P. M. Howley (eds.) Fields Virology. Third Edition. Philadelphia, Pa.: Lippincott-Raven.

Melnick, J. L., and C. P. Gerba. 1980. The ecology of enteroviruses in natural waters. CRC Critical Review in Environmental Control 10:65–93.

Meng, J., P. Dubreuh, and J. Pillot. 1997. A new PCR based seroneutralization assay in cell culture for diagnosis of hepatitis E. Journal of Clinical Microbiology 35:1373–1377.

Meng, X-J., P. G. Halbur, M. S. Shapiro, S. Govindarajan, J. D. Bruna, I. K. Mushahwar, R. M. Purcell, and S. U. Emerson. 1998. Genetic and experimental evidence for cross-species infection by swine hepatitis E virus. Journal of Virology 72:9714–9721.

Mento, S. J., C. Weeks-Levy, J. M. Tatem, E. J. Gorgacz, and W. F. Waterfield. 1993. Significance of a newly identified attenuating mutation in Sabin 3 oral poliovirus vaccine. Developments in Biological Standardization 78:93.

Mohadjer, S., and S. Mehrabian. 1975. Studies on the survival of *Shigella flexneri* in river and tap water. Archives Roumaines de Pathologic Experimentales et de Microbiologie 34:307–12.

Morgan, U. M., and R. C. Thompson. 1998. Molecular detection of parasitic protozoa. Parasitology 117(Suppl.):S73–85.

Morgan, U. M., P. T. Monis, R. Fayer, and P. Deplazes. 1999a. Phylogenetic relationships among isolates of *Cryptosporidium*: Evidence for several new species. Journal of Parasitology 85(6):1126–1133.

Morgan, U., L. Xiao, I. Sulaiman, R. Weber, A. A. Lal, R. C. Thompson, and P. Deplazes. 1999b. Which genotypes/species of *Cryptosporidium* are human susceptible to? Journal of Eukaryotic Microbiology 46(5):42S–43S.

Morgan, U., R. Weber, L. Xiao, I. Sulaiman, R. C. Thompson, W. Ndiritu, A. A. Lal, A. Moore, and P. Deplazes. 2000. Molecular characterization of *Cryptosporidium* isolates obtained from human immunodeficiency virus-infected individuals living in Switzerland, Kenya, and the United States. Journal of Clinical Microbiology 38(3):1180–1183.

Morrow, R. H., and J. H. Bryant. 1995. Health policy approaches to measuring and valuing human life: Conceptual and ethical issues. American Journal of Public Health 85:1356–1360.

Muela, A., J. M. Garcia-Bringas, I. Arana, and I. Barcina. 2000. The effect of simulated solar radiation on *Escherichia coli*: The relative roles of UV-B, UV-A, and photosynthetically active radiation. Microbial Ecology 39(1):65–71.

Nataro, J. P., and J. B. Kaper. 1998. Diarrheagenic *Escherichia coli*. Clinical Microbiology Reviews 11(1):142–201

Neal, R. A. 1985. Chemicals and safe drinking water: National and international perspective. Pp.1–8 (Ch.1) in Rice, R. G. (ed.) Safe Drinking Water: The Impact of Chemicals on a Limited Resource. Chelsea, Mich.: Lewis Publishers.

Neumann, N. F., L. L .Gyürek, L. Gammie, G. R. Finch, and M. Belosevic. 2000. Comparison of animal infectivity and nucleic acid staining for assessment of *Cryptosporidium parvum* viability in water. Applied and Environmental Microbiology 66(1):406–412.

Nigrovic, L. E., and V. W. Chiang. 2000. Cost analysis of enteroviral polymerase chain reaction in infants with fever and cerebrospinal fluid pleocytosis. Archives of Pediatrics and Adolescent Medicine 154:761–768.

NLM (National Library of Medicine). 2000. TOXNET (Toxicology Data Network). Available online at http://toxnet.nlm.nih.gov/.

NRC (National Research Council). 1988. Enhancing Human Performance: Issues, Theories, and Techniques. Washington, D.C.: National Academy Press.

NRC. 1992. In the Mind's Eye: Enhancing Human Performance. Washington, D.C.: National Academy Press.

NRC. 1996. Understanding Risk: Informing Decisions in a Democratic Society. Washington, D.C.: National Academy Press.

NRC. 1997. Safe Water from Every Tap: Improving Water Service to Small Communities. Washington, D.C.: National Academy Press.

NRC. 1999a. Setting Priorities for Drinking Water Contaminants. Washington, D.C.: National Academy Press.

NRC. 1999b. Identifying Future Drinking Water Contaminants. Washington, D.C.: National Academy Press.

NRC. 1999c. Tooele Chemical Agent Disposal Facility: Update on National Research Council Recommendations. Washington, D.C.: National Academy Press.

Nriagu, J. O. (ed.). 1994. Arsenic in the environment. Part I: Cycling and characterization. Advances in Environmental Science and Technology Series 26.

O'Brien, R. T., and J. S. Newman. 1977. Inactivation of polioviruses and coxsackieviruses in surface water. Applied and Environmental Microbiology 33:334–340.

O'Donoghue, P. J. 1995. *Cryptosporidium* and cryptosporidiosis in man and animals. International Journal for Parasitology 25(2):139–195.

Okhuysen, P. C., C. L. Chappell, J. H. Crabb, C. R. Sterling, and H. L. DuPont HL. 1999. Virulence of three distinct *Cryptosporidium parvum* isolates for healthy adults. Journal of Infectious Diseases 180(4):1275–1281.

Okun, D. A. Historical overview of drinking water contaminants and public water utilities. Pp. 22–32 in Identifying Drinking Water Contaminants. Washington, D.C.: National Academy Press.

Oreskes, N. 1998. Evaluation (not validation) of quantitative models. Environmental Health Perspectives 106(Suppl. 6):1453–1460.

Orlandi, P. A., and K. A. Lampel. 2000. Extraction-free, filter-based template preparation for rapid and sensitive PCR detection of pathogenic parasitic protozoa. Journal of Clinical Microbiology 38:2271–2277.

Pallansch, M. A., and L. J. Anderson. 1998. Coxsackievirus, echovirus, and other enteroviruses. Chapter 258 in Gorbach, S. L, J. G. Bartlett, and N. R. Blacklow (eds.) Infectious Diseases. Philadelphia, Pa.: W.B. Saunders.

Palmer, M. 1988. Bacterial loadings from resuspended sediments in recreational beaches. Canadian Journal of Civil Engineering 15:450–455.

Pankow, J. F., and J. A. Cherry. 1996. Dense Chlorinated Solvents and Other DNAPLs in Groundwater: History, Behavior, and Remediation. Portland, Oreg.: Waterloo Press.

Parkin, R. T., and J. M. Balbus. 2000. Variations in concepts of susceptibility in risk assessment. Risk Analysis 20(5)603–611.

Parkin, R. T., J. O. Davies-Cole, and J. M. Balbus. 2000. Chronic sequelae associated with waterborne pathogens: A definition and review of human evidence. Paper presented at the Annual Meeting of the American Public Health Association, Boston, November. Washington, D.C.: American Public Health Association.

Perhac, R. M. 1998. Comparative risk assessment: Where does the public fit in? Science, Technology, and Human Values 23:221–241.

Peters, E., and P. Slovic. 1996. The role of affect and worldviews as orienting dispositions in the perception and acceptance of nuclear power. Journal of Applied Social Psychology 26:1427–1453.

Pina, S., J. Jofre, S. U. Emerson, R. H. Purcll, and R. Girones. 1998. Characterization of a strain of infectious hepatitis E virus isolated from sewage in an area where hepatitis E is not endemic. Applied and Environmental Microbiology 64:4485–4488.

Pontius, F. W. and S. W. Clark. 1999. Drinking water quality standards, regulations and goals. Chapter 1 in Water Quality and Treatment: A Handbook of Community Water Supplies, Fifth Edition. New York: McGraw-Hill.

Quinn, T. C., and R. E. Chaisson. 1998. International epidemiology of the human immunodeficiency virus. Pp. 1063–1081 in Gorbach, S. L., J. G. Bartlett, and N. R. Blacklow (eds.) Infectious Diseases. Philadelphia, Pa.: W.B. Saunders Co.

Ravel, J., I. T. Knight, C. E. Monahan, R. T. Hill, and R. R. Colwell. 1995. Temperature-induced recovery of *Vibrio cholerae* from the viable but nonculturable state: Growth or resuscitation? Microbiology 141(Pt. 2):377–383.

Ravetz, J. 1999. Models as metaphors. ULYSSES WP-99-3. Germany: Darmstadt University of Technology, Center for Interdisciplinary Studies in Technology.

Rayner, S., and R. Cantor. 1987. How fair is safe enough? The cultural approach to societal technology choice. Risk Analysis 7:3–13.

Redlinger, T., K. O'Rourke, L. Nickey, and G. Martinez. 1998. Elevated hepatitis A and E seroprevalence rates in a Texas/Mexico border community. Texas Medicine 94:68–71.

Regli, S., J. B. Rose, C. N. Haas, and C. P. Gerba. 1991. Modeling risk for pathogens in drinking water. Journal of the American Water Works Association 83(11):76–84.

Ren, R. B., E. G. Moss, and V. R. Racaniello. 1991. Identification of two determinants that attenuate vaccine-related type 2 poliovirus. Journal of Virology 65:1377–1382.

Renn, O., T. Webler, H. Rakel, P. Dienel, and B. Johnson. 1993. Public participation in decision making: A three-step procedure. Policy Sciences 26:189–214.

Rigsbee, W., et al. 1997. Detection of the viable but nonculturable state in *Escherichia coli O157:H7*. Journal of Food Safety 16:255–262.

Robertson, L. J., A. T. Campbell, and H. V. Smith. 1992. Survival of *Cryptosporidium parvum* oocysts under various environmental pressures. Applied and Environmental Microbiology 58:3494–3500.

Rochelle, P. A., D. M. Ferguson, T. J. Handojo, R. De Leon, M. H. Stewart, and R. L. Wolfe. 1997a. An assay combining cell culture with reverse transcriptase PCR to detect and determine the infectivity of waterborne *Cryptosporidium parvum*. Applied and Environmental Microbiology 63(5):2029–2037.

Rochelle, P. A., R. De Leon, M. H. Stewart, and R. Wolfe. 1997b. Comparison of primers and optimization of PCR conditions for detection of *C. parvum* and *G. lamblia* in water. Applied Environmental Microbiology 63(1):106–114.

Roivainen, M., M. Knip, H. Hyoty, P. Kulmala, M. Hiltunen, P. Vahasalo, T. Hovi, and H. K. Akerblom. 1998. Several different enterovirus serotypes can be associated with prediabetic autoimmune episodes and onset of overt IDDM. Childhood Diabetes in Finalnd (DiMe) Study Group. Journal of Medical Virology 56:74–78.

Rollins, D. M., and R. R. Colwell. 1986. Viable but nonculturable stage of *Campylobacter jejuni* and its role in survival in the natural aquatic environment. Applied and Environmental Microbiology 52(5):531–538.

Rose, J. B., C. N. Haas, and S. Regli. 1991a. Risk assessment and the control of waterborne giardiasis. American Journal of Public Health 81:709–713.

Rose, J. B., C. P. Gerba, and W. Jakubowski. 1991b. Survey of potable water supplies for *Cryptosporidium* and *Giardia*. Environmental Science and Technology 25:1393–1400.

Roszak, D. B., and R. R. Colwell. 1987. Survival strategies of bacteria in the natural environment. Microbiological Reviews 51(3):365–379.

Rowe, G., and L. J. Frewer. 2000. Public participation methods: A framework for evaluation. Science, Technology, and Human Values 25:3–29.

Sabin, A. B. 1985. Oral poliovirus vaccine: History of its development and use, and current challenge to eliminate poliomyelitis from the world. Journal of Infectious Diseases 151:420.

Sanchez, J. L., and D. N. Taylor. 1997. Cholera. Lancet 349:1825–1830.

Sawyer, M. H. 1999. Enterovirus infections: Diagnosis and treatment. Pediatric Infectious Diseases Journal 18:1033–1040.

Schaub, S. A., and R. K. Oshiro. 2000. Public health concerns about caliciviruses as waterborne contaminants. Journal of Infectious Diseases 181(Suppl. 2):S374–380.

Selevan, S. G., C. A. Kimmel, and P. Mendoza. 2000. Identifying critical windows of exposure for children's health. Environmental Health Perspectives 108(Suppl. 3):451–455.

Shieh, Y. S., R. S. Baric, and M. D. Sobsey. 1997. Detection of low levels of enteric viruses in metropolitan and airplane sewage. Applied and Environmental Microbiology 63(11):4401–4407.

Shorter, J. 1973. Correlation Analysis in Organic Chemistry: An Introduction to Linear Free-Energy Relationships. Oxford: Clarendon Press.

Sibille, I., T. Sime-Ngando, L. Mathieu, and J. C. Block. 1998. Protozoan bacterivory and *Escherichia coli* survival in drinking water distribution systems. Applied and Environmental Microbiology 64(1):197–202.

Slovic, P., T. Malmfors, D. Krewski, C. K. Mertz, N. Neil, and S. Bartlett. 1995. Intuitive toxicology. II. Expert and lay judgments of chemical risks in Canada. Risk Analysis 15:661–675.

Smith, E. M., C. P. Gerba, and J. L. Melnick. 1978. Role of sediment in the persistence of enteroviruses in the estuarine environment. Applied and Environmental Microbiology 35(4):685–688.

Smith, J. L. 2001. A reviwe of Hepatitis E virus. Journal of Food Protection 64(4):572–586.

Snacken, R., A. P. Kendal, L. R. Haaheim, and J. M. Woods. 1999. The next influenza pandemic: Lessons from Hong Kong, 1997. Emerging Infectious Diseases 5:195–203.

Sobsey, M., and B. Olson. 1983. Microbial agents of waterborne disease. In Berger, P. S., and Y. Argaman (eds.) Assessment of Microbiology and Turbidity Standards for Drinking Water. Washington, D.C.: U.S. Environmental Protection Agency.

Sowby, F. D. 1965. Radiation and other risks. Health Physics 11:879–887.

Starr, C. 1969. Social benefit versus technological risk. Science 1965:1232–1238.

Steiner, T. S., N. M. Thielman, and R. L. Guerrant. 1997. Protozoal agents: What are the dangers for the public water supply? Annual Review of Medicine 48:329–340.

Steinert, M., L. Emody, R. Amann, and J. Hacker. 1997. Resuscitation of viable but nonculturable *Legionella pneumophila* Philadelphia JR32 by *Acanthamoeba castellanii.* Applied and Environmental Microbiology 63 (5):2047–2053.

Stollerman, G. H. 1998. *Streptococcus pyogenes* (Group A streptococci). Pp. 1703–1719 in Gorbach, S. L., J. G. Bartlett, and N. R. Blacklow (eds.) Infectious Diseases. Philadelphia, Pa.: W.B. Saunders.

Strebel, P. M., R. W. Sutter, S. L. Cochi, R. J. Bielik, E. W. Brink, O. M. Kew, M. A. Pallansch, W. A. Orenstein, and A. R. Hinman. 1992. Epidemiology of poliomyelitis in the United States one decade after the last reported case of indigenous wild virus-associated disease. Clinical Infectious Diseaes 14:568–579.

Sturbaum, G. D., Y. R. Ortega, R. H. Gilman, C. R. Sterling, L. Cabrera, and D. A. Klein. 1998. Detection of *Cyclospora cayetanemsis* in wastewater. Applied and Environmental Microbiology 64(6):2284–2286.

Sulaiman, I. M., L. Xiao, and A. Lal. 1999. Evaluation of *C. parvum* genotyping techniques. Applied and Environmental Microbiology 65(10): 4431–4432.

Sulaiman, I. M., U. M. Morgan, R. C. A. Thompson, A. A. Lal, and L. Xiao. 2000. Phylogenetic relationships of *Cryptosporidium* parasites based on the 70-kilodalton heat shock protein (HSP70) gene. Applied and Environmental Microbiology 66:2385–2391.

Swanson, M. B., and A.C. Socha (eds.). 1997. Chemical Ranking and Scoring: Guidelines for Relative Assessments of Chemicals. Proceedings of the Pellston Workshop on Chemical Ranking and Scoring. Pensacola, Fla.: Society of Environmental Toxicology and Chemistry Press.

Swerdlow, D. L., B. A. Woodruff, R. C. Brady, P. M. Griffin, S. Tippen, H. D. Donnell, Jr., E. Geldreich, B. J. Payne, A. Meyer, Jr., J. G. Wells, et al. 1992. A waterborne outbreak in Missouri of *Escherichia coli* O157:H7 associated with bloody diarrhea and death. Annals of Internal Medicine 117(10):812–819.

Tan, W., X. Fang, J. Li, and X. Liu. 2000. Molecular beacons: A novel DNA probe for nucleic acid and protein studies. Chemistry: A European Journal 6:1107–1111.

Tesh, S. N. 1999. Citizen experts in environmental risk. Policy Sciences 32:39–58.

Ticehurst, J. R. 1999. Hepatitis E virus. In Murray, P. R., E. J. Baron, M. A. Pfaller, et al. (eds.) Manual of Clinical Microbiology. Seventh Edition. Washington, D.C.: American Society for Microbiology.

Tratnyek, P. G. 1998. Correlation analysis of the environmental reactivity of organic substances. Pp. 167–194 in Macalady, D. L. (ed.) Perspectives in Environmental Chemistry. New York: Oxford University Press.

Tsang, T. H. F., E. K. Denison, H. V. William, L. V. Venczel, M. M. Ginsberg, and D. J. Vugia. 2000. Acute hepatitis E infection acquired in California. Clinical Infectious Diseases 30:618–619.

Tsarev, S. A., L. N. Binn, P. J. Gomatos, R. R. Arthur, M. K. Monier, H. vanCryck-Gandre, C. F. Longer, and B. L. Innis. 1999. Phylogenetic analysis of hepatitis E virus isolates from Egypt. Journal of Medical Virology 57:68–74.

Tuttle, T. Gomez, M. P. Doyle, J. G. Wells, T. Zhao, R. V. Tauxe, and P. M. Griffin. 1999. Lessons from a large outbreak of *Escherichia coli* O157:H7 infections: Insights into the infectious dose and method of widespread contamination of hamburger patties. Epidemiology and Infection 122(2):185–192.

Vapnik, V. N. 1995. The Nature of Statistical Learning Theory. New York: Springer-Verlag.

Vesey, G., N. Ashbolt, E. J. Fricker, D. Deere, K. L. Williams, D. A. Veal, and M. Dorsch. 1998. The use of a ribosomal RNA targeted oligonucleotide probe for fluorescent labeling of viable *Cryptosporidium parvum* oocysts. Journal of Applied Microbiology 85:429–440.

Webler, T., D. Levine, H. Rakel, and O. Renn. 1991. A novel approach to reducing uncertainty: The group Delphi. Technological Forecasting and Social Change 39:253–263.

Webster, R. G., W. J. Bean, O. T. Gorman, T. M. Chambers, and Y. Kawaoka. 1992. Evolution and ecology of influenza A viruses. Microbiological Reviews 56:152–179.

Weichart, D., and S. Kjelleberg. 1996. Stress resistance and recovery potential of culturable and viable but nonculturable cells of *Vibrio vulnificus*. Microbiology 142(Pt 4):845–53.

Weiss, J. B., H. van Keulen, and T. E. Nash. 1992. Classification of subgroups of *Giardia lamblia* based upon ribosomal RNA gene sequence using the polymerase chain reaction. Molecular Biochemical Parasitology 54:73.

Weiss, S. M., and C. A. Kulikowski. 1990. Computer Systems That Learn: Classification and Prediction Methods from Statistics, Neural Nets, Machine Learning, and Expert Systems. San Mateo, Calif.: Morgan Kaufmann Publishers.

WHO (World Health Organization). 1998. Zoonotic Non-O157 Shiga Toxin Producing *Escherichia coli* (STEC). Report of a WHO Scientific Working Group Meeting.

Widmer, G., S. Tzipori, C. Fichtenbaum, and J. K. Griffiths. 1998. Genotypic and phenotypic characterization of *Cryptosporidium parvum* isolates from people with AIDS. Journal of Infectious Diseases 178:834–840.

Widmer, G., E. A. Orbacz, and S. Tzipori. 1999. β-tubulin mRNA as a marker of *Cryptosporidium parvum* oocyst viability. Applied and Environmental Microbiology 65:1584–1588.

Wiedenmann, A., P. Krüger, and K. Botzenhart. 1998. PCR detection of *Cryptosporidium parvum* in environmental samples—a review of published protocols and current developments. Journal of Industrial Microbiology and Biotechnology 21:150–166.

Wommack, K. E., and R. R. Colwell. 2000. Virioplankton: Viruses in aquatic ecosystems. Microbiology and Molecular Biology Reviews 64(1):69–114.

Xiao, L., U. Morgan, J. Limor, A. Escalante, M. Arrowood, W. Shulaw, R. Thompson, R. Fayer, and A. Lal. 1999a. Genetic diversity within *Cryptosporidium parvum* and related *Cryptosporidium* species. Applied and Environmental Microbiology 65(8):3386–3391.

Xiao, L., L. Escalante, Ch. Yan, I. Sulaiman, A. A. Escalante, R. J. Montali, R. Fayer, and A. A. Lal. 1999b. Phylogenetic analysis of *Cryptosporidium* parasites based on the small-subunit rRNA gene locus. Applied and Environmental Microbioliology 65(4):1578–1583.

Xiao, L., Morgan, U. M., Fayer, R. C. Thompson, and A. A. Lal. 2000. *Cryptosporidium* systematics and implications for public health. Parasitology Today 16(7):287–292.

Yearley, S. 1999. Computer models and the public's understanding of science: A case-study analysis. Social Studies of Science 29:845–866.

Zupan, J., and J. Gasteiger. 1993. Neural Networks for Chemist: An Introduction. New York: VCH Publishers.

Acronyms and Abbreviations

A/E	attaching and effacing
AIDS	acquired immune deficiency syndrome
AWWA	American Water Works Association
AWWARF	AWWA Research Foundation
BMD	benchmark dose
bp	base pair
CCL	Drinking Water Contaminant Candidate List
CDC	Centers for Disease Control and Prevention
CIM	contaminant identification method
COMMPS	Combined Monitoring-Based and Modeling-Based Priority Setting
CPF	cancer potency factor
DALY	disability adjusted life-year
DNA	deoxyribonucleic acid
DOE	U.S. Department of Energy
DYNAMEC	dynamic mechanism for selecting and prioritizing hazardous substances
EC	European Commission
EDPSD	Endocrine Disruptor Priority-Setting Database
EDSTAC	Endocrine Disruptor Screening and Testing Advisory Committee (EPA)
ELISA	enzyme-linked immunosorbent assay
EPA	U.S. Environmental Protection Agency
FDA	U.S. Food and Drug Administration

FISH	fluorescent in situ hybridization
GRAS	generally recognized as safe (FDA)
HEV	hepatitis E virus
HIV	human immunodeficiency virus
HPC	heterotrophic plate count
IARC	International Agency for Research on Cancer
IMS	immunomagnetic separation
IRIS	Integrated Risk Information System (EPA)
LEE	locus for enterocytic effacement
LFER	linear free energy relationship
LOAEL	lowest observed adverse effect level
MCL	maximum contaminant level
MCLG	maximum contaminant level goal
mRNA	messenger ribonucleic acid
MTBE	methyl-t-butyl ether
NCHS	National Center for Health Statistics
NCOD	National Drinking Water Contaminant Occurrence Database (EPA)
NDWAC	National Drinking Water Advisory Council
NIAID	National Institute of Allergy and Infectious Diseases
NLM	National Library of Medicine
NLV	Norwalk-like caliciviruses
NOAEL	no observed adverse effect level
NPDWR	National Primary Drinking Water Regulation
NRC	National Research Council
ORD	Office for Research and Development (EPA)
OW	Office of Water (EPA)
PCCL	preliminary CCL
PCR	polymerase chain reaction
POP	persistent organic pollutant
PTB	persistent, toxic, or liable to bioaccumulate
PWS	public water system

QALY	quality adjusted life-year
QSAR	quantitative structure-activity relationship
RFD	reference dose
RFLP	(PCR) restriction fragment length polymorphism
RNA	ribonucleic acid
rRNA	ribosomal RNA
SAB	Science Advisory Board (EPA)
SAR	structure-activity relationship
SDWA	Safe Drinking Water Act
SDWIS	Safe Drinking Water Information System
STX	Shiga toxin
TCID	tissue culture infectious dose
TIGR	Institute for Genomic Research
UCM	unregulatored contaminant monitoring
UCMR	Unregulated Contaminant Monitoring Regulation (Rule)
USGS	U.S. Geological Survey
VAR	virulence-activity relationship
VFAR	virulence-factor activity relationship
WMG	"Waterborne Microbial Genomics" project

Appendix A
The European Prioritization Schemes
"COMMPS" AND "DYNAMEC"

INTRODUCTION

This appendix provides an overview of two European rule-based schemes for identifying and prioritizing substances (primarily chemicals) that may pose risks to freshwater and marine environments and human health through these aquatic environments. Although neither scheme exclusively addresses drinking water contaminants, they are provided to illustrate how the complex and often contentious task of identifying, ranking, and culling multitudes of substances to much smaller numbers that will receive regulatory and research consideration has recently been approached in Western Europe. For example, they serve as two very clear and relevant examples of how expert judgment is vital and integral to the design, implementation, and validation of these types of prioritization schemes. In a broader capacity, several facets of their design can be compared and contrasted with the chemical prioritization schemes reviewed in the committee's first report (NRC, 1999a) and the approach recommend in this report for the development of future Drinking Water Contaminant Candidate Lists (CCLs).

COMBINED MONITORING-BASED AND
MODELING-BASED PRIORITY SETTING (COMMPS)

Currently 15 countries belong to the European Union, which is becoming increasingly important in its role of environmental protection through the European Commission (EC). Among other requirements, Article 16 of the (1999) European Parliament and Council Directive requires the commission to establish a List of Substances based on their risk to the aquatic environment and to human health through the aquatic environment. To create such a list expediently, the EC decided that a simplified risk-based assessment procedure was needed that would account for the intrinsic health and environmental hazards of substances of concern based on monitoring and modeling data. More specifically, the approach should consider the aquatic ecotoxicity and human toxicity of a substance through various aquatic exposure routes and other related factors that may indicate the possibility of widespread environmental contamination, such as chemical production volume and use patterns.

On this basis, the COMMPS procedure was developed in collaboration with the (German) Fraunhofer Institute for Environmental Chemistry and Ecotoxicology and subsequently accepted by the European Commission to establish the priority list. The current Version 2 of COMMPS is based on an approach that combines automated risk-based ranking with subsequent expert judgment for the final selection of priority substances. That is, the procedure is essentially a series of simplified substance-by-substance risk assessments. (Notably, only chemicals were assessed and included on the first priority list.) The report, *Proposal for a European Parliament and Council Decision Establishing the List of Priority Substances in the Field of Water Policy* (EC, 2000) summarizes the background, design, development, intended uses, and other related information concerning COMMPS. Further information about the European Commission and COMMPS is available on the Web at http://www.europa.eu.int.

In brief, the automated risk-based assessment results in two different types of ranking lists—one type based on monitored exposure levels and the other on modeled exposure estimates—which are in turn based on production volumes, use patterns, environmental distribution, and biodegradation as input parameters. More specifically, the first use of the COMMPS procedure comprised the following five steps:

1. *Selection of candidate substances for the ranking procedure.* For this step, a "list-based" approach was used in which the original candidate substances were selected from eight existing official lists and monitoring programs. (The committee notes that this approach is very similar to the approach used by the EPA to develop the draft 1998 CCL; EPA, 1997; NRC, 1999b.)

2. *Calculation of exposure scores.* In this step, two ranked lists were established for organic chemicals in the aquatic compartment, one

based on surface water monitoring data and the other on modeling data. Further lists were established for pollutants adsorbed by sediments and for metals based exclusively on monitoring data.

3. *Calculation of health effect scores.* One or more such lists were established for organic pollutants in the aquatic compartment, for sediments, and for metals based on test data.

4. *Computation of the risk-based priority index.* Ranked lists were calculated by multiplying the exposure and the corresponding health effects index for each substance. Two lists were ultimately developed for organic chemicals based on aquatic monitoring and modeling data, respectively. One list was obtained based on sediment monitoring data, and several lists were obtained for metals.

5. *Recommendation of priority substances.* For this purpose, a two-step procedure was applied. In the first step, the ranked lists were screened to cull a subset of candidate priority substances from each of the lists. These highly ranked substances were further screened and reorganized based on two criteria: (1) the grouping of substances that normally occur as mixtures and (2) the elimination of candidate substances if their marketing and use are already severely restricted or prohibited in Western Europe (i.e., "historic" pollution). In the second step, expert judgment was used on a substance-by-substance basis to make a final decision on whether a particular candidate priority substance would be included or excluded from the list.

In general, candidate substances selected based on monitoring exposure data were accepted for inclusion in the List of Priority Substances unless there was strong evidence against their high relative rank. In contrast, substances taken from the modeling list were accepted only if additional information was available (e.g., additional monitoring data) that supported the high relative rank of the substance. In all, 658 substances were compiled and evaluated using this approach. In June 2000, the European Parliament and Council adopted a total of 32 chemicals (e.g., pesticides, solvents, metals) that were selected and recommended through use of the COMMPS procedure and expert judgment.

A DYNAMIC MECHANISM FOR SELECTING AND PRIORITIZING HAZARDOUS SUBSTANCES (DYNAMEC)

The OSPAR Commission was founded as a result of the 1992 Oslo and Paris (OSPAR) Convention for the protection of the Northeast Atlantic marine environment. It includes 16 Western European countries together with the European Community (represented by the European Commission). In addition, participants and observers from more than two dozen nongovernment organizations representing various environmental groups and industry also contribute to OSPAR's activities. One of the major goals of OSPAR is to develop programs and measures to identify, prioritize, monitor, and control the emissions, discharges, and losses of hazardous substances that may reach the Northeast Atlantic Ocean. In this regard, in 1998 the OSPAR Commission established an Ad Hoc Working Group on the development of a dynamic mechanism for selecting and prioritizing hazardous substances (hereafter referred to as DYNAMEC) to update the existing 1998 OSPAR List of (15) Chemicals (and groups of related chemicals) for Priority Action.

In brief, the purpose of DYNAMEC is to serve as a tool to enable the OSPAR Commission—in a transparent manner and using sound information—to identify and select those hazardous substances that have to be addressed by the commission as a whole. The tool is then used to determine those hazardous substances that should be given priority in OSPAR's activities. In broader terms, DYNAMEC should help the OSPAR Commission as a first step in the implementation of its long-term strategy on the elimination of anthropogenic inputs of hazardous and radioactive substances to the Northeast Atlantic Ocean "within one generation," that is, by 2020. The DYNAMEC mechanism consists of several interrelated steps and procedures that are summarized below and illustrated in Figure A-1.

The OSPAR report *Briefing Document on the Work of the DYNAMEC and the DYNAMEC Mechanism for the Selection and Prioritisation of Hazardous Substances* (OC, 2000) provides an introduction and description of the DYNAMEC mechanism and other related information. Further information about the OSPAR Commission, its policies on hazardous substances, and DYNAMEC is available on the Internet at www.ospar.org.

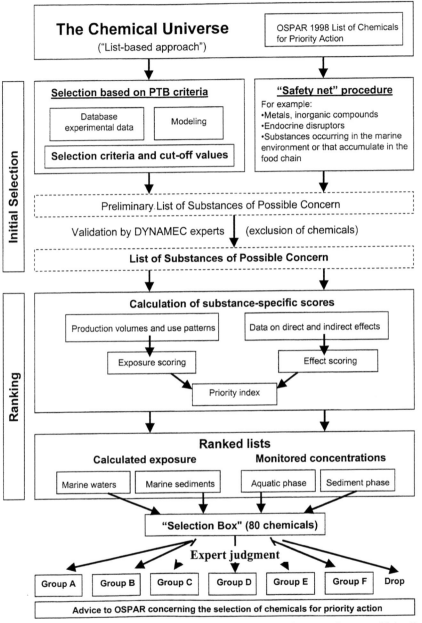

FIGURE A-1   Simplified overview of steps and procedures within the DYNAMEC mechanism and work carried out under DYNAMEC. NOTE: PTB = substance that is persistent (P), toxic (T), or liable to bioaccumulate (B). SOURCE: Adapted from EC, 1999.

The Chemical Universe

DYNAMEC considered that there are approximately 250,000 man-made chemicals in the so-called chemical universe. Thus, it would clearly not be possible to assess and rank all of these chemicals in a substantive manner. Moreover, the vast majority would invariably not be of concern in the marine environment. Therefore, as a first step, DYNAMEC incorporated the chemicals included in three large and well-established European environmental databases: (1) the Nordic Substance Database (approximately 18,000 substances); (2) the Danish Environmental Protection Agency quantitative structure-activity relationship (QSAR) database (more than 166,000 substances); and (3) the database of the Netherlands' BKH/Haskoning report (approximately 180,000 substances) for initial assessment. Thus, DYNAMEC also relied on a list-based approach for the initial identification of chemicals for subsequent consideration.

Initial Selection of Substances

DYNAMEC identified three intrinsic criteria to assess all the substances compiled in the initial selection step. The working group then established five sets of cutoff values (ranging from the most to the least restrictive) to be applied to these criteria. In brief, the criteria assess whether a substance is persistent (P), toxic (T), or liable to bioaccumulate (B). However, after taking into account the overall structure and purpose of DYNAMEC, the least stringent selection criteria and corresponding cutoff values were ultimately applied to the hazardous substances under consideration. After establishing and applying the PTB criteria, the criterion for persistency was developed further to render it more specific to the marine environment. In a separate validation exercise, the cutoff criteria were also applied to the 246 substances (or groups of related substances) included on the OSPAR 1998 List of Candidate Substances. The outcome of this exercise indicated that only 61 of the substances were identified as being of possible concern, while the remaining 185 were not—due mainly to a lack of data and a very low potential for bioaccumulation.

The Safety Net Procedure

Under DYNAMEC, "hazardous substances" refers not only to substances or groups of related substances that are toxic, persistent, and liable to bioaccumulate, but also to those that are deemed by OSPAR to require a similar assessment approach—even if they do not meet the criteria for toxicity, persistence, and bioaccumulation. To help select substances with an "equivalent level" of concern, DYNAMEC agreed to supplement the initial selections by a "safety net" procedure. Specifically, DYNAMEC experts reviewed proposals from interested parties to include substances on the preliminary List of Substances of Possible Concern that they felt achieved such an equivalent level of concern. Thus, several substances were ultimately included on the preliminary list using this mechanism. The safety net procedure is also intended to address those substances (e.g., metals, inorganic compounds, endocrine disruptors) for which the criteria of persistency and bioaccumulation are generally not applicable.

Quality Assurance/Validation

The results of the initial selection of substances were examined by a group of experts established by DYNAMEC in order to check the plausibility and consistency of the substance-specific data and exclude those substances that had been incorrectly selected.

List of Substances of Possible Concern

The ultimate outcome of the initial selection procedure was a List of Substances of Possible Concern for the marine environment. However, DYNAMEC noted that the status of this list is not definite and could change as further information becomes available and in light of improved knowledge.

Fact Sheets

DYNAMEC decided that fact sheets should be prepared to aid further assessment of all listed substances of possible concern. These fact sheets would provide comprehensive but concise background information, such as physical-chemical properties and production/use volume information (where available). After producing and distributing the first set of fact sheets, subsequent work focused on expanding the fact sheets for 80 chemicals and groups of related chemicals that were later determined to require priority action (i.e., so-called "selection box" substances described later in this appendix). DYNAMEC noted that additional related work would be necessary to complete fact sheets for all remaining substances of possible concern and to help locate and ascertain relevant data to fill gaps on the existing fact sheets.

Flagging Substances

For a variety of reasons, the substances and groups of related substances identified by the initial selection, process will give rise to differing levels of concern. In particular, a given substance may (1) have intrinsic properties similar to persistent organic pollutants (POPs) and fulfill the most restrictive set of cutoff points for PTB criteria; (2) have suspected endocrine disrupting properties; and (3) already be adequately addressed in other forums. Regarding the latter, OSPAR could then evaluate whether to await the outcome of any relevant action or to initiate specific OSPAR action. Since DYNAMEC sought to produce a comprehensive and feasible list of substances that are a threat to the marine environment, OSPAR agreed that any substances falling into one or more of these three categories should be "flagged" to ensure consideration in the revision of the existing List of Chemicals for Priority Action.

Ranking

In order to rank all substances or groups of related substances on the Preliminary List of Substances of Possible Concern, each was characterized with respect to its production volumes, use patterns, and/or measured occurrence in the environment. The level of potential concern for each substance was assessed through use of an effect score (relative toxicity and liability to bioaccumulate) and an exposure score (relative level of predicted or measured occurrence in the environment). The mathematical product of these two scores was used to help determine the relative risk for each listed substance. This process included automated data processing and was followed by expert judgment (e.g., on the basis of chemical fact sheets). In addition, DYNAMEC decided that calculated exposure estimations and monitored freshwater concentrations, both for the aquatic phase and in sediment, should be accounted for in the ranking process.

It is important to note that these ranking algorithms were based on those that had already been established for use in the previously reviewed COMMPS procedure. However, some algorithms or weighting factors were modified to render them more suitable for the marine environment. In some cases, conservative default values were used when certain substance-specific data were not known or available. In addition, a significant obstacle that DYNAMEC had to overcome concerned restricted access to some data on production/use volumes for certain substances for reasons of confidentiality. This meant that the application of the ranking algorithms, assessment of the outcome of the ranking, and the data used could be undertaken and validated only by a limited number of experts with unrestricted access to the data.

For substances without sufficient information available to carry out the ranking, further action could not be undertaken until either adequate information became available or some other approach for determining the status of such substances was developed. The ranking of the List of Substances of Possible Concern resulted in four lists:

1. substances associated with marine waters based on measured environmental concentration and the properties of the substances;

2. substances associated with marine waters based on modeled exposure scores (in turn based on calculation from production volume and use patterns);

3. substances associated with marine sediments based on measured environmental concentration and the properties of the substances; and

4. substances associated with marine sediments based on modeled exposure scores (in turn based on calculation from production volume and use pattern).

Although final selection of substances for priority action is ultimately a policy decision by the OSPAR Commission itself, it was agreed that DYNAMEC should continue to provide information and expert advice to support revision of the existing OSPAR List of Chemicals for Priority Action.

"Selection Box" of 80 substances

To facilitate these discussions, a selection box of 80 substances (all chemicals) was extracted by combining the 48 top-ranked substances from the four ranked lists (excluding certain substances already included on the 1998 OSPAR List of Chemicals for Priority Action) with all initially selected substances that could fulfill the most stringent cutoffs for the PTB criteria or those that were previously flagged as endocrine disruptors.

Grouping of Selection Box Substances

DYNAMEC experts examined the 80 selection box substances on the basis of their expanded chemical fact sheets and established a basis for grouping these substances that is described in Table A-1. A complete listing of selection box substances by group is provided in Appendix 4 of the briefing document for DYNAMEC (OC, 2000).

Based on these groupings, DYNAMEC recommended that the OSPAR Commission consider adding the 12 substances included in Groups A and B when it revises the OSPAR List of Chemicals for Priority Action. Regarding the 20 total Group A and B substances that might be in doubt, DYNAMEC recommended that they should not presently be considered priority substances. However, interested parties were invited to provide more reliable data for these substances in 2000-2001 so that they might be considered with the rest of the Group A and B substances. DYNAMEC further recommended that the 15 substances in Groups C and D should not be considered as priority substances unless new data could be provided expeditiously to support their consideration.

Lastly, DYNAMEC recommended that OSPAR consider initiating monitoring activities with respect to some of the heavily regulated substances in Group E to help determine whether concentrations observed in the environment result from historic uses, unintended or by-product emissions and discharges, or long-range (atmospheric) transport. No recommendations were made in the DYNAMEC report (EC, 2000) concerning Group F endocrine disruptors; however, OSPAR has established a separate List of Priority Research and Development Actions for Endocrine Disruptors within its overall strategy for hazardous substances.

TABLE A-1 Selection Box Groups

Group	Contents	Description
A	5 (13)[a]	Substances of very high concern (i.e., POP-like substances or substances with severe PTB profile) and indication of production, use, or occurrence in the environment
B	7 (7)[a]	Other initially selected substances with less severe PTB profile and indication of use or exposure
C	8	Substances of very high concern (i.e., POP-like substances or substances with severe PTB profile) but with no indication of use or exposure
D	7	Other initially selected substances with no indication of use or exposure
E	20	Substances with PTB properties that are already heavily regulated or withdrawn from the market
F	6	Endocrine disruptors that do not meet P or B criteria and are not natural hormones
Drop	7	Substances that do not meet the initial selection criteria and should be deleted from the Draft Preliminary List of Substances of Possible Concern

[a]These substances were initially selected as a result of reliance on QSAR data or experimental data; thus, the confidence in the assessment might be in doubt.
SOURCE: Adapted from OC, 2000.

REFERENCES

EC (European Commission). 2000. Proposal for a European Parliament and Council Decision Establishing the List of Priority Substances in the Field of Water Policy Study on the Prioritisation of Substances Dangerous to the Aquatic Environment. Document 500PC0047 online at http://europa.eu.int/eur-lex/en/com/dat/2000/en_500PC0047.html.

EPA (U. S. Environmental Protection Agency). 1997. Announcement of the Draft Drinking Water Contaminant Candidate List; Notice. Federal Register 62(193):52194-52219.

NRC (National Research Council). 1999a. Setting Priorities for Drinking Water Contaminants. Washington, D.C.: National Academy Press.

NRC. 1999b. Identifying Future Drinking Water Contaminants. Washington, D.C.: National Academy Press.

OC (OSPAR Commission for the Protection of the Marine Environment of the North-East Atlantic). 2000. Briefing Document on the Work of the DYNAMEC and the DYNAMEC Mechanism for the Selection and Prioritization of Hazardous Substances. Reference Number:1998-16.

Appendix B
Matlab Programs for Contaminant Classification

This appendix contains the Matlab[1] programs that were used to conduct the classification exercises described in Chapter 5 of this report.

class_init.m	-- initialization code
lin_class.m	-- code to train a linear classifier
nn_class.m	-- code to train a neural network classifier
class_error.m	-- code for error analysis
lin_predict.m	-- code to predict classification using the linear classifier
nn_predict.m	-- code to predict classification using the neural network classifier

```
%  -------------------------------------------------
% NRC Committee on Drinking Water Contaminants

% Filename: class_init.m

% Matlab code to initialize the classification
problem.
% Data are loaded and attributes are analyzed.
% After running this, run either lin_class.m or
nn_class.m.

%  -------------------------------------------------
% Load the training data set and set up data
variables
```

---

[1] Matlab 6 ©The MathWorks, Inc. 3 Apple Hill Drive, Natick, MA 01760-2098; http://www.mathworks.com/products/matlab/.

```matlab
S = load('caldata.txt');     % the name of the
calibration data file
id = S(:,1);
t = S(:,2);                  % class labels (target)
X = S(:,3:7);                % attributes

fid=fopen('caldata_id.txt','r'); % the file
containing the contaminant names
names=[];
for i=1:length(t)
    if i==1
        names=str2mat(fscanf(fid,'%s',1));
    else
        names=str2mat(names, fscanf(fid,'%s',1));
    end
end
fclose(fid);

X1=[]; X0=[];
for i=1:length(t)
    if t(i)==1
        X1 = [X1;X(i,:)];
    end
    if t(i)==0
        X0 = [X0;X(i,:)];
    end
end
aaa = size(X1); NT1 = aaa(1);      % The number of
contaminants with T=1
aaa = size(X0); NT0 = aaa(1);      % The number of
contaminants with T=0


% --------------------------------------------------------
% Plot correlation analysis of attributes

figure(1)
str(1) = {'Severity'};
str(2) = {'Potency'};
str(3) = {'Prevalence'};
str(4) = {'Magnitude'};
str(5) = {'Persist/Mob'};
fs=12;
for i=1:5
```

```
   subplot(5,5,i),
plot(X1(:,i),X1(:,1),'kx',X0(:,i),X0(:,1),'ko','LineW
idth',1)
   axis square
   set(gca,'LineWidth',1)
   text(0,12,str(i),'FontSize',fs)
   if i==1
      text(-3,0,str(1),'Rotation',90,'FontSize',fs)
   end
end
for i=2:5
   subplot(5,5,i+5),
plot(X1(:,i),X1(:,2),'kx',X0(:,i),X0(:,2),'ko','LineW
idth',1)
   axis square
   set(gca,'LineWidth',1)
   if i==2
      text(-3,0,str(2),'Rotation',90,'FontSize',fs)
   end
end
for i=3:5
   subplot(5,5,i+10),
plot(X1(:,i),X1(:,3),'kx',X0(:,i),X0(:,3),'ko','LineW
idth',1)
   axis square
   set(gca,'LineWidth',1)
   if i==3
      text(-3,0,str(3),'Rotation',90,'FontSize',fs)
   end
end
for i=4:5
   subplot(5,5,i+15),
plot(X1(:,i),X1(:,4),'kx',X0(:,i),X0(:,4),'ko','LineW
idth',1)
   axis square
   set(gca,'LineWidth',1)
   if i==4
      text(-3,0,str(4),'Rotation',90,'FontSize',fs)
   end
end
for i=5:5
   subplot(5,5,i+20),
plot(X1(:,i),X1(:,5),'kx',X0(:,i),X0(:,5),'ko','LineW
idth',1)
   axis square
```

```
    set(gca,'LineWidth',1)
    if i==5
        text(-3,0,str(5),'Rotation',90,'FontSize',fs)
    end
end
% -------------------------------------------------
% End of program
% -------------------------------------------------


% -------------------------------------------------
% NRC Committee on Drinking Water Contaminants

% Filename: lin_class.m

% Matlab code to build a linear classifier on the
training data set.
% After this, run class_error.m and lin_predict.m.


% -------------------------------------------------
% Linear Regression y = Xw where w is the weight
vector

Xlin = [X ones(length(t),1)]; % Add a column of ones
to fit bias/intercept.
X1lin = [X1 ones(NT1,1)];  % Add a column of ones to
fit bias/intercept.
X0lin = [X0 ones(NT0,1)];  % Add a column of ones to
fit bias/intercept.
w = pinv(Xlin)*t;

disp('The weights (five attributes plus offset)
are:');
disp(w);

y = Xlin*w;
y1= X1lin*w;
y0= X0lin*w;

meanse = sum((y-t).^2)/length(t);
disp('The mean squared error is:')
disp(meanse);

% -------------------------------------------------
% End of program
```

```
% ----------------------------------------------------


% ----------------------------------------------------
% NRC Committee on Drinking Water Contaminants

% Filename: nn_class.m

% Matlab code to build a neural network classifier on
the training data set.
% After this, run class_error.m and nn_predict.m.


% ----------------------------------------------------
% Set up Neural Network with two feed forward layers.
% The first is a hidden layer containing two nodes.
% The second is an output layer with a single node.
% Both layers have biases.
% The hidden layer has a hyperbolic tangent sigmoid
transfer function.
% The output layer has a linear transfer function.
% The training algorithm uses a conjugate gradient
search method.
% Network performance is measured according to the
mean of squared errors.

figure(2)
Xminmax = [1 10; 1 10; 1 10; 1 10; 1 10];
tranfuns = {'tansig' 'purelin'};
net = newff(Xminmax, [2 1], tranfuns, 'traincgb',
'learngdm', 'mse');
net.trainParam.min_grad = 1e-10;
net.trainParam.epochs = 1000000;
net.trainParam.minstep = 1.0e-10;
net = train(net,X',t');
disp('Input weight matrix, bias, and transfer
function in first layer');
net.IW{1,1}
net.b{1}
net.layers{1}.transferFcn
if net.numLayers>1
    for i = 2:net.numLayers
        disp('Layer weight matrix, bias, and transfer
function for next layer');
        net.LW{i,i-1}
```

```
      net.b{i}
      net.layers{i}.transferFcn
   end
end

y = sim(net,X'); y = y';
y1= sim(net,X1'); y1 = y1';
y0= sim(net,X0'); y0 = y0';
% -----------------------------------------------------
% End of program
% -----------------------------------------------------

% -----------------------------------------------------
% NRC Committee on Drinking Water Contaminants

% Filename: class_error.m

% Matlab code to determine classification error and
optimize the threshold.
% After this, run either lin_predict.m or
nn_predict.m.


% -----------------------------------------------------
% Classification error in training data set

minthresh=min(0,min(min(y1),min(y0)));
int=.05;
Threshrange=minthresh:int:max(max(y1),max(y0));

idxZero = (t==0);
idxOne = (t>0);
E0=[]; E1=[];
N0misclass=[]; N1misclass=[]; Nmisclass=[];
for thresh = Threshrange
   classOne = (y>thresh);
   classZero = (y <= thresh);
   N0mc = sum(idxZero & classOne);
   N1mc = sum(idxOne & classZero);
   Nmc = N0mc + N1mc;
   N0misclass = [N0misclass N0mc];   %The number of
T=0 misclassified
   N1misclass = [N1misclass N1mc];   %The number of
T=1 misclassified
```

```
    Nmisclass = [Nmisclass Nmc];   %The total number
misclassified
    e00 = N0mc/sum(idxZero);
    e11 = N1mc/sum(idxOne);
    E0 = [E0 e00]; % The fraction of T=0 contaminants
that are misclassified as 1
    E1 = [E1 e11]; % The fraction of T=1 contaminants
that are misclassified as 0
end
figure(3)
plot(Threshrange,100*E0,'ko--
',Threshrange,100*E1,'kx:','Markersize',8,'LineWidth'
,1.5)
set(gca,'LineWidth',2,'fontsize',fs);
xlabel('Threshold','FontSize',fs)
ylabel('Classification Error (%)','FontSize',fs)
legend('error for T=0 contaminants','error for T=1
contaminants',0)

figure(4)
plot(Threshrange,N0misclass,'ko--
',Threshrange,N1misclass,'kx:',Threshrange,Nmisclass,
'k+-','Markersize',8,'LineWidth',1.5)
set(gca,'LineWidth',2,'fontsize',fs);
xlabel('Threshold','FontSize',fs)
ylabel('Classification Error (number that are
misclassified)','FontSize',fs)
legend('number of misclassified T=0
contaminants','number of misclassified T=1
contaminants','total number of misclassified
contaminants',0)


% --------------------------------------------------
% Find the threshold that minimizes the total number
of misclassified contaminants
inda = find(Nmisclass==min(Nmisclass));
threshes = Threshrange(inda);
sthreshes = size(threshes);
if sthreshes(2)>1    % If there are more than one
threshold values ...
    indb =
find(E0(inda)+E1(inda)==min(E0(inda)+E1(inda)));
    thresh = threshes(indb);    % ... fine the one the
minimizes the total percent error
```

```
else
    thresh = threshes;
end
sthresh = size(thresh);
if sthresh(2)>1        % If there are still more than
one threshold values ...
    thresh = min(thresh);    % ... choose the smallest
one.
end

disp('The optimal threshold is:');
disp(thresh);
indc = find(Threshrange==thresh);
disp('The percent error in misclassifying T=1
contaminants is:');
disp(100*E1(indc));
disp('The percent error in misclassifying T=0
contaminants is:');
disp(100*E0(indc));
disp('The total number of misclassified contaminants
is:');
disp(Nmisclass(indc));
mis_y1 = find(y1<thresh);
mis_y0 = find(y0>thresh);
disp('Misclassified T=1 contaminants are:');
for i=1:N1misclass(indc)
    disp(names(mis_y1(i),:));
    disp([mis_y1(i), y1(mis_y1(i))]);
end
disp('Misclassified T=0 contaminants are:');
for i=1:N0misclass(indc)
    disp(names(NT1+mis_y0(i),:));
    disp([mis_y0(i), y0(mis_y0(i))]);
end


% ----------------------------------------------------
% Plot classification results as a histogram

figure(5)
fs=12;
T1col = 'w'; T0col = 'k';
histax=Threshrange+int;
[n,xout] = hist(y1,histax);
bar(xout,n,.4,T1col);
```

```
h = findobj(gca,'Type','patch');
set(h,'LineWidth',2)
if max(n)>30
   set(gca,'ylim',[0 30])
   upval = num2str(max(n));
   text(1.025, 29, '\uparrow');
   text(1.025, 27.5, upval);
else
   yset=max(n)+1;
   set(gca,'Ylim',[0 yset]);
end
hold on
[n,xout] = hist(y0,histax-int/2);
bar(xout,n,.4,T0col)
xlabel('{\itY}_{\iti}','FontSize',fs)
ylabel('Number of contaminants','FontSize',fs)
set(gca,'LineWidth',2,'fontsize',fs);
xx = get(gca,'xlim');
yy = get(gca,'ylim');
line([thresh, thresh],[0,
.9*yy(2)],'color','k','LineStyle',':','LineWidth',2);
ymul=.9; ymo=.1;
labxpos = xx(1)+.04*(xx(2)-xx(1));
labypos = .9*yy(2);
boxx=[labxpos labxpos; labxpos+int/2 labxpos+int/2;
labxpos+int/2 labxpos+int/2; labxpos labxpos];
boxy=[ymul*labypos (ymul+ymo)*labypos; ymul*labypos
(ymul+ymo)*labypos; ymul*labypos+.05*labypos
(ymul+ymo)*labypos+.05*labypos;
ymul*labypos+.05*labypos
(ymul+ymo)*labypos+.05*labypos];
patch(boxx(:,1), boxy(:,1),T0col)
patch(boxx(:,2), boxy(:,2),T1col,'linewidth',2)
text(labxpos+int, (ymul+ymo)*labypos,
'T=1','Verticalalignment','bottom','fontsize',fs)
text(labxpos+int, ymul*labypos,
'T=0','Verticalalignment','bottom','fontsize',fs)
strg(1)={'Classifier \rightarrow'};
strg(2)={'Threshold     '};
text(thresh,.6*yy(2),strg(1),'horizontalalignment','r
ight','Fontsize',fs)
text(thresh,.53*yy(2),strg(2),'horizontalalignment','
right','Fontsize',fs)
hold off
% ----------------------------------------------------
```

```
% End of program
% ----------------------------------------------------

% ----------------------------------------------------
% NRC Committee on Drinking Water Contaminants

% Filename: lin_predict.m

% Matlab code to predict classification for test
cases using linear classifier.
% Run this after running lin_class.m and
class_error.m.


% ----------------------------------------------------
% Prediction for test cases

SP = load('testdata.txt'); % the name of the data
file containing test cases
idP = SP(:,1);
XP = SP(:,2:6);
XP = [XP ones(length(idP),1)];

YP = XP*w;
disp('The predicted values for the test cases are:');
for i=1:length(idP)
    disp([idP(i), YP(i)]);
end
% ----------------------------------------------------
% End of program
% ----------------------------------------------------

% ----------------------------------------------------
% NRC Committee on Drinking Water Contaminants

% Filename: nn_predict.m

% Matlab code to predict classification for test
cases using neural network classifier.
% Run this after running nn_class.m and
class_error.m.


% ----------------------------------------------------
% Prediction for test cases
```

```
SP = load('testdata.txt'); % the name of the data
file containing test cases
idP = SP(:,1);
XP = SP(:,2:6);

YP = sim(net,XP');
disp('The predicted values for the test cases are:');
for i=1:length(idP)
   disp([idP(i), YP(i)]);
end
% ------------------------------------------------------
% End of program
% ------------------------------------------------------
```

Appendix C
Biographical Information

COMMITTEE MEMBERS

DEBORAH L. SWACKHAMER, Chair, is a professor in the Division of Environmental and Occupational Health in the School of Public Health at the University of Minnesota. Her research involves assessment of contaminants in the environment and associated risks to public health and the environment. She has published dozens of papers on topics ranging from inventories of xenobiotic organic compounds in the Great Lakes, to analytical methods for contaminant detection, to bioaccumulation of organochlorine compounds in fish and multimedia approaches for modeling human exposure. She has served on the executive committee of the Division of Environmental Chemistry of the American Chemical Society, the Board of Directors of the International Association for Great Lakes Research, and the Science Advisory Committee of the U.S. Environmental Protection Agency's (EPA's) Great Waters program. She is currently a member of the Science Advisory Board of the International Joint Commission of the U.S. and Canada. She previously served on the National Research Council (NRC) Committee on Coastal Oceans. Dr. Swackhamer received her B.A. in chemistry from Grinnell College in Iowa, and her M.S. in water chemistry and Ph.D. in oceanography and limnology from the University of Wisconsin, Madison.

R. RHODES TRUSSELL, Vice Chair, is the lead drinking water technologist and director for corporate development at Montgomery Watson, Inc. Dr. Trussell chairs the EPA Science Advisory Board's Committee on Drinking Water. He has served on several NRC committees, is currently a member of the Water Science and Technology Board, and is a member of the National Academy of Engineering. Dr. Trussell received his B.S. in civil engineering and his M.S. and Ph.D. in sanitary engineering from the University of California, Berkeley.

FRANK J. BOVE is a senior epidemiologist for the Epidemiology and Surveillance Branch of the Division of Health Studies, Agency for Toxic Substances and Disease Registry. Dr. Bove has published several papers and reports on the epidemiology of exposure to drinking water contaminants and related adverse health effects. He received a B.A. in political science and philosophy from the University of Pennsylvania and an M.S. in environmental health science and Sc.D. in epidemiology from the Harvard School of Public Health.

LAWRENCE J. FISCHER is a professor in the Department of Pharmacology and Toxicology and is the director of the Institute for Environmental Toxicology at Michigan State University. He serves as chairperson of the Michigan Environmental Science Board. His primary research interest is biochemical toxicology. Specific research includes absorption, distribution, metabolism, and excretion of drugs and chemicals and toxicity of chemicals to the endocrine pancreas. Dr. Fischer received his B.S. and M.S. in pharmacy from the University of Illinois and his Ph.D. in pharmaceutical chemistry from the University of California, San Francisco.

WALTER GIGER is a professor at the ETH Zurich and at the University of Karlsruhe. He is the director of the Division for Chemical Pollutants at the Swiss Federal Institute for Environmental Science and Technology, Zurich. His research, teaching, and consulting activities focus on organic compounds in the environment and in the geosphere. Research topics include development of analytical techniques for identification of organic pollutants in drinking water, wastewater, and natural waters; investigation of sources, occurrences, and fate of organic pollutants in wastewater and drinking water; and evaluation of chemical, physical, and biological processes that determine the environmental fate of chemicals. Dr. Giger received his B.S. and Ph.D. in chemistry from ETH Zurich.

JEFFREY K. GRIFFITHS is director of the Graduate Programs in Public Health and an associate professor of family medicine and community health at Tufts University School of Medicine. His research is focused on the biology and epidemiology of the emerging waterborne disease cryptosporidiosis and the use of micronutrients to boost the immune systems of malnourished children. He currently serves on the

EPA's National Drinking Water Advisory Council and has represented the National Association of People with AIDS to the EPA Drinking Water Microbial Disinfection and Byproducts Committee. Dr. Griffiths received an A.B. in chemistry from Harvard College, his M.D. from Albert Einstein College of Medicine, and his M.P.H.&T.M. from the Tulane University School of Public Health and Tropical Medicine. He is board certified in pediatrics, internal medicine, and infectious diseases.

CHARLES N. HAAS is the Betz Chair Professor of Environmental Engineering at Drexel University. He was formerly a professor and acting chair in the Department of Environmental Engineering at the Illinois Institute of Technology. His areas of research involve microbial and chemical risk assessment, hazardous waste processing, industrial wastewater treatment, waste recovery, and water and wastewater disinfection processes. He has chaired a number of professional conferences and workshops, has served as a member of several advisory panels to the EPA, and is currently on an advisory committee to the Philadelphia Department of Health. Dr. Haas has served on several NRC committees, including the Committee on the Evaluation of the Viability of Augmenting Potable Water Supplies with Reclaimed Water and the Committee to Review the New York City Watershed Management Strategy. He currently serves on the NRC Committee on Toxicants and Pathogens in Biosolids Applied to Land. Dr. Haas received a B.S. in biology and an M.S. in environmental engineering from the Illinois Institute of Technology and a Ph.D. in environmental engineering from the University of Illinois.

NANCY K. KIM is director of the Division of Environmental Health Assessment of the New York State Department of Health and an associate professor in the School of Public Health at the State University of New York, Albany. Her research interests include chemical risk assessment, exposure assessment, toxicological evaluations, structure-activity relationships, and quantitative relationships among toxicological parameters. She received her B.A. in chemistry from the University of Delaware and her M.S. and Ph.D. in chemistry from Northwestern University.

DAVID M. OZONOFF is a professor in and chair of the Department of Environmental Health in Boston University's School of Public Health. His research centers on health effects on communities exposed to various kinds of toxic chemicals, new approaches to understanding the results of small case-control studies, and the effects of exposure misclassification in environmental epidemiology. He has studied public health effects resulting from exposure to a number of contaminated sites. Dr. Ozonoff received his M.D. from Cornell University in 1967 and his M.P.H. from the Johns Hopkins School of Hygiene and Public Health.

REBECCA T. PARKIN is an associate research professor in the Department of Environmental and Occupational Health in the School of Public Health and Health Services at the George Washington University. Previously, Dr. Parkin was director of scientific, professional, and section affairs at the American Public Health Association and assistant commissioner of the Division of Occupational and Environmental Health at the New Jersey Department of Health. Her areas of expertise include environmental epidemiology, public health policy, risk assessment, and risk communication. She is a former member of the NRC's Water Science and Technology Board. Dr. Parkin received her A.B. in sociology from Cornell University and her M.P.H. in environmental health and Ph.D. in epidemiology from Yale University.

CATHERINE A. PETERS is an associate professor in the Program of Environmental Engineering and Water Resources in the Department of Civil and Environmental Engineering at Princeton University. Her areas of expertise include environmental chemistry, engineering statistics, and environmental risk assessment. Her research combines experimental investigation and mathematical modeling to understand the processes governing the behavior of organic contaminants that are complex chemical mixtures. She is particularly interested in tractable mathematical and analytical methods that adequately describe the chemistry of complex mixtures and provide meaningful information that can be used in risk assessment. Dr. Peters received her B.S.E. in chemical engineering from the University of Michigan and her M.S. in civil engineering and Ph.D. in civil engineering-engineering and public policy from Carnegie Mellon University.

JOAN B. ROSE is a professor in the College of Marine Science at the University of South Florida. Her research interests include methods for detection of pathogens in wastewater and the environment, water treatment for removal of pathogens, wastewater reuse, and occurrence of viruses and parasites in wastewater sludge. Dr. Rose served on the NRC Committee on Wastewater Management for Coastal Urban Areas and the Committee on Potable Water Reuse. She is currently the vice chair of the NRC's Water Science and Technology Board and is a member of the

Board on Life Sciences. Dr. Rose received a B.S. in microbiology from the University of Arizona, an M.S. in microbiology from the University of Wyoming, and a Ph.D. in microbiology from the University of Arizona.

PHILIP C. SINGER is a professor in the Department of Environmental Sciences and Engineering in the School of Public Health at the University of North Carolina, Chapel Hill, where he is also director of the School's Drinking Water Research Center. Dr. Singer was formerly a member of NRC's Water Science and Technology Board and served on the Committee on U.S. Geological Survey Water Resources Research. A member of the National Academy of Engineering, he has published more than 150 papers and reports principally concerned with aspects of water chemistry and drinking water quality. He is currently a member of the Drinking Water Committee of EPA's Science Advisory Board. Dr. Singer received his B.S. in civil engineering from Cooper Union and his M.S. and Ph.D. in environmental sciences and engineering from Harvard University.

PAUL G. TRATNYEK is an associate professor in the Department of Environmental Science and Engineering and the Department of Biochemistry and Molecular Biology at the Oregon Graduate Institute of Science and Technology. He is also an affiliated scientist with the Center for Coastal and Land-Margin Research and the Center for Groundwater Research. His research primarily involves a wide range of oxidation-reduction reactions that can occur in the environment and the contribution of these reactions to the fate of organic pollutants. Examples include oxidations by chlorine dioxide and oxidations of gasoline oxygenates, such as methyl-t-butyl ether (MTBE). Dr. Tratnyek received his B.A. in chemistry from Williams College and his Ph.D. in applied chemistry from the Colorado School of Mines.

STAFF

MARK C. GIBSON is a staff officer at the NRC's Water Science and Technology Board and the study director for this report. As a research associate, he has supported this study since its inception and helped prepare the committee's first two reports, *Setting Priorities for Drinking Water Contaminants* and *Identifying Future Drinking Water Contaminants*. He is also study director for the Committee to Improve the USGS National Water Quality Assessment (NAWQA) Program. Mr. Gibson received his B.S. in biology from Virginia Polytechnic Institute and State University and his M.S. in environmental science and policy in biology from George Mason University.

ELLEN A. DE GUZMAN is a senior project assistant at the NRC's Water Science and Technology Board. She received her B.A. degree from the University of the Philippines. She has worked with a number of studies including *Watershed Management for Potable Water Supply, Issues in Potable Reuse, Valuing Ground Water, New Directions in Water Resources Planning for the U.S. Army Corps of Engineers,* and *Improving American River Flood Frequency Analyses.* She co-edits the WSTB newsletter and manages the WSTB homepage.